RUSSIA IN PERSPECTIVE

Hayden Series In Social Studies

RUSSIA IN PERSPECTIVE

FRED SCHULZE

HAYDEN BOOK COMPANY, INC., NEW YORK

Library of Congress Catalog Card Number 67-21725

Printed in the United States of America

ACKNOWLEDGMENTS

I am indebted to Holland Hunter for introducing me to the study of the Soviet Union and for his assistance in the conception and preparation of this book. I have had many occasions to be grateful for his advice and friendship. John Emerson's encouragement and thoughtful criticisms were of great value. He was a helpful guide in adapting material to the high school level. My wife Maya was alternately patient and firm, and always grammatical.

PREFACE

Students today need wider horizons than ever before. They need to know not only about their own communities and their own states but also how their lives are shaped by events throughout the United States and beyond our shores to the ends of the earth. It used to be sufficient for an educated person to know how American ideas and values came down to us across the ages from the Near East, from Greece, and from Rome. The main thread of the story ran through Europe, whence most of us came.

Now, in the latter part of the twentieth century, an educated person requires a much broader perspective. Latin America, Africa, and Asia touch our lives much more closely than was true before World War II. A purely Atlantic focus is not enough. As the processes of modernization reach out to societies that previously were on the edge of the world's stage, we need to learn about the past experience and the present outlook of these non-Western peoples.

This book serves such a purpose. The modern history of Russia provides a valuable case study of the way a large society has reacted to the pressures of modernization. Russia, located on the eastern edge of Europe but extending also into Asia, has been a latecomer. Compared to many countries today, premodern Russia was neither very poor nor very backward. Nevertheless, it is instructive to see how the Russian people, with all their vigor and diversity, have sought to catch up with Western Europe and North America. This book gives a balanced and perceptive review of the record.

As the countries of Western Europe followed England in the industrial revolution during the nineteenth century, there was a tendency for each to place more reliance on the State in its efforts to develop. The role of the State was larger in German industrialization, for example, than it had been in France. The Russian government took an even larger hand before World War I, and as we all know, the USSR since 1917 has been a testing ground for highly centralized and systematic efforts to catch up rapidly. How well have Soviet methods worked? Were Stalin's methods the best ones available? Now that there are scores of other countries eager to modernize themselves rapidly, what can they learn from the USSR? These are important questions. The present study will enable students to form their own judgments as to the lessons of Soviet experience.

American life has been shaped by rapid, continuous change, and history has been kind to most of us. It is hard for young Americans to see the world as it appears to most of the human race. In a traditional society, change is feared. In the recent experience of Asia, Africa, and Latin America, history has not been kind. To a young person in these countries, the world is likely to look grim and the future to appear ominous.

It is a healthy exercise for thoughtful young Americans to imagine how they would feel if, instead of living in the United States, they were living in one of the many low-income countries that is now trying to overcome its backwardness. Youth in these countries feel a mixture of admiration for, and bitterness towards, the wealthy peoples of North America and Northwestern Europe. Often their bitterness arises out of past racial or national grievances. Often they burn with resentment against social and economic and political injustices in the traditional society around them. Eager for prompt reform, they may willingly be swept into mass movements. For such people in many parts of the world, the Russian revolution and the present power of the Soviet Union appear like a great beacon.

As you go through Fred Schulze's review of the Soviet record in the following chapters, ask yourself how you would have felt if you had grown up in Soviet society and lived through these events. Try to imagine how a Russian your age would feel about this record, and what outlook on the world he or she is likely to have. Have in mind also the reaction to this national experience that might be expected from a young Indian, or Nigerian, or Brazilian. The effort will stretch your imagination and deepen your understanding.

Holland Hunter
Haverford College

CONTENTS

Chapter 1

THE PROCESS OF MODERNIZATION

Soviet leaders frequently point to the rapid development of the Soviet Union since the 1917 revolution as proof that the Communist system is a success. They claim that in the course of half a century a backward country of illiterate peasants has been transformed into a modern nation, a scientific, industrial, and military leader of the world. Many people in the underdeveloped countries of Africa, Asia, and Latin America have been attracted by the promise that the Soviet example offers the quickest and fairest way to create a modern industrial society. The Soviet government appears confident that more and more countries will choose the Soviet Union as a model for their economic and political development.

Some newly independent countries that are not in sympathy with the Soviet Union politically nevertheless look to the Soviet economic system for aid and guidance. They may copy certain features of the economy, such as centralized planning or government ownership of industry; or they may welcome Soviet aid in the form of teachers, engineers, and technicians. In 1960 the Soviet Union established Friendship University (now Patrice Lumumba University) in Moscow, for African, Asian, and Latin American students. Several thousand students attend the University at present, studying mainly scientific and technical subjects. They pay no tuition and receive large scholarships from the Soviet government.

Even the U. S. government was surprised by the high rate of Soviet industrial growth, more rapid in the 1950's than that of American industry. For many years under Stalin the Soviet Union boasted of fantastic progress and expansion, and the Russians claimed to have invented everything from the airplane to baseball. Americans believed this was all propaganda, and much of it was.

When the first Soviet space satellite, "Sputnik," went up in 1957, however, we began to realize that at least some of the Soviet claims were merely exaggerations rather than outright lies.

The Soviet Union had indeed changed tremendously and was rapidly growing into a major world power. Soviet scientific and technical achievements are now respected throughout the world, although it is widely recognized that other aspects of Soviet life, for example agriculture and general living standards, have not made similarly rapid progress.

The decision to industrialize the Soviet Union as rapidly as possible was made in 1928 and caused changes in the entire society. Even the political ideas of the Communist leaders were altered by this desire for industrialization, and the priority given to the development of heavy industry drastically affected the lives of the people.

Factors in Industrialization

To understand the Soviet Union better it is necessary to know something about the process of industrialization and what happens when a primarily agricultural country begins to industrialize. (By "industrialize" we mean creating a society in which a large part of the population is working in factories, producing such things as steel, cars, refrigerators, oil, etc.) Actually the problem is not just a question of economics—of manufacturing cars, for example, instead of growing wheat or rice. The problem is that of modernizing an entire society—the political, educational, and social system, as well as the economic system. The creation of an industrial nation presupposes certain favorable conditions. There must be natural resources available and the knowledge required to develop them. Modernization also requires changes in government machinery and in the attitudes of the people.

There are many ways of achieving a modern industrial society. Conditions in every country are different, and each industrial country has overcome its backwardness in its own way. There are, however, certain basic problems common to all. Much of the current competition between the Soviet Union and the United States concerns their respective beliefs that socialism or capitalism is the best way to solve these problems.

Features of Underdeveloped Nations

One important characteristic of an underdeveloped nation is the dominance of an agricultural way of life; the great majority of the people are engaged in farming. They produce most of what they need themselves, or they trade in a local village market. Each peasant household is nearly self-sufficient. Farming and domestic skills are taught by one generation to the next and may have changed little in many centuries. This is especially true today for large parts of Africa, Asia, and Latin America. In such a traditional agricultural society, local interests tend to be more important than national ones. People are sometimes unaware even of the name of the country in which they live.

Another important feature of an industrially underdeveloped society is the very limited means of communication and transportation. The lack of contact between different areas of the country tends to make the attitude of the peasants very traditional and conservative. People who have seen only their own village or province are likely to be suspicious of new or strange ideas and to resist changes which would mean doing things in a different way. Factory work and city life seem confusing and dangerous. One good example of this attitude was the nineteenth-century Chinese fear of railroads. Although they greatly needed a nationwide transportation system for trade and defense, the Chinese distrusted the strange, smoky steam locomotives and refused to allow railroads to be built in their country until 1890.

Lack of education is partially responsible for such resistance to change. In many underdeveloped nations the peasantry is largely illiterate. Literacy is a most important condition for economic and social progress and the development of a modern society. People who cannot read or write do not make very effective workers or citizens.

In a modern industrial society at least half of the population works at nonagricultural jobs. The work of producing food, clothing, and other goods is divided into specialized tasks. Instead of producing all his own food, clothing, and shelter, each industrial worker makes only one product or part of a product, or does one of many operations necessary to its production. In return for his labor, he receives wages with which he buys what he needs for his own use at stores; these goods may have been produced hundreds or thousands of miles away. Most workers live in towns and cities rather than in rural areas. Those who remain in agriculture, using machines, chemicals, and new farming techniques, produce far more than they themselves need; their surplus is sold to the people in cities. In the United States, for example, one farmer produces enough food for 25 people, which helps to explain our great national surplus.

Need for Agricultural Revolution

The emergence of industry is dependent to a considerable degree on an agricultural revolution. A large increase in food production is of crucial importance for two reasons. First, there must be food available for the workers of the new factories in the towns and cities; they obviously cannot grow their own food. Second, the new factories must get workers from somewhere. Most of them must be former peasants who are attracted into, or forced into, the cities. Consequently, the number of people on the farms will become smaller, but they must still produce as much, or more, food in order to free others for industrial work.

Need for Education

The peasant who becomes an industrial worker requires education and technical training. Even the least skilled workers will have to know how to read. The factory managers, engineers, and technicians need even greater education in order to supervise a modern industrial society. If a country wants to make rapid industrial progress, it must spend a great deal of money and effort to establish a system of general education. Most of the population must be taught to read, and an increasing number must be given advanced technical training. We will see later (in Chapters 7 and 11) that this was one of the major challenges facing the Russians after the 1917 revolution.

Need for Transportation

Industry cannot grow without transportation. Raw materials (iron ore, cotton, wood, various minerals, and the like) must be moved to factories along with the fuels (oil, gas, and coal) that will supply the power to run them. Often these resources are located at great distances from one another. Transportation is necessary to bring them together and also to deliver the finished products to the people who will buy them. The country must be connected by railroads, canals, and highways.

Finding Capital

Enormous amounts of money must also be invested in the development of natural resources—to purchase oil drilling equipment, for example, or to build a large dam to produce hydroelectric power. The construction of a nationwide transportation system is staggeringly expensive. In addition, large sums of money must be invested in basic machinery. The ability to find this necessary capital determines a country's rate of growth.

Here again agriculture is important. If enough food can be raised, the surplus can be exported in exchange for money, heavy machinery, or raw materials. On the other hand, if agricultural production declines, food may have to be imported. Money that could have been used to build factories will have to go to buy food abroad.

The sources of capital available for investment in industry vary from country to country. Money must not only exist in large quantities, but the men who control it must be willing to invest it in factories, mines, railroads. The noble, living chiefly on what is produced on his own estate, may live in luxury, but he may not contribute anything to his country's industrial growth. His wealth is in land rather than money. By contrast, a merchant who has become wealthy in trade might put some of his money into a new factory, or he might loan it to another to build a new enterprise. Even if he places his money in a bank, this capital may be of help, since it will enable the bank to make loans to businessmen to construct factories or buy new machines.

If a country is extremely backward, its rich men few, and its banks negligible, there may be no means of finding capital within its borders. Money must be procured from foreign businessmen and governments, or from the United Nations and other international organizations.

Importance of Social Attitudes

None of these steps can be taken without important changes in the attitudes of the people, particularly toward industrialization and the very idea of change itself. It is essential that some powerful group in the country, the merchants, the political leaders, or the nobility, decide that industrialization will be good for the nation. The motivation is usually political: a desire to become an important world power, to expand one's influence or territory.

Once the decision to industrialize has been made, the general population must somehow be convinced of the necessity of changing its traditional way of life. People must be given some reason for leaving their homes and making other sacrifices. They may either be forced to do these things by their own poverty or government decree, or they may be persuaded that industrial development will eventually bring them higher living standards.

The significance of social attitudes is illustrated by the contrasting experiences of China and Japan in the nineteenth century. In China, the merchants were regarded as the lowest class in society. They had no influence on the development of the country. The traditional prejudice against merchants and trade resulted in the refusal of the government to support the growth of business and industry. Consequently, very few ambitious and intelligent Chinese went into business. By the time this opposition was broken down in the late nineteenth century, China had been left behind by other nations and was a weak and second rate power. Japanese merchants, on the other hand, had long been at the top of the social order; their political and social influence made it possible for Japan to change her traditional way of life relatively easily. Before 1900 Japan had become the first industrial and military power in Asia.

Importance of the Managers of Capital

How the process of industrialization is carried out depends somewhat on the stage of economic development of the particular country. In England individual merchants and landlords played a major role. They not only had capital but were interested in expanding industry and trade. Banks were not important, and the government aided the process mainly by not interfering. In Germany, however, the banks had to assume more of the responsibility, since wealthy private investors were scarcer. There was only a very primitive banking system in Russia in the nineteenth century, and very few rich men were willing to invest in industry. Therefore, the government itself took the lead in constructing railroads and factories and in developing coal and iron mines. In many cases the more backward a nation has been, the more active is the role its government plays in starting and nurturing the process of industrialization.

The British Pattern

England was the first country to pass through the so-called "Industrial Revolution" and was sooner or later followed by many others in Europe and Asia. Looking back over the past two centuries, one can see the British experience as the model that other countries have imitated or revised, according to their own local conditions. A brief discussion of what happened in England in the period 1780 to 1830 will provide a pattern with which Russian experience can be compared. The differences are striking and show much about present Soviet society.

Britain emerged as the first industrial power because of a unique coincidence of circumstances. In the eighteenth century British landowners gained control of Parliament and passed the Enclosure Laws, which resulted in the gradual concentration of land in the hands of fewer and fewer lords and rich gentry. The poorer peasants were deprived of their land and became migratory laborers, searching the country for work. The rich farmers could afford to experiment with new farming techniques and thus developed new agricultural machinery. Using these new methods, fewer and fewer farm workers could produce more and more food, a development that forced still more peasants from the land. The growing number of unemployed laborers were willing to move around the country to find work. In fact, they were compelled by poverty to go almost anywhere and to accept almost any wage.

During these years Britain was also expanding her empire throughout the world. Trade with these new colonies grew rapidly, and a wealthy merchant class developed. There was a great demand for British goods, especially textiles. In order to take advantage of this demand, the merchants and some rich landowners were prepared to invest their money in the textile industry. Until this time textiles had been produced mainly by hand; the spinning and weaving were done by villagers in their own homes. The invention within a few years of such machines as the cotton gin, flying shuttle, spinning jenny, and steam engine caused a revolutionary change in the industry.

Textiles could now be produced by machine in large mills and factories. New towns and cities grew up that were centers for industry. The unemployed peasants were naturally attracted to these factories and took jobs in them at very low pay. Within a few decades there was a mass movement from the country to the city. The combination of a rise in food production, a supply of cheap labor, adequate money for investment, a desire to industrialize, numerous technical inventions, and abundant raw materials, such as rich deposits of coal and iron ore, all resulted in a profound change in English society.

Political and Social Consequences

This basic transformation of English life was accompanied by serious problems and severe hardships. Economic changes are never without political and social consequences. Within a century the population of England tripled and became concentrated in the cities. These cities, crowded with more and more uneducated workers from the country, became areas of drabness, dirt, and dire want. Since there were so many laborers looking for work, factory owners could pay the lowest possible wages. It is difficult to imagine working conditions in England a century and a half ago. Children as young as

A London slum in the nineteenth century

Overcrowding was a serious problem as thousands of peasants moved into the cities and towns to take factory jobs. (Courtesy, The Bettmann Archive)

Boy and girl working at a spinning machine in an American textile factory, 1909
Children this age and younger worked in factories well into the twentieth century. (Courtesy, The Bettmann Archive)

six years old were employed in mines and factories. A work day of fourteen to sixteen hours was common.

Pressure for reforms built up throughout the nineteenth century, but progress was slow. The first laws passed for the protection of the workers show the harsh conditions of the time. The Factory Act of 1833 prohibited children under nine from working in textile mills. By a similar act in 1842, boys under ten and women were forbidden to work underground in coal mines. The Ten Hours Act of 1847 established the ten-hour work day in factories, but only for women and children. These laws represented what was then thought of as the ideal, the best possible conditions; in practice, the laws were often disregarded.

All modern countries, including the Soviet Union and the United States, have gone through a difficult period of economic development. There is no easy way to industrialize; it is a painful process, at least temporarily. Many people have reacted strongly against the suffering and injustices of industrialization. One consequence was the growth of trade unions, organizations of workers who joined together to demand better pay and working conditions from their employers. Another reaction was the development of socialist and revolutionary ideas, protesting violently against the evils of low pay and poor working conditions. Karl Marx, although a German, lived in England in the middle of the nineteenth century and analyzed the poverty and

Workers ready to start the day in a New England textile factory
(Courtesy, The Bettmann Archive)

misery of the urban workers. The ideas he developed have since had an enormous influence throughout the world, particularly in Europe and in Russia.

You may wonder what all this has to do with the Soviet Union. Until the Communist Revolution in 1917, Russia was one of the most backward countries in Europe, with an underdeveloped industry and a population of largely illiterate peasants. Today the Soviet Union is the major rival of the United States as an industrial and military power. How did this change come about? That story is the subject of this book.

PROJECTS

A. Research

(1) Trace the development of specific industries in the United States, for example, steel, oil, textiles, automobiles. How did each industry start? Where did the money come from? What role did the government play?

(2) How did the government support the building of American railroads?

(3) What is the state of industrialization today in such countries as Egypt, China, Guinea, Mexico, Cuba, Rhodesia, Indonesia?

(4) Describe American agriculture today: the number of family farms; migrant farm workers; farm surpluses; government subsidies.

B. Activities

(1) Make a model or diagram illustrating how the cotton gin works.

(2) Make population density maps of England, the United States, and the Soviet Union before and after industrialization. How does this show the movement to the cities?

(3) Make a map of the world showing which nations are primarily agricultural, which are primarily industrial. Make maps to scale according to population, not physical size. Also, make maps to scale according to percentage of the world's income. The *United Nations Bulletin* is a good source for such information.

(4) Using graphs or charts, show the growth of major American, English, and Soviet cities. Also show the increase in literacy. Compare the literacy figures to those for selected underdeveloped nations.

(5) Take the nearest major city and describe how it gets its food supplies. What would happen if all transportation workers went on strike?

C. Further Reading

Hay, Samuel P., *Response to Industrialism 1885-1914* (University of Chicago Press)—American reactions to the problems of industrialization in the United States.

Rostow, W. W., *Stages of Economic Growth* (Cambridge University Press)—A description of the stages a country passes through on the way from an agricultural to an industrial economy.

Chapter 2

KARL MARX: THE CRYSTALLIZATION OF THE COMMUNIST IDEAL

It is important to realize that in many ways Karl Marx and his ideas were typical of European and American reactions to the Industrial Revolution of the nineteenth century. As was mentioned in the first chapter, industrialization meant tremendous changes in the old way of life. The use of machines promised future wealth and abundance for all; but it also meant growing cities plagued by slums, disease, poverty, and a short, miserable life for millions of industrial workers. Not a few people of the time, especially writers and intellectuals, were shocked by the new and seemingly worsening conditions. They protested against them with all the powers at their disposal, deploring the fact that technological progress was being paid for by so much human suffering.

Dissenting Authors

Industrialization occurred first in England, then spread gradually to France, Germany, Italy, the United States, and finally to Russia. In every case it evoked dissenting voices. One of the first to describe the plight of the city poor was Charles Dickens; industrial poverty was a theme of many of his novels, including *Hard Times*. In France, works such as *Les Miserables* by Victor Hugo and *Germinal* by Émile Zola described the suffering of the workers. In the United States, Frank Morris, Theodore Dreiser, Upton Sinclair, and many others registered their protests.

In Russia, industrialization came late in the nineteenth century, and the social protests of writers such as Maxim Gorky were similar to those made earlier. Gorky, one of the greatest of Russian authors, had experienced years of terrible poverty as a boy and never had more than a few years of schooling. His real name was Peshkov, but he adopted the name Gorky, which means "bitter" in Russian. His three-volume autobiography, his short stories, and his novels picture life in Russia for the poorest classes as bitter indeed.

Young boys working in a Russian coppersmith's shop in the nineteenth century
Maxim Gorky, the writer, worked in such shops during his early childhood. (Courtesy, The Bettmann Archive)

Appalled by existing conditions, he implied that something must be done to improve them.

Growth of Labor Unions

Protests against the problems caused by industrialization took many forms. Some men rejected the new way of life entirely, desiring to return to the traditional agrarian existence. Others tried to carry out social reforms to improve working and living conditions for the factory workers. From such efforts, labor unions grew up in Europe and the United States in the second half of the nineteenth century. Unions originally were means of getting workers together to make joint protests about wages and working conditions. The growth of unions was violently resisted at first by factory owners, who were sometimes aided by the government. Strikes were broken up by privately hired gangs of toughs, or on occasion, by the army. By winning the right to strike and to bargain with employers for better working conditions and higher wages, labor unions began to play a major role in the United States and most of Europe. (Significantly, unions did not play as important a role in Russia, as we shall see in Chapter 4.)

Early Socialist Ideas and Experiments

Some men, however, came to the conclusion that drastic changes were necessary and that the entire system had to be changed. They blamed the poverty of the workers on the private ownership of industry. A particular object of much criticism was the economic idea of *laissez-faire:* "let things alone." This doctrine held that there should be no public or government control over private business, no government regulation of prices, working conditions, or wages. Critics compared the large and luxurious houses of the factory owners with the overcrowded tenements of the workers and made various proposals for eliminating this inequality, by both peaceful and violent means. Tentatively, we can give the name "socialist" to any of these ideas for a system in which there is little or no private ownership of industry. (It would be as if Ford, General Motors, DuPont, and the like, were all owned and run by the government.) There were many French and English socialists who preceded Karl Marx and from whom he borrowed ideas. Marx, however, became the most influential and the one who is best known today.

Many socialistic experiments were carried out in Europe and the United States. Small communities (farms) were established, often by religious groups, where all property was owned and shared equally. Perhaps these experiments were based on too idealistic a view of human nature; in any case, they all failed, some immediately, others after several decades. One well-known experiment was Brook Farm, in Massachusetts, which lasted from 1841 to 1847 and attracted such famous American writers as Emerson and Thoreau. Several of these communal societies are described in an interesting book by William Hinds, *American Communities*.

One attempt at peaceful change came from a businessman, Robert Owen (1771-1858), manager of an English cotton mill. Owen was appalled by the conditions in which his workers lived and spent most of his life working for reforms and improved working and living conditions. He finally developed an idea for a perfect community of 3,000 people, who would work and live together, sharing equally. His inspiration led to the founding (1825) of such a model community in Indiana, called "New Harmony," but it too failed eventually. Owen was influential in putting pressure on the English Parliament to pass reform legislation (described in Chapter 1). His proposals were read in England and in Europe and encouraged the later development of labor unions.

Hardening of the Socialist Position

Socialism became a strong movement first of all in France. The rise of socialist ideas was the result not only of industrialization but also of the political revolution of 1789. The French Revolution had proclaimed the equality of all men, that is, that all men were citizens with equal legal rights. But it became clear in the following years that to this legal equality some measure of economic equality had to be added. If these changes could not be obtained peacefully, it was argued that violent revolution would be necessary.

There was a great variety of opinion among socialists, but they were united in the belief that *laissez-faire* capitalism was the cause of poverty and social discontent. (Remember that *laissez-faire* capitalism was opposed to *any* government intervention in business matters and accordingly opposed all taxes and labor laws, such as minimum wage laws.) Socialists agreed on the need to reorganize the economic system and to replace private ownership with some kind of public, cooperative, governmental, or state control. They felt that such control would eliminate the social evils of the Industrial Revolution.

Emergence of Marx

Karl Marx was born in Germany in 1818 of Jewish parents who had become Protestants. Industrialization was beginning to affect Europe after its start in England. Marx studied philosophy at the Universities of Berlin and Jena, receiving his Ph.D. at the age of twenty-three. He turned to the study of politics and economics, read socialist literature, and debated political and economic questions. In 1841 he began writing for a small radical newspaper. For several years he was engaged in journalistic work in Germany, Paris, and Belgium. In his newspaper articles, Marx criticized conservative governments and businessmen and called for the workers to revolt against them. Frequently governments censored or even closed down these extremely critical and revolutionary newspapers.

Among the French socialists whose works Marx read were St. Simon and Fourier. St. Simon had been the first to emphasize economic relationships as the determining factor of history. He viewed man's past as a continual conflict between different economic classes, usually those who "had" and those who "had not." Through conflict, society had evolved throughout history. Fourier violently attacked the policy of *laissez-faire* and also opposed central authority, proposing instead the creation of small self-governing units in which all land resources and machinery were to be owned in common. Each group was to plan its work and divide the tasks equally among its members.

Marx was also influenced by the ideas of a German philosopher, Feuerbach, who developed a theory of "materialism." According to Feuerbach, ideas and individual men are not important in history; they do not cause men to act in certain ways. Rather, men's actions are determined by *material* conditions, such as the kind of work they do and the amount of property they own.

Another German philosopher from whom Marx borrowed was Hegel, who was neither a socialist nor an economist. From Hegel, however, Marx took the idea of the "dialectic" and applied it to economic history. The dialectic refers to a method of development. Hegel wrote mainly of the way in which ideas develop; Marx used his own version of the dialectic method to examine history and claimed to have discovered how society develops.

Marx's Dialectic

Basically, the dialectic consists of three parts: thesis, antithesis, and synthesis. Suppose you have an idea, any idea; the statement of this idea is the *thesis*. This thesis will naturally bring up the statement of an opposing or contradictory idea, which Hegel called the antithesis. When the thesis and the antithesis clash, the result is something new, an idea which is neither thesis nor antithesis, but which contains part of each. Hegel called this new idea the synthesis.

The dialectical process constantly repeats itself; each synthesis becomes a new thesis, which evokes a new antithesis. Again, a synthesis is produced. In this way, ideas continually develop by a process of conflict.

You may be able to guess how Marx combined the ideas of St. Simon and Feuerbach with those of Hegel to provide a method of analyzing society and explaining history. In Marx's dialectic, instead of two ideas clashing, thesis and antithesis, he saw two social classes in conflict, the workers and the factory owners, for example. Out of such a

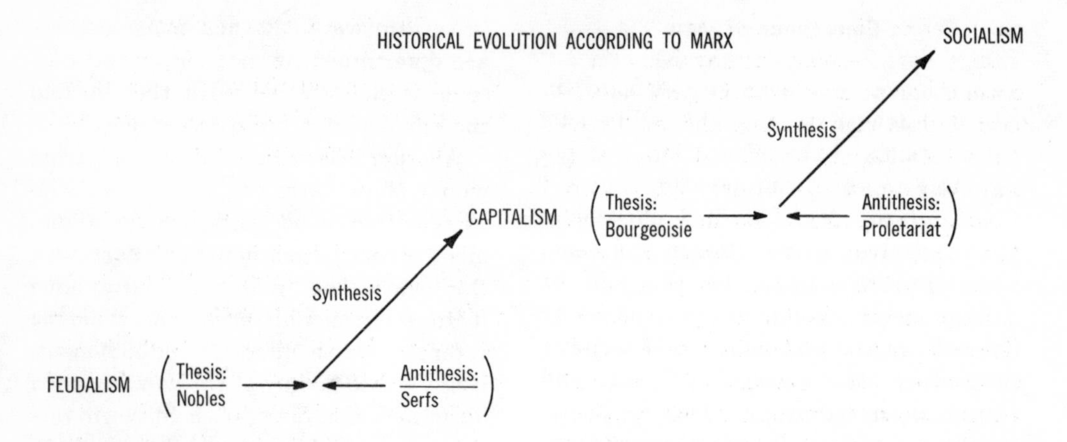

clash would come a new (socialist) society, a new way of life which Marx would call a synthesis.

One example of the way in which the dialectic operates is the following: *Capitalism* developed as a few men accumulated great wealth and property and built factories. The construction of these factories, however, led to the creation of an opposing force, the workers. (Naturally, workers were necessary to run a factory.) The class struggle between the capitalists (the factory owners) and the workers, or in Hegel's terms, between thesis and antithesis, would end in the socialist revolution, Marx predicted. This would be something new, a synthesis growing out of the old institutions, a new way of organizing and running industry.

The diagram above may give an idea of how the "dialectic" worked, in Marx's theories. During the stage of feudalism the nobles came into increasing conflict with the serfs (thesis and antithesis). From this clash came a new stage, bourgeois capitalism, in which the power belonged to the middle class—merchants, factory owners, and the like. This class in turn came into conflict with the growing working class, or proletariat—the people who worked in their factories. Out of this clash would come the stage of socialism, in which there would be no conflicts because the people as a whole would own the factories and all national wealth.

Marx was only one of many socialists writing in the 1840's and was almost totally unknown at that time. Other socialists proposed the abolition of private property through the violent revolution of the workers. Marx read their pamphlets, articles, and books, wrote attacks on their ideas, argued vehemently with those he knew personally, and at the same time, borrowed bits and pieces from their works. Few of Marx's ideas were original; his genius was in the way he combined them. He created a system of thought which claimed to explain all past history and to predict its future course. Marx felt that he had discovered certain "scientific laws of history" that provided a basis for the analysis and understanding of human history.

"The Communist Manifesto"

The earliest and most famous expression of Marx's views was *The Communist Manifesto,* written in 1848. Marx had met Friedrich Engels, another German radical, in 1844, and they had found themselves in general agreement on most issues. They worked together until Marx died in 1883, and the two names have become inseparable. (It is interesting to note that Engels' family owned factories in England and that for years Engels supported the penniless Marx and his family while they lived in the slums of London.) In late 1847 they were asked to write a *manifesto* (a public statement of policy) for a tiny secret revolutionary group of German exiles in London, who called themselves the "Communist League." In this short document, which was not widely read until many years later, Marx and Engels put forward their basic ideas. The *Manifesto* is an attack on existing society and a call to the working classes of the world to revolt and overthrow the capitalists.

Essential to Marx's viewpoint is the belief that economic factors are of primary importance in determining human behavior, and, therefore, in the development of history. This development proceeds according to definite, knowable "laws" (such as the dialectic). History progresses through a series of precise stages, each of which can be defined in economic terms. One stage follows inevitably from another. The transitions between stages are marked by violent revolutions.

To understand any stage in history, a follower of Marx would ask, "Who owns the means of production?" The phrase "means of production" refers to all types of wealth and property that can be used to produce more goods. Thus, land, factories, transportation, mines, and electrical power are all means of production. By looking at which members of a society own these various kinds of wealth, Marxists would divide history into five stages: primitive, slave-holding, feudal, bourgeois (middle class) capitalistic, and socialistic.

The Five Stages of History

Here are brief definitions of each of the five stages of history as Marx and Engels set them up:

(1) *The primitive stage of development*—At this first stage no state or government yet exists; there is no social organization and no private property. All property is owned by the tribe, as in the time of the cave men or in some primitive jungle tribes.

(2) *The slave-holding stage*—The important means of production in this stage are human beings, held as slaves. A few men own many other men and live on what is produced by the work of these slaves. For example, ancient Egypt, Greece, and Rome.

(3) *Feudalism*—Land is the important means of production and is concentrated in the hands of a few men. The masses of people are serfs, bound to the land to work it for the profit of the nobles who own it. Europe in the Middle Ages is an example.

(4) *Bourgeois capitalism*—Factories and mines are the means of production in an industrialized society; they are owned by a few wealthy men (capitalists) and worked by the proletarian (non-property owning) masses. Profits go to the capitalists, who pay the workers as little as possible.

(5) *Socialism*—The workers, or proletariat, take over the means of production and operate them for their own benefit. Social classes are eliminated, and communism is gradually established. This final development leads to the abolition of the state (that is, of government), a classless society (no rich, no poor), and an abundance of goods for all, which are distributed "communally" (that is, "according to one's needs.")

Working Definitions

Capital—productive wealth (mines, factories, machines, and the like) which can be used to manufacture other goods. *Capitalism* is an economic system in which most of the capital is privately owned.

Bourgeoisie—the middle class (originally a French word—pronounced "boorzh-wah-zee"—describing people who were neither peasants nor nobles).

Proletariat—originally this word meant the lowest class in a community; later it came to mean the workers, especially factory workers.

Socialism—an economic system in which capital, means of production, and land are owned and controlled by the public as a whole and administered for the general welfare of the community. Society is organized according to the principle, "From each according to his ability, to each according to his contribution."

Communism—an economic system in which all property and wealth is owned in common. Society is organized according to the principle, "From each according to his ability, to each according to his need."

In each of these stages, according to Marx and Engels, a class struggle develops between those who own and control the means of production and those who do not, who only work on the land and in the factories and mines. The conflict leads eventually to a revolution in which the controlling class is overthrown. Then a new class dominates society, until it too is overthrown. The movement from stage to stage is slow, but inevitable, and the direction cannot be reversed. A single stage may last for decades or even for centuries. Only when the proper conditions exist, when the society is "ready," will it move on to the next stage through violent revolution. For example, the stage of capitalism will last until the working class becomes stronger than the capitalist class and so poor that it is forced to revolt.

The Final Stage

This "dialectical" progress continues until the final stage of socialism is reached. Once the workers take over all the means of production and use them for the common good, class differences will be eliminated. Private property will be abolished; no individuals will own factories or mines; the "public"—all the people—will own them communally. As classes are eliminated, socialism will evolve into its final and perfect form, communism.

Marx was extremely vague in his description of this final stage. His papers contain a few general statements but almost no specific details about the future communist society. Since it will be classless, since all the people will both own and work the means of production, they will therefore

Monument to Karl Marx opposite the Bolshoi Theater in Moscow

Built in 1961, the monument carries the famous closing words from the Communist Manifesto: *"Proletarians of all countries, unite!" Statues and portraits of Marx are a familiar sight in the Soviet Union. (Courtesy, Sovfoto)*

be without conflict and will not need a state or government nor even money. (For example the just distribution of material goods will abolish crime and hence make the police unnecessary.) Such are the outlines of the vision that Marx left behind. He was even less definite on the subject of exactly *how* socialism would eventually become communism. (This is a question which has been left to current Soviet leaders to solve. The Soviet Union claims to have already built "socialism" and to have begun building "communism." Soviet leaders say they are working toward it but are not there yet.)

"Das Kapital"

Marx's major work, a massive three-volume political and economic study, *Das Kapital* (Capital), was the result of an entire life of research and study. *Das Kapital* elaborates the ideas sketched earlier in the *Manifesto.* It gives detailed illustrations and proofs for these ideas. Only the first volume was published while Marx lived; the other two were edited and published by Engels. Before the first volume was printed in 1867, Marx wrote to Charles Darwin, the famous biologist who developed the theory of evolution, offering to dedicate the work to him. Marx felt that he was doing for economics what Darwin had done for biology. Darwin described the evolution of animal and plant life; Marx was trying to show how human society also evolved according to scientific laws. Darwin declined the honor of the dedication.

Although few people paid attention to Marx's writings at first, their influence gradually spread among workers and intellectuals. Many groups throughout Europe adopted his theories or variations of them as a basis for their own actions. Most of his followers began to call themselves Marxists, but different men emphasized different parts of his writings.

The Workers' International

In 1864, the Workers' International was established, a combination of many labor unions and other working class groups from all of Europe. By cooperating, they hoped to win basic reforms from the capitalists or even to carry out the international, proletarian (workers') revolution called for in the *Communist Manifesto.* Marx did not actually establish this international organization, but he soon joined and took over its leadership. He was more extreme than many of the other leaders in the International, and disputes over tactics were frequent. While Marx and Engels encouraged violent revolution, others were increasingly in favor of reforms and legal changes through political action, voting, etc. These moderates gradually left; by 1876 the International had split and dissolved.

The fame of Karl Marx has increased steadily since his death. He was totally unknown in 1848 when he and Engels wrote the *Manifesto.* By the 1860's and 1870's his was the most respected name among socialists and revolutionaries, but he was still not generally known. His influence has grown continually, however, even up to the present. His ideas have been taken up by many different groups and have gone through various changes and revisions. (Lenin, the most important revisor of Marx, is discussed in Chapter 5.) Followers of Marx have been arguing for nearly a century about the correct interpretation of his theories. The best current example of this kind of rivalry is the disagreement between the Soviet leaders, Brezhnev and Kosygin, and the Chinese leader Mao Tse-tung as to who is the "true Marxist" (see Chapter 13).

PROJECTS

A. Research

(1) Who supported reform legislation in England, such as the Factory Act of 1833 or the Ten Hour Act of 1847? Who opposed these laws? When and how were laws passed in the United States affecting child labor, minimum wages, unemployment, social security?

(2) Labor unions developed in the United States in the face of determined, sometimes bloody, opposition from business and government (for example, the famous Haymarket Square riot of 1886, in which eight people were killed and many wounded). Unions ranged in philosophy and tactics from the terrorist miners' group, the Molly Maguires, and the later, socialist I.W.W. (Industrial Workers of the World, often called Wobblies) to the relatively conservative Knights of Labor and its successor, the American Federation of Labor. What tactics did the moderate and extreme unions use to overcome resistance to the organizing of labor? Which were most successful?

(3) Hershey, Pennsylvania—the "chocolate town"—was planned as a model community for workers. How did it compare to Robert Owen's efforts on behalf of workers in his cotton mill?

(4) The communities of Brook Farm and New Harmony were founded with great enthusiasm and optimism; why did they quickly fail? Were other American attempts at communal living any more successful? (Hinds' book, *American Communities,* is one source of information.)

B. Activities

(1) Make a graph showing what part of our national income goes to the wealthiest, poorest, and middle segments of our population. Compare this distribution of income to that in the Soviet Union and also to that in a developing Latin American, Asian, or African country. (Helpful sources would be Michael Harrington's *The Other America* and United Nations pamphlets on world income distribution.)

(2) Debate the following question: "Resolved: The United States government should guarantee an adequate annual income to all its citizens, whether or not they work." This controversial proposal was made in a report to the President by the National Commission on Technology, Automation, and Economic Progress in February, 1966. (This report should be available from the United States Government Printing Office, in Washington, D. C. The idea is also discussed in Robert Theobold's *Free Men and Free Markets.*)

C. Further Reading

All of the following books deal, at least in part, with working conditions and problems caused by industrialization:

Dickens, Charles, *David Copperfield* (Washington Square Press, N.Y.); *Hard Times* (Harper & Row, N.Y.)

Dreiser, Theodore, *The Financier* (Dell, N.Y.); *The Titan* (Dell, N.Y.)

Gorky, Maxim, *Autobiography* (Collier, N.Y.); *Foma Gordeyev* (Delta, N.Y.); *Mother* (Collier, N.Y.)

Hugo, Victor, *Les Miserables* (Washington Square Press, N.Y.)

London, Jack, *The Iron Heel* (Hill and Wang, N.Y.)

Norris, Frank, *The Octopus* (Bantam, N.Y.)

Sinclair, Upton, *The Jungle* (Signet, N.Y.)

Steffens, Lincoln, *Shame of the Cities* (Hill and Wang, N.Y.)

Steinbeck, John, *Grapes of Wrath* (Viking Press, N.Y.); *In Dubious Battle* (Bantam, N.Y.)

Zola, Émile, *Germinal* (Bantam, N.Y.)

One of the best short biographies of Karl Marx is by Isaiah Berlin, *Karl Marx: His Life and Environment* (Oxford University Press, N.Y.). See also the chapters on Marx in Edmund Wilson's *To The Finland Station* (Doubleday & Co., Garden City, N.Y.).

The best collection of the works of Marx and Engels is *Basic Writings on Politics and Philosophy: Karl Marx and Friedrich Engels,* edited by Lewis Feuer (Doubleday & Co., Garden City, N.Y.).

Chapter 3

RUSSIA: THE LAND AND ITS RESOURCES

The Soviet Union is a country of extremes and contrasts, especially with regard to geography, climate, and natural resources. Cold weather and vast distances are its two most striking physical features. The coldest place in the world, except for the polar regions, is a tiny town in eastern Siberia, Verkhoyansk, where temperatures as low as −94°F have been recorded. Even in the European part of the Soviet Union the winters are severe and the variations in temperature very great. The area around the Caspian Sea has summer temperatures over 115°F, but winter recordings reach as low as −20°F. (For Russian place names mentioned in the text, see Map 1.)

Natural Resources

Equal in size to the United States, Canada, and Mexico combined (or nearly three times the size of the U.S.A.), the Soviet Union possesses what is probably the largest supply of natural resources in the world. Adequate amounts of almost every necessary mineral are to be found in the Soviet Union, making it the most self-sufficient country in the world. The harsh climate, however, and the tremendous distances make it difficult to develop some of these resources. More than one-third of the Soviet Union (an area equal to the entire United States) is too cold for any kind of agriculture, one-third is overly mountainous, one-quarter too dry, and many areas too windy or too wet. For one reason or another, nearly three-fourths of the country is unattractive for habitation and impractical for raising food.

A nation is not a world power merely because it has great deposits of mineral and fuel resources. These are important, but there are other factors. It must also possess the technical knowledge needed to develop these resources, and the resources must be located within reasonable distance of existing cities and transportation. For example, there are quite large coal deposits near Verkhoyansk, but they are so far from any large town and the climate is so frightful that it seems very doubtful that this coal will ever be used. Beside

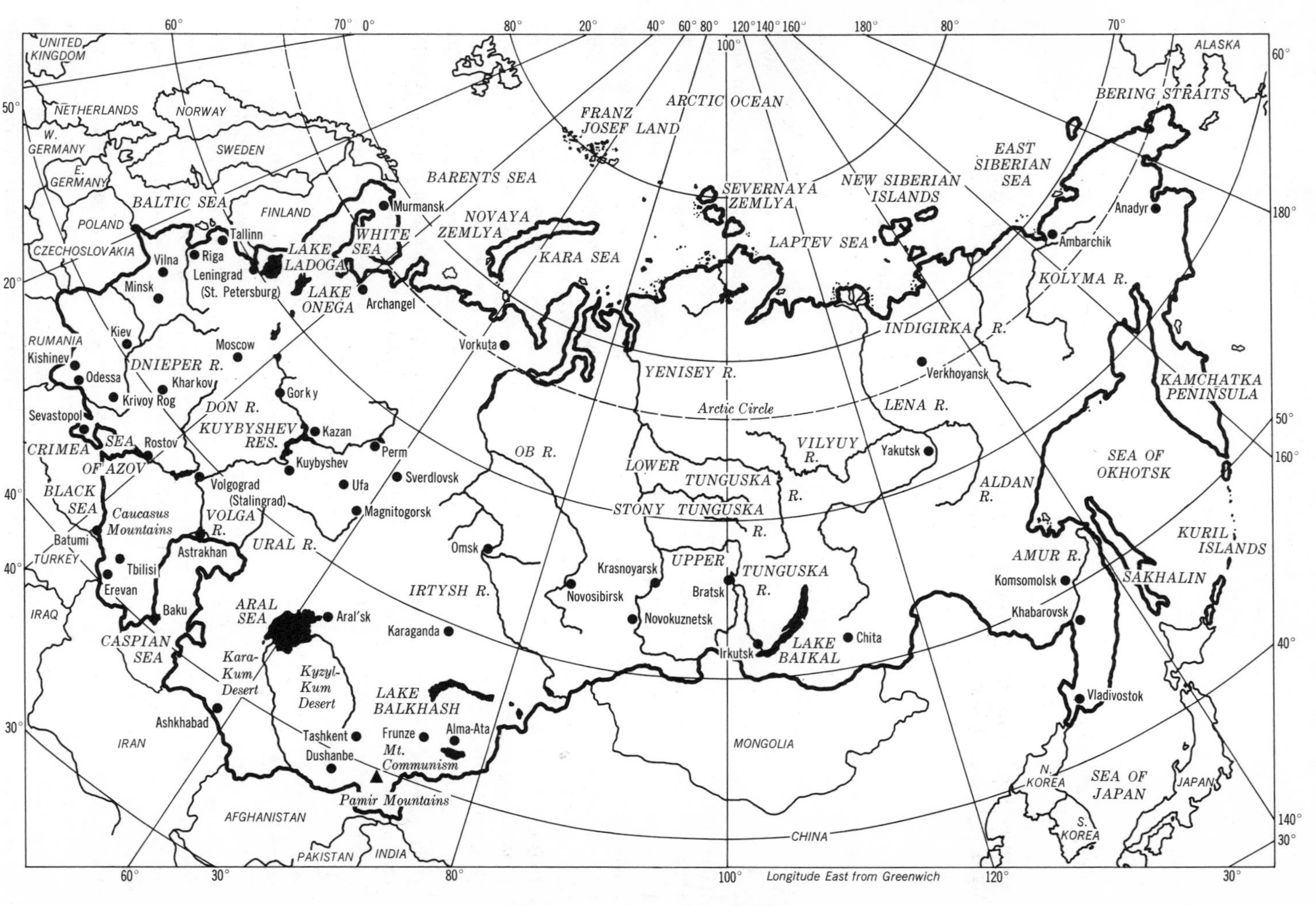

Map 1 Russian place names

considerations of this sort, the natural wealth of a nation is, to some degree, relative. Today coal is much less important than it was a century ago, and in another century it may be completely replaced by atomic power. A country that seems poor today may become important twenty years from now because of the discovery of a way to use some material previously thought worthless.

From Poland in the west, the Soviet Union stretches over 6,000 miles to the Pacific Ocean, a distance roughly equal to that between San Francisco and London. Some idea of what this means is suggested by the fact that the express train from Moscow to Vladivostok—a port city on the Pacific—takes nine days for the trip (see Map 2).

Navigation

The Soviet coastline is the longest, and the most useless, in the world. No port, except Murmansk, on the Barents Sea (part of the Arctic Ocean) is free from ice all year round. Some of the harbors on the Arctic and Pacific Oceans are frozen as much as ten months of the year, while even the ports on the Black Sea are closed by ice for one or two of the winter months.

The problem of ice is even more serious as it affects the navigation of the major rivers. The Volga, the most important river, is blocked by ice for three or four months. The great rivers of Siberia—the Ob, Lena, Irtysh, and Yenisei, among the world's longest—are frozen at least six months. They all flow north into the Arctic Ocean, which is now navigable for as many as 150 days per year only by constant use of icebreakers.

Climate

In comparing the United States and the Soviet Union, it should be remembered that the Black and Caspian Seas, located in the extreme south of the Soviet Union, actually lie on the same latitude as the Great Lakes. Almost all of the Soviet Union is north of the American-Canadian border. For this reason, one should compare Soviet natural conditions and climate to those of Canada, not to those of the U.S.A.

One of the major obstacles to Soviet growth in Siberia is *permafrost,* a common phenomenon in the Arctic regions of Canada and Alaska as well. Permafrost, which affects 47 per cent of the area of the Soviet Union, keeps the ground permanently frozen to a depth of anywhere from 5 to 1,000 feet. In the summer the top few feet may thaw out (as much as 10 feet in southern Siberia), but the rest remains frozen. As a result, the melting ice and snow cannot soak into the ground, and a vast swamp of mud, many feet deep, is created. Agriculture is obviously impossible under such conditions. Permafrost also severely hinders the development of Siberia's resources, causing countless problems in the construction of factories, houses, roads, and wells. It is not surprising that some quite large Siberian cities have only dirt roads and streets; it is just not possible to build an ordinary road on ground that is a sea of mud during several months of the year.

The climate of the Soviet Union is governed by two main influences, moisture from the Atlantic and the Baltic and cold dry air from the Arctic. The extreme cold of Siberia is due to the fact that there are no natural barriers to the southward movement of the Arctic air masses. The effect of this cold Arctic air is felt in European Russia also, since most of the western two-thirds of the Soviet Union consists of broad plains. The Ural mountains

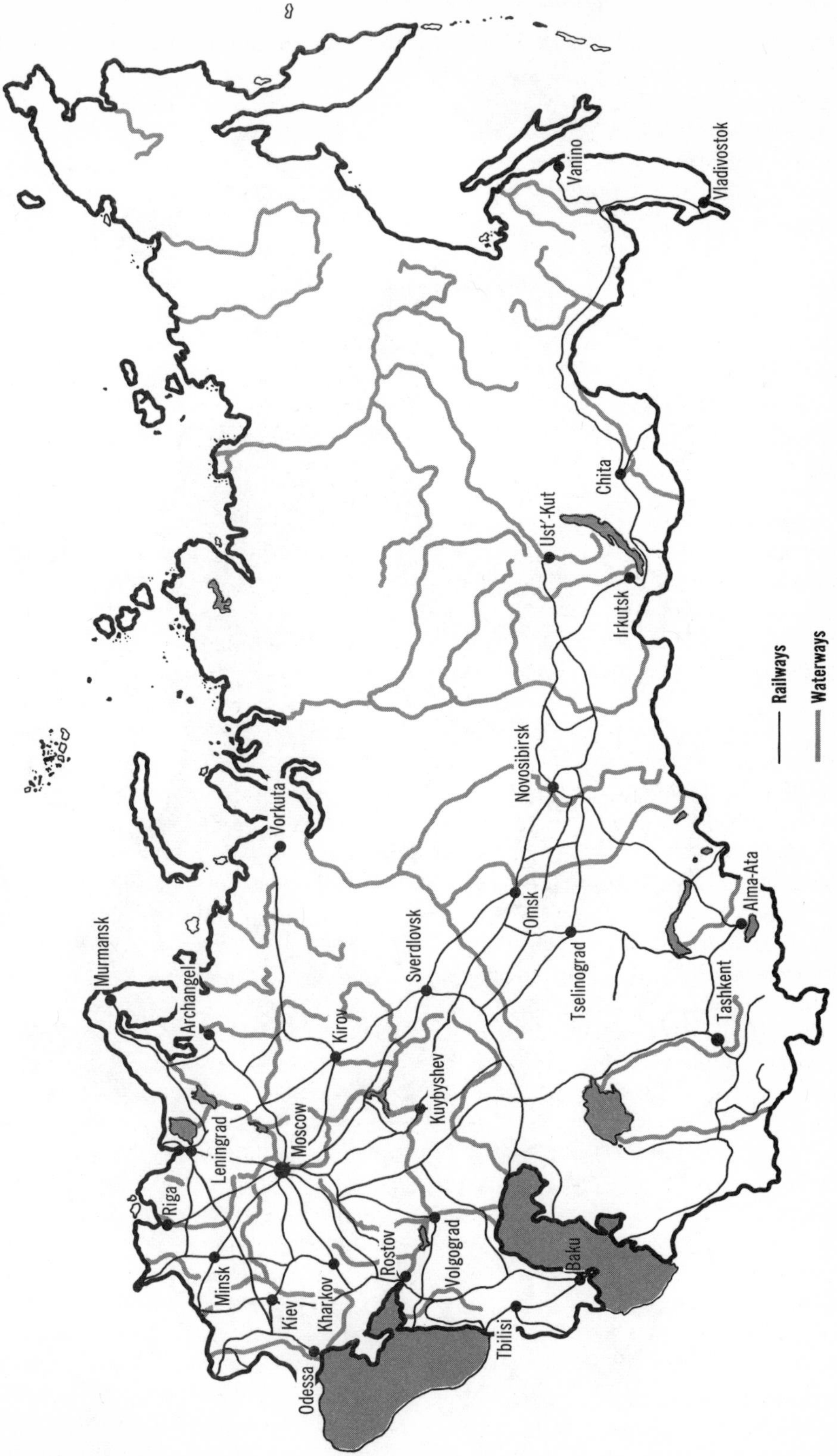

Map 2 Railways and Navigation in the Soviet Union

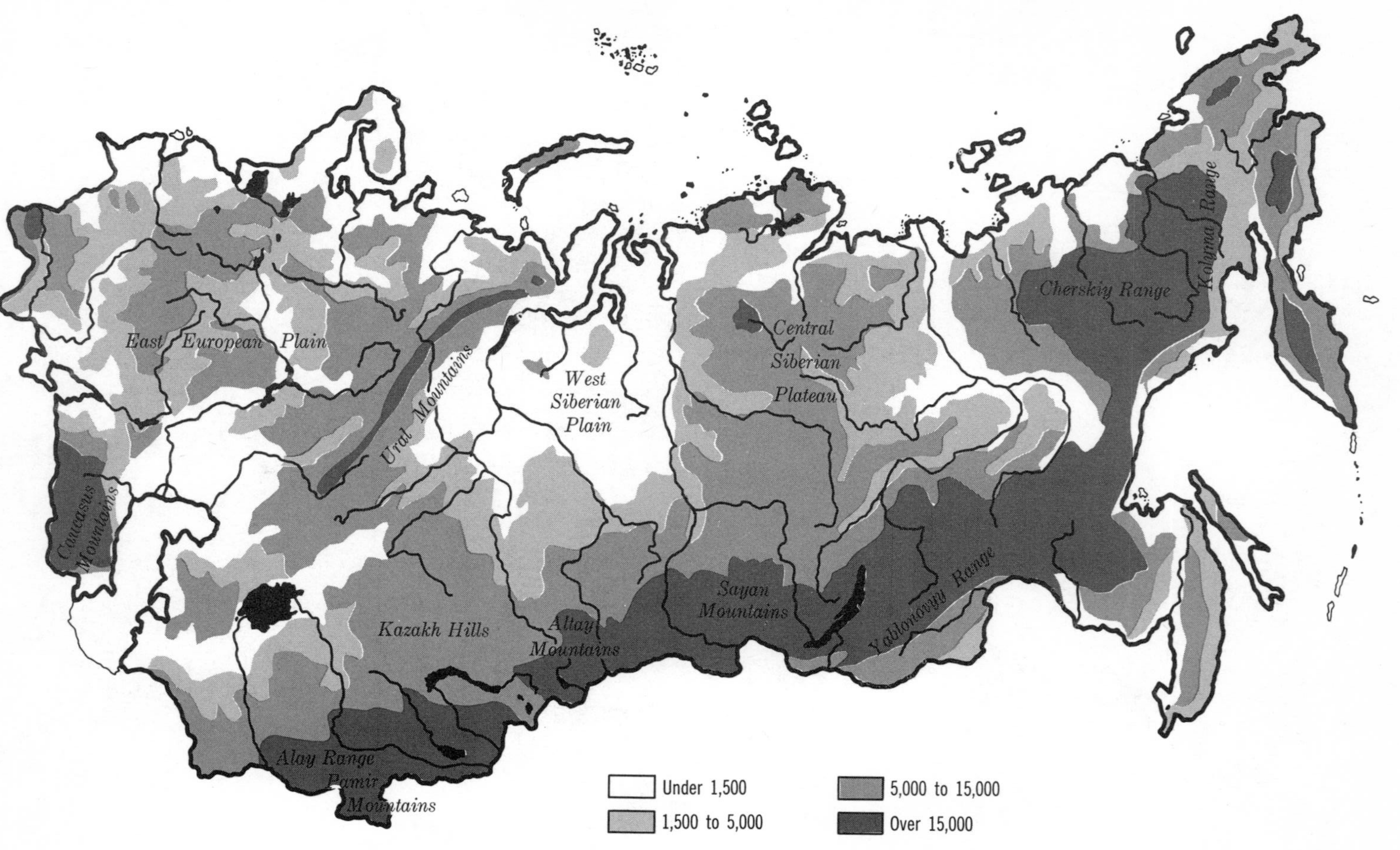

Map 3 Topographical features of the Soviet Union

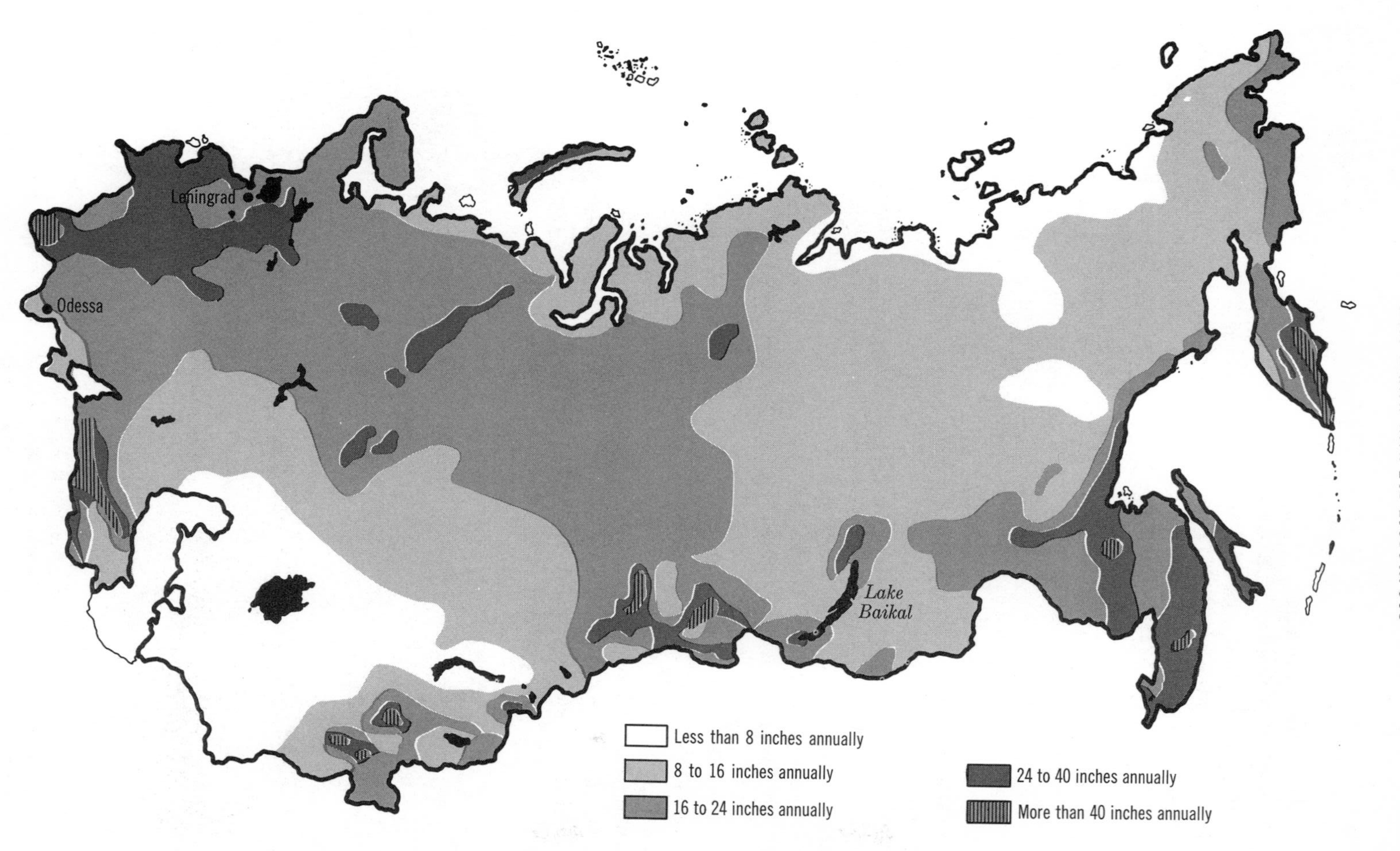

Map 4 Precipitation in the Soviet Union

are really only high hills and do little to keep out the cold winds from Siberia. This mass of Arctic air is able to dominate the climate of most of Siberia and European Russia because a continuous chain of high mountains along the southern border, from the Caspian to the Pacific, blocks out completely the warm, wet air from India and the Pacific. (Take a look at Map 3 to understand this phenomenon clearly.)

The moist air that penetrates European Russia from the Atlantic through the Baltic Sea and Poland is the main moderating influence on the climate but gradually loses influence as it moves eastward. The area that it affects forms an approximate triangle between Odessa, Lake Baikal, and Leningrad (see Map 4). North of the Leningrad-Baikal line the growing season is too short for anything but experimental agriculture. South of the Odessa-Baikal line the rainfall is generally inadequate for agriculture. It is not too surprising then that within this wedge, which constitutes only 10 per cent of the total area of the Soviet Union, can be found 95 per cent of Soviet agriculture, industry, and population.

Natural Zones

The Soviet Union can be divided horizontally (Map 5) into five basic natural zones. From north to south they are the tundra, the taiga, the mixed forest, the steppe (or prairie), and the desert. The fertile agricultural wedge runs approximately from the southern edge of the taiga to the beginning of the desert.

The Tundra

The *tundra* is a rather narrow zone along the northern border of the Soviet Union, near the Arctic Circle. It is quite similar to the far northern regions of Alaska, Canada, and Scandinavia. Only mosses, shrubs, and small bushes are able to grow on this flat, frozen land, where summer lasts barely a month. This area is naturally very sparsely populated. A few Lapps, Eskimos, and other non-Russian tribes live here by hunting, fishing, and herding reindeer.

The frozen arctic tundra

Flat and treeless, the tundra stretches across northern Siberia, Canada, and Alaska. Its few inhabitants are similar to the eskimos. (Courtesy, Sovfoto)

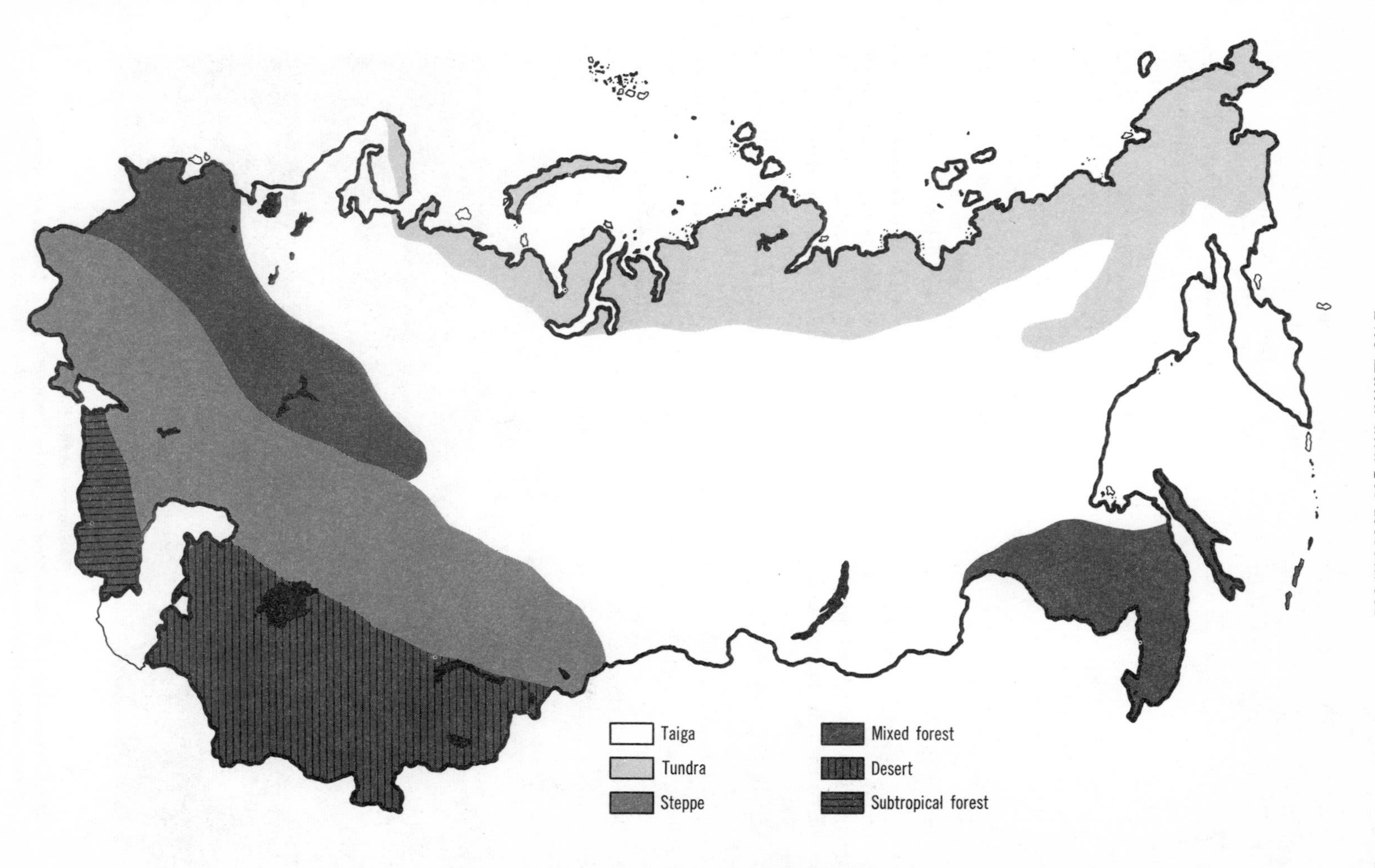

Map 5 The five basic natural zones of the Soviet Union

The Taiga

South of the tundra lies an area equal to the entire United States, the *taiga* (a Yakut word meaning forest). It is the largest coniferous forest in the world, consisting mainly of pine, fir, and spruce trees. Most of the taiga is located in Siberia, although it extends into the European part of the Soviet Union also. Much of the western part of the taiga has been cleared for farming, though the soil is poor, but the eastern part of this forest is largely untouched.

The Mixed Forest

Although the coniferous forest covers most of Siberia, in European Russia it gradually gives away to an area of mixed forests. The winters in this area are less severe, and the soil is richer than in the areas further north. This mixed forest region is where the history of the Russian people began; it contains some of the oldest cities, such as Moscow, Kiev, and Gorky.

The Steppe

The mixed forest region is not large, and it soon begins to merge into the famous steppe. The *steppe* is mainly flat grassland, with some trees in the north, fading away into desert in the south. It could be compared with Montana and Saskatchewan—dry and hot in the summer, cold and wind-swept in the winter. The soil here is very

Aerial view of the taiga

Stretching over thousands of miles of Siberia, the forests of the taiga cover an area equal in size to the United States. (Courtesy, Sovfoto)

A Turkmen shepherd with his sheep
His pasture lies in the Kara-Kum desert. (Courtesy, Sovfoto)

dark and fertile, and the steppe is thus often referred to as the "black-earth" region. Except when there is a serious drought, this is the richest agricultural area in the Soviet Union. Most of the wheat and corn for the entire country is grown here.

In recent years, particularly under Khrushchev, attempts were made to cultivate more and more of this region, especially the driest areas in the east and south. This "virgin lands program," which will be discussed in detail later (Chapter 7), was a risky project because of the very unpredictable rainfall, and it has been partially abandoned. A rich harvest one year may be followed by a year in which there is almost no rain and therefore an extremely poor harvest. There is also the danger that the area will turn into a dust bowl, as happened in Oklahoma and Kansas in the 1930's.

The Desert

The Central Asian deserts to the south of the steppe lack sufficient rainfall to be naturally productive. Both the Kara-Kum and the Kyzyl-Kum deserts, east and south of the Aral Sea, are sandy, but other areas of this zone have quite fertile soils. The major crop is cotton, grown mainly in the Uzbek Republic.

With proper irrigation, large parts of this region could become productive. The Soviet government is making some progress in the development of a system of canals and irrigation reservoirs, but the cost of such an effort is exceedingly high. This situation is met with frequently in the Soviet Union—difficult physical conditions hindering the development of potentially rich natural resources.

Subtropical Areas

In addition to the five major natural zones, there are many smaller areas with unique features. Of great agricultural significance are the subtropical shores of the Crimea and the eastern Black Sea Coast. These shores of the Black Sea receive the largest amount of rainfall of any region in the Soviet Union—in places over 100 inches per year. Some parts of this region are too wet and swampy, but many others have been drained and cultivated with tea, grapes, tobacco, and citrus fruits—crops that cannot be grown elsewhere in the Soviet Union.

Other Unique Areas

Another unique area is the Kamchatka peninsula in the Pacific. It is covered with very rugged, recently formed mountains and some of the most active volcanoes in the world. The highest range of mountains in the Soviet Union is the Pamirs, in the Central Asian republic of Tadzhikistan. The Caucasus mountains, between the Black and Caspian Seas, include the highest peaks in Europe, rising up to 19,000 feet. On

The Pamir mountains in Central Asia, the highest in the Soviet Union
This is Red Army Peak. (Courtesy, Sovfoto)

the gentler slopes one can find rich meadows and Alpine pastures similar to those of Austria and Switzerland.

Mineral Deposits

It is difficult to form accurate estimates of the size of Soviet reserves of oil, coal, iron, and other minerals (see Map 6). Some of the recently discovered deposits in Siberia have not yet been carefully explored, and it may prove impractical and too costly to develop some of them. The situation is somewhat similar to our own in Alaska, where, for example, large oil deposits have been discovered, but no way yet found to make their development worthwhile.

Wealth of the Ukraine

In Russian industrial development, both before and after the Revolution, a major advantage has been the location of large supplies of iron ore and coal close together. Until the start of the Second World War, the most important area of heavy industry was the Donets Basin (the Donbas) in the southern Ukraine. Only the Ruhr valley, on whose industry Hitler built his war machine, and the British Midlands have such excellent combinations of basic resources. Within a small area there is Donets coal, high grade iron ore from Krivoy Rog, hydroelectric power from the Dnieper River, and local deposits of minerals needed for making steel, such as manganese. The Donbas was the industrial center of prerevolutionary Russia and is to a lesser degree of the Soviet Union also. Before 1914, the Donbas produced nearly ninety per cent of Russian coal and seventy-five per cent of Russian iron ore. It still accounts for about forty per cent of Soviet coal and iron today, but it is gradually losing out to the newer regions of the east, in the Urals and in Siberia.

The Ukraine, however, is still the leading industrial area of the Soviet Union, producing steel, trucks, farm machinery, locomotives, rails, chemicals, cement, and many kinds of heavy equipment. When one recalls that the Ukraine is also the grain-producing center of the Soviet Union, the economic significance of this republic can be understood more clearly. The Soviet defeat of the Nazi invasion of 1941 seems even more remarkable in view of the fact that the Germans occupied almost all of the Ukraine for several years. One of the reasons the Soviet Union survived this loss was the rapid growth during the 1930's and 1940's of new industry in the Urals and farther east in Siberia.

Wealth of the Urals

The greatest Soviet reserves of iron ore are in the Ural Mountains, in the region of Magnitogorsk. The Urals are also a source of almost every mineral needed for heavy industry, except coal, making it a region of rare value. The exploitation of the natural wealth of the Urals was begun under Peter the Great (see Chapter 4), but the most rapid expansion came in the 1930's and 1940's under Stalin. For example, Magnitogorsk did not exist in 1926. Today it is a city of over 300,000 people. During the 1930's many American engineers went to Russia to help plan and build these new industrial enterprises. During the Second World War, many Soviet factories were moved to the Urals from the western part of the country to escape German attack. When the war was over they remained there, emphasizing the new importance of the "East" to the Soviet economy.

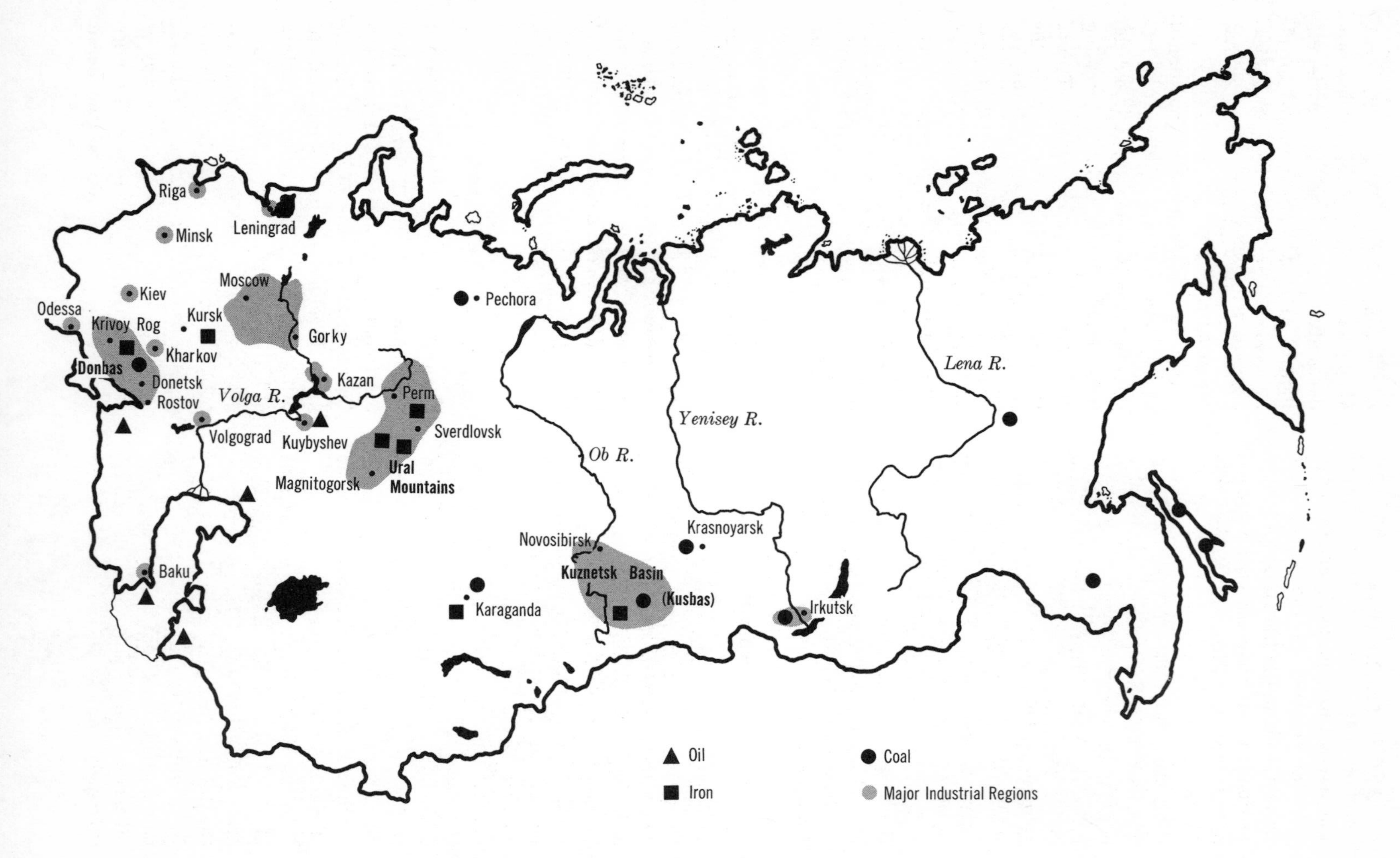

Map 6 Natural Resources of the Soviet Union

Coal Reserves

The Soviet Union probably has the largest coal reserves in the world. The Donets fields in the Ukraine still lead in production, but they are losing ground quickly to the Kuznetsk Basin (the Kusbas), several thousand miles east, near the beginning of the Ob River. The coal in the Kuzbas is approximately equal to the combined deposits of Pennsylvania, West Virginia, Kentucky, and Ohio. The deposits around Karaganda, in Western Siberia, are almost as large. When the recently discovered coalfields near Krasnoyarsk, several hundred miles east of the Kuzbas, are fully examined they will probably prove to be the largest of all. Other large sources of coal are located in the far east, near Vladivostok and on the Pacific island of Sakhalin.

Oil Deposits

In American industry, coal is gradually being replaced by oil and natural gas. The same is true of the Soviet Union, although the Russians have been slower to change over. For many years the words oil and Baku were almost synonymous to the Russian citizen, in the way oil and Texas are linked in American minds. The rich oil fields of Baku, on the shore of the Caspian Sea, were first developed in the 1870's, and by 1900 they were producing half of the world's oil. They continued to be the most important Russian oil deposits for most of the twentieth century.

In the 1930's oil was discovered east of the Volga in the Bashkir republic, near Kuibyshev and Ufa. As soon as the German Army threatened to capture Baku during the years 1942-43, these new deposits took on tremendous significance. They have been developed extremely rapidly in the period since the Second World War. This area, known as the "Second Baku," now produces about two-thirds of all Soviet oil. Central Asia has been surveyed for oil in recent years, and there are indications that large reserves exist in that region also.

Due to the "oil boom" mentioned above, the population of Kuibyshev has tripled in the last thirty years, and the whole Middle Volga region is becoming an important industrial center. Two of the largest hydroelectric dams in the world have been built on the Volga river in the past decade, at Kuibyshev and Volgograd. The city of Volgograd will appear only on the most recent maps; until 1961 it was called Stalingrad. (In 1961 all cities named for Stalin were renamed, and most monuments to him were taken down. See Chapter 7 for a discussion of why this was done.) Many new factories have been attracted to this area, and it has the fastest industrial growth rate in the country. The two large dams have also created artificial lakes of considerable size, which help to irrigate this dry land. The Middle Volga region should play an increasingly important industrial and agricultural role in the future.

Natural Gas

Natural gas deposits are scattered throughout the Soviet Union. The richest found so far are in the northern Caucasus and in the Middle Volga region. Pipelines are now being built to bring this gas to the industrial centers of European Russia. New deposits have recently been tapped in the Uzbek republic, and others have been discovered in eastern Siberia, near Yakutsk. It will be many years before a way is found to use this rich source of energy because of the problem of the harsh

Tapping oil under the Caspian Sea near Baku

A whole town for oil workers, including stores and apartments, has been built on piers that jut out several miles into the sea. (Courtesy, Sovfoto)

Siberian weather. Even then, the deposits are located at such a distance from existing centers of industry that they may never be worth developing.

Hydroelectric Power

The present Soviet leaders place great emphasis on the hydroelectric power potential of their country. Five of the twelve largest rivers in the world are located in Siberia and may provide a source of much future energy. The dam at Bratsk on the Angara River (a tributary of the Yenisei) produces more electric power than any other dam in the world—4½ million kilowatts, compared to 2 million for Hoover Dam. (Bratsk will eventually be surpassed by Grand Coulee Dam in the state of Washington, now being enlarged to a capacity of over 5½ million.)

Often, however, it is cheaper to produce electric power by some other means, such as burning coal or oil. Huge dams like that at Bratsk are perhaps valuable as symbols but not necessarily the most economical source of power. Total Soviet electric power today is about one-third that of the United States.

A favorite slogan of Lenin's that can still be seen today in newspapers and on posters is: "Communism equals Soviet power plus electrification of the whole country!" The present importance attached to the development of electric power is almost as great as it was the year the statement was made (1919). At the time of the revolution, electricity was available only in the cities of Russia. The ordinary peasant regarded it as a wonder of modern science, a promise of the future Communist society. Although most of the country today has electric power, continued Soviet industrial growth depends on the development of new sources.

Peoples of the Soviet Union

One of the most important resources of a country is its people. Reserves of minerals and fuels are valuable only if there is a sufficient number of trained and qualified workers in the population. While the natural wealth of the Soviet Union is distributed throughout the country, the population is largely concentrated in the European section. Over three-fourths of the Soviet people live west of the Urals, the traditional dividing line between Europe and Asia. This is where most of the "fertile triangle" is, the area where soil and climate are most favorable. (See Map 7.)

Americans often assume that most of the 233 million inhabitants of the Soviet Union are Russians. In fact, only 55 per cent of the population is Russian. There are over 200 individual national groups and more than 80 separate languages.

Some of these groups are very small Siberian tribes consisting of only a few thousand people. There are, however, twenty-five nationalities with at least half a million members each. Many of these peoples were incorporated into the Russian empire before or during the nineteenth century, while Russia was expanding into Siberia, Central Asia, and the Caucasus.

The RSFSR

According to the constitution, the Soviet Union is a union of fifteen independent republics (see Map 8). The largest by far is the Russian Soviet Federated Socialist Republic, or the RSFSR. Clustered around it are fourteen national republics, symbolizing Russian expansion before and after the Revolution.

Ukrainians and Belorussians

Of these, the most important is the Ukraine, the "breadbasket" of the USSR. After the Russians, the Ukrainians are the second largest nationality, numbering over thirty seven million people. Their language is similar to Russian, and they are historically connected with both the Russians and the Poles. (Ex-premier Khrushchev was from the Ukraine.) Another closely related group is the Belorussians, who live near the Polish border and number nearly eight million. They are even closer to the Russians in language and culture than the Ukrainians.

Baltic Republics

Before the Second World War, the Soviet Union resumed control over the Baltic nations of Estonia, Latvia, and Lithuania, and incorporated them as separate Soviet Republics. This area on the Baltic Sea had been one of the targets of Russian expansion in the late seventeenth century. The Russian desire for a port on the Baltic was the main reason for a long war with Sweden in the early eighteenth century (see Chapter 4). Except for a brief period of national independence between the two World Wars, Estonia, Lithuania, and Latvia have been continually under Russian rule since the end of the eighteenth century.

The Lithuanians, who comprise nearly two and a half million people, are one of the few Roman Catholic groups in the USSR. The Latvians and Estonians, who number about one and a half million and one million respectively, are predominantly Lutheran. (Almost all church-affiliated Russians belong to the Greek Orthodox Church. For more on

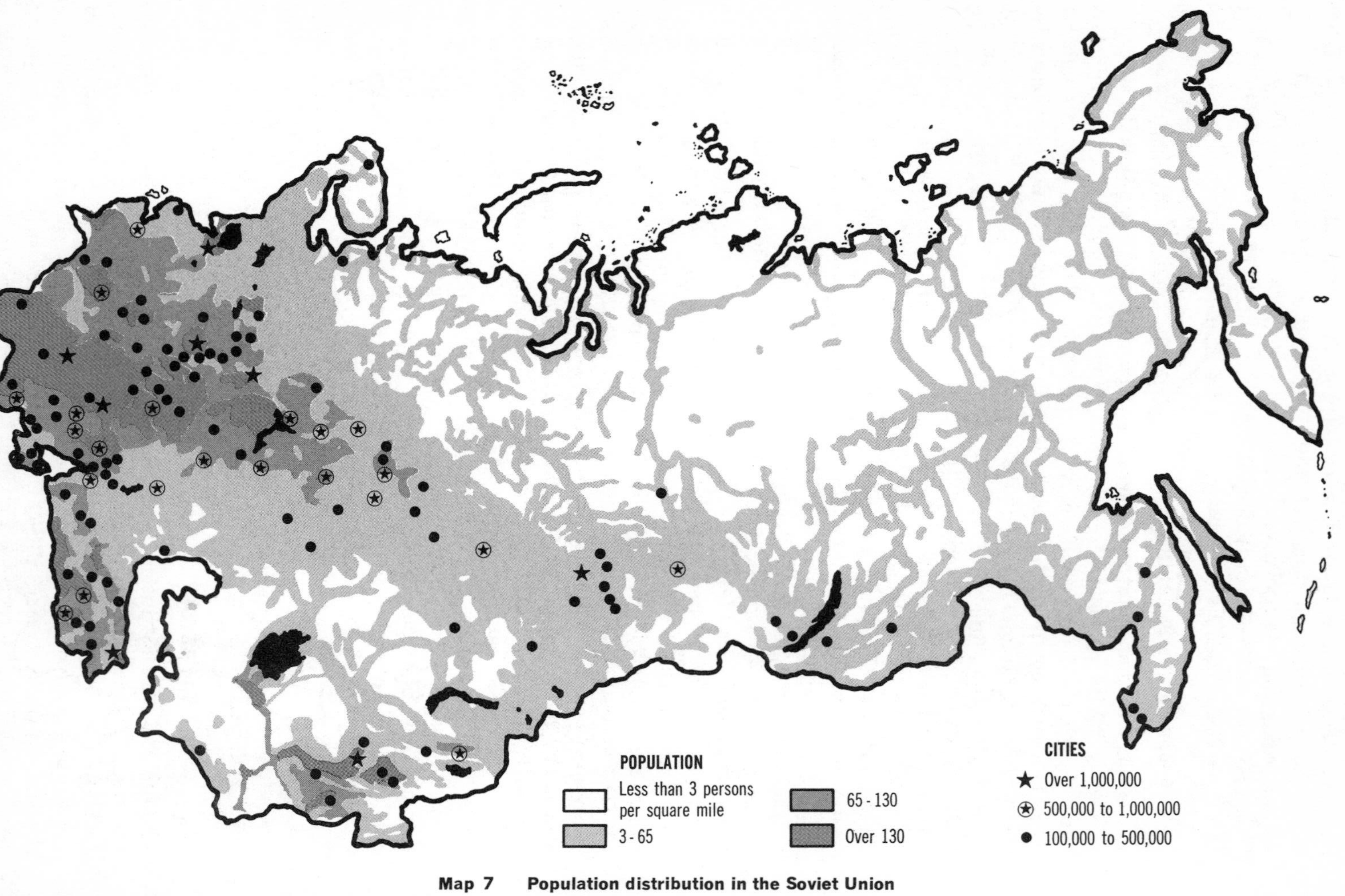

Map 7 Population distribution in the Soviet Union

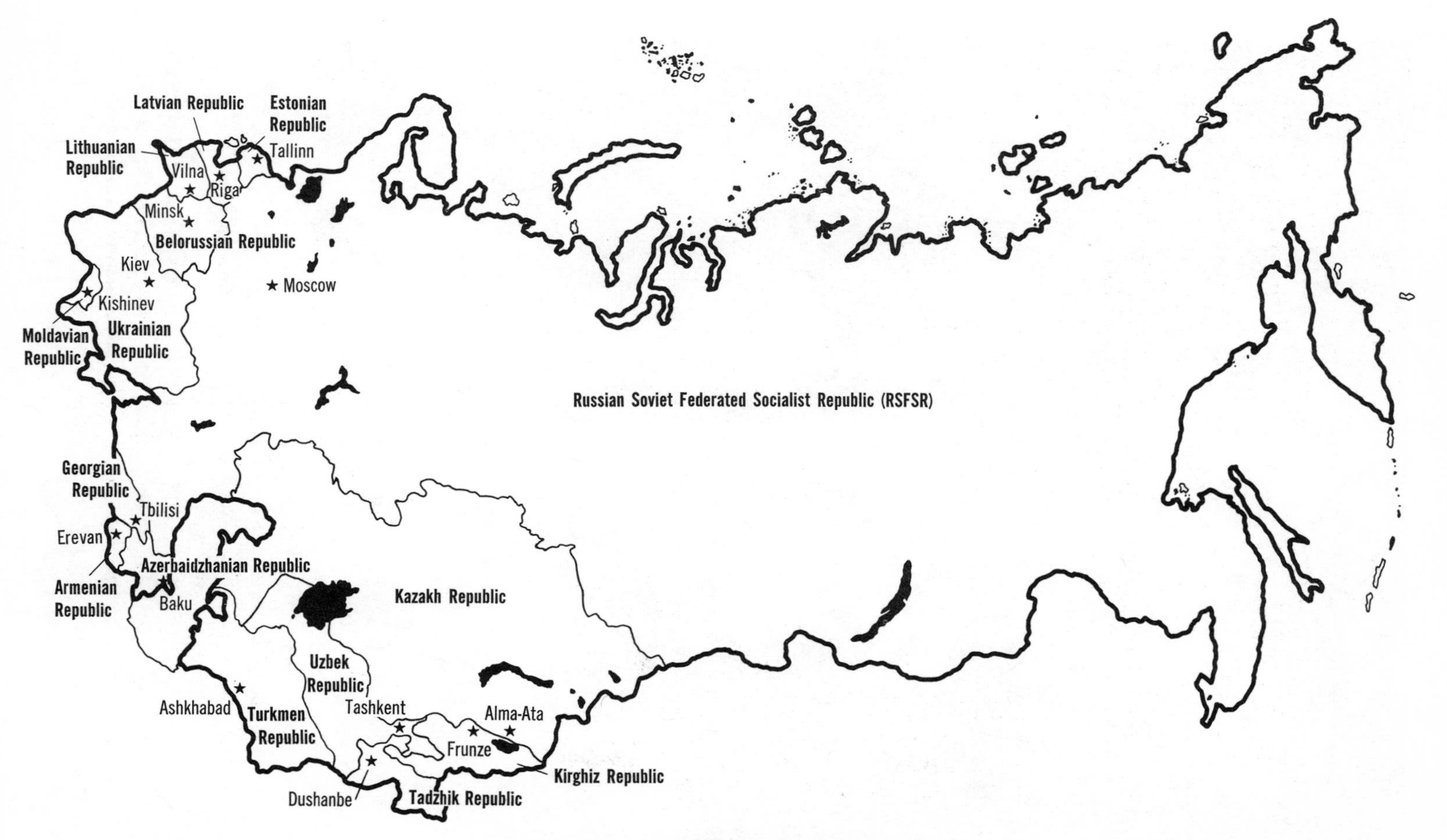

Map 8 The fifteen republics of the Soviet Union

People of the far north of European Russia

Similar to the Lapps of northern Scandinavia, they raise reindeer and hunt and trap for a living. (Courtesy, Sovfoto)

religion, see Chapter 12.) All three peoples have been more closely related to West European culture than the Russians have. Even today the Baltic republics are well-known for their architecture, clothing styles, and the high quality and craftsmanship of their manufactured products. Most Soviet citizens are still unable to travel outside the USSR, so that a trip to the Baltic republics is as close as they can get to Europe, spiritually as well as geographically. The old Baltic cities of Tallin and Riga are especially popular with Soviet youth because of their West European atmosphere.

Turkic Peoples

Within the central area of the RSFSR there are many non-Russian nationalities, including several Turkic ones. The largest group is the Tatars, who number about five million and live around

Kazan. These people are the descendants of the Mongols who conquered Russia in the twelfth century and ruled for nearly two hundred years (see Chapter 4). In the same area live one and a half million Chuvash, a closely-related people who are also of Turkic origin. Another Turkic people is the Bashkirs, who number about one million and live near Ufa. Nearby are the Mordvians, a people related to the Finns with a census of about one and a quarter million. An equal number of Poles are scattered throughout the western part of the Soviet Union.

Georgians, Armenians, Azerbaidjani

The composition of the population becomes even more varied and complex on the southern borders. There are dozens of small races and tribes in the Caucasus Mountains, many living in almost total isolation in mountain villages. The three major groups, each with a separate republic, are the Georgians (Stalin was a Georgian), the Armenians, and the Azerbaidjani. The Azerbaidjani are Moslem, speak a language close to Turkish, and are related to the Persians. They number about three and three-fourths million. There are approximately four million Georgians and one and three-fourths million Armenians.

Both the Georgians and the Armenians have extremely old civilizations (dating from the first centuries A.D.). Each people has its own kind of Christian church, unallied with Protestant,

Camels hauling grain on a state farm in the Uzbek Republic

These beasts of burden are still used in many parts of Central Asia. (Courtesy, Sovfoto)

Roman Catholic, or Greek Orthodox Christianity. Georgia was a powerful state long before Russia even existed. Since both the Armenian and Georgian civilizations are much older than that of Russia, some Armenians and Georgians look down on the Russians. Their sense of cultural superiority is based on a longer tradition.

Uzbeks and Kazakhs

The largest non-European group is the Uzbek, about six million people, living in central Asia. Uzbek culture is also very old, influenced by Persian culture, and highly developed. The Uzbeks were a great power in the twelfth to fourteenth centuries. Under the rule of Tamerlane in the fourteenth century they controlled all of central Asia and southern Russia and attacked India, east Europe, Iran, and Iraq. The Uzbek Republic is now the center of Soviet cotton farming.

The Kazakhs are historically a nomadic people, related to the Mongols. They are excellent horsemen. Today there are about three and a half million Kazakhs, most of them settled and working in agriculture. Of all national groups the Kazakhs were the most violent in their opposition to the Communist policy of collectivization in the 1930's (see Chapter 7). It is estimated that about one million out of a total population of four million were killed while resisting the Communists. In the past two decades, rich natural resources have been discovered in the Kazakh Republic, especially iron ore, chromium, nickel, copper, and lead. The area is changing rapidly as new industry is developed to take advantage of its deposits.

A Turkmen geologist (left) and a Russian topographer

The two are at work on a survey in the desert. (Courtesy, Sovfoto)

Tadjik, Kirghiz, Turkmen

The three smaller Central Asian republics are the Tadjik, Kirghiz, and Turkmen Republics. These areas, sparsely inhabited by Moslem tribes, were absorbed into the Russian empire during the second half of the nineteenth century. In the first few years following the Revolution, there was considerable agitation among the Central Asian peoples and those of the Caucasus for national independence. None of these peoples, however, succeeded in breaking away from Russian control (see Chapter 6). It is interesting to note that the territory of the Soviet Union today is almost exactly that of the old Russian empire.

Soviet War Losses

The population of the Soviet Union would be much greater today if it were not for World War II. It is difficult to comprehend Soviet war losses, they are so overwhelming. Nearly ten million soldiers were killed, plus fifteen million civilians, including women and children. In the city of Leningrad, surrounded by the Germans for two and a half years, almost one million people lost their lives. That number alone is more than the total American dead for the entire war. By including the losses of World War I, the Revolution, and Civil War, Russian war dead in this century have been estimated at fifty million people.

As a result, there are now twenty million fewer men than women in the Soviet Union. Some of the heavy physical work usually performed by men in the United States is thus done by women. They work on construction jobs, drive tractors, and clean streets.

The rural-urban balance of the Soviet population reflects the scope of the changes that have occurred since 1917. At the time of the Revolution, more than 80 per cent of the population lived in the country. Today, nearly 55 per cent lives in towns and cities. The number of industrial workers has risen from three to thirty million. Although the Soviet Union is still a more rural nation than the United States, where over 80 per cent of the people live in towns and cities, the contrast with prerevolutionary Russia is striking.

PROJECTS

A. Research

(1) Find areas in the United States and Canada that have approximately the same annual rainfall, temperature, or vegetation as the major natural regions of the Soviet Union.

(2) Is there an area in the United States similar to the Leningrad-Odessa-Lake Baikal triangle in population and agriculture?

(3) What American river might be compared with the Volga both in length and in importance for the transportation of goods? Compare the two rivers and find out whether the American river is still as important to our commerce as the Volga is to Russian commerce.

(4) Compare relief maps of the United States and the Soviet Union. How do major mountain ranges affect the climate by obstructing the movement of cold or warm air? Are the similarities or the differences between the two countries more significant?

B. Activities

(1) Make a map showing the location of major natural resources in the United States, including Alaska. Are these resources as difficult to exploit as those of the Soviet Union?

(2) Follow the 40th, 50th, and 60th parallels through the United States and the Soviet Union. Make a list of the major cities located near each parallel in both countries.

(3) Stage a friendly argument between a Russian and an Armenian or Georgian about whose culture and civilization are superior. The Russian can obviously point to many recent accomplishments. The Armenian or Georgian, however, can cite cultural achievements dating back centuries before Russia existed.

(4) Debate whether or not a specific non-Russian people (Estonian, Georgian, Uzbek, or the like) is better off under Soviet rule. Take into account economic progress, desire for national independence, and historical factors such as when and how Russian or Soviet rule was established.

C. Further Reading

Cressey, George B., *Soviet Potentials: A Geographic Appraisal* (Syracuse University Press, Syracuse, N.Y.)—An excellent introduction to Soviet geography, with many good photographs and maps.

Fullard, Harold (ed.), *Soviet Union in Maps* (Denoyer-Geppert)—An inexpensive booklet of maps, showing climate and natural resources.

Hooson, David J. M., *A New Soviet Heartland?* (D. Van Nostrand Co., Princeton, N.J.)—A discussion of the recent development of the area from Lake Baikal to the Middle Volga, with several good maps.

Jackson, W. A. Douglas, *Russo-Chinese Borderlands* (D. Van Nostrand, Princeton, N.J.)—A study of the areas in Central Asia and Siberia where Russians and Chinese have come into conflict, today and in the past. Good maps are included.

Kingsbury, R. C., and Taaffe, R. N., *An Atlas of Soviet Affairs* (Praeger, N.Y.).

Miller, Wright, *Russians As People* (Dutton, N.Y.)—Chapter 2, "Hibernation and Awakening," is a graphic description of the Russian winter and early spring.

Rywkin, Michael, *Russia in Central Asia* (Collier Books, N.Y.)—A brief history of Russian expansion into Central Asia.

Chapter 4

RUSSIA BEFORE THE REVOLUTION

Russian history begins in Kiev, not in Moscow. During the fifth century, the Slavic peoples began to move into the western and southern parts of the present day Soviet Union, settling mainly in the forest areas and establishing towns along the major rivers. (The Slavic peoples gradually separated into the following groups that we know today: the Russians, Ukrainians, Belorussians, Poles, Czechs, Slovaks, Bulgarians, Serbs, and Croats.) One of the most important of the early Slavic cities was Kiev, on the Dnieper river.

The Rise and Fall of Kiev

In this early medieval period there was no single Russian nation or state; each large city and the area around it was ruled by a prince and his family. These noble families were constantly at war with each other. Every prince wanted power not only over his own city, but over other cities also. The warring princes united only against some common enemy, such as the many nomadic tribes from Asia which frequently attacked the Slavic peoples. Many of the princes were actually Vikings who had been traveling on Russian rivers for many years, since these rivers formed a major trade route between Scandinavia and the Middle East.

By the ninth century, however, Kiev was generally recognized as the first among Russian cities. The grand prince of Kiev was acknowledged the leader of all Russia. But even he had very little direct control over the areas distant from Kiev. Each prince still ruled his own territory as he wished, although he allowed the grand prince of Kiev to speak for the whole country in foreign relations. The Russian state was really an agglomeration of small states and cities, rather than a unified country, and the territory it covered was still no larger than that of France.

Kiev continued to dominate Russia until the time of the Mongol invasion (1236-1240). During the eleventh century, Kiev was probably the largest city in all Europe, and one of the most magnificent. The population was over

A view of Kiev from a hill overlooking the Dnieper River

100,000, and there were more than 400 churches in the city. Kievan power declined in the next century, however, and the many Russian princes fell to fighting each other again, each one hoping to replace the grand prince of Kiev as the leader of Russia. The entire country was so weakened by these conflicts that it was unable to defend itself successfully against the Mongol invaders.

The Establishment of Greek Orthodoxy

Perhaps the most significant event of the Kievan period was the baptism of Vladimir, prince of Kiev, in 988. Up to this date, the Russians had not had an organized religion. Valdimir sent men from his court to travel around and observe the various religions of the world so that he could choose the most beautiful one for Russia. He decided to choose the Greek Orthodox branch of Christianity.

The Christian Church had begun to split into two separate branches, the Roman Catholic, or Western, and the Greek Orthodox, or Eastern. Rome was the center of the Western Church; Byzantium (later called Constantinople and now called Istanbul) was the center of the Eastern Church. (In 1965, at the Ecumenical Council, Pope Paul announced the beginning of the end of this 900-year split in the Church.)

This decision to accept the Eastern type of Christianity had important consequences. Since most of Europe belonged to the Western Church, Russia sometimes found her relations with other European countries complicated by religious hostilities as well as by political disagreements. One reason for the traditional conflict between Russians and Poles is the fact that Poland was Roman Catholic, Russia, Orthodox.

Consequences of the Mongol Conquest

There was close contact with Europe in the Kievan period. Russian nobility married into the royal families of Europe, especially that of England. Russian achievements in art and architecture were equal to any of early medieval Europe. This valuable contact was broken off by the Mongol conquest, completed in 1240. Kiev was totally destroyed, as were other major cities. Mongol rule was harsh and destructive, but the most tragic consequence was the fact that Russia was isolated from Europe for more than two centuries.

Although Russia did not adopt Mongol customs or become an "Asiatic" country, she was prevented from participating in the great social and cultural changes occurring in Europe at that time and as a consequence was almost totally stagnant for over two hundred years. It is impossible to imagine Western civilization without the Renaissance, the Reformation, the period of exploration, or the discovery of the scientific method. These events and ideas of the fifteenth and sixteenth centuries failed to touch Russia at the time they happened. Their results did not begin to reach her until the seventeenth century and later. Russia thus had to spend the next centuries trying to catch up with the West, especially in science and technology. More important, some modern Western political and social ideas, such as individualism and democracy, never did develop there as strongly as they did in other European countries.

The Rise of Moscow

With Kiev destroyed, the center of Russian history moved to the north. The first mention of Moscow is in 1147 (almost 350 years before Columbus). At that time a tiny trading village on the Moscow river, it grew rapidly as a center of trade under the Mongols. Toward the end of the Mongol occupation, Moscow began to assert control over some of the other nearby Russian cities. The prince of Moscow gradually assumed a position of power and influence

View of the Kremlin showing the Moscow River in the foreground
Originally the walls enclosed and protected the early town of Moscow.

St. Basil's cathedral in Red Square

The cathedral was built by Ivan the Terrible to celebrate the defeat of the Mongols at Kazan. According to legend, Ivan had the eyes of the chief architect put out so that he could not build another church as beautiful as this one.

similar to that of the Kiev princes in earlier centuries. (Although the Mongols occupied Russia with troops and collected heavy tribute, they never bothered to govern Russian internal affairs directly. As long as the Russians paid their levies, they were permitted to rule themselves.)

Gradually the other Russian princes were forced to submit to the authority of the Moscow prince. Some were defeated in battle, some were won over by promises, and some simply wanted the protection that Moscow could offer. One by one the old Russian cities of Vladimir, Suzdal, Pskov, Novgorod, and Ryazan all gave in to Moscow.

Under Muscovite leadership, the combined Russian forces became stronger than the Mongols, who had fallen to fighting among themselves. The Mongol rule was finally broken in 1480, although for the next hundred years small bands of Mongols lived on the eastern and southern borders of Russia, occasionally destroying towns and villages.

The sixteenth century witnessed the complete triumph of the prince of Moscow as the ruler of all of Russia, and the beginning of absolute autocracy. Ivan IV, usually called Ivan the Terrible, was the first ruler to take the title of Tsar. (This title, also spelled Czar, comes from the Latin *Caesar*. Its German form is *Kaiser*.) The cruelty of Ivan, who reigned from 1547 to 1584, is famous. He concentrated all power in his own hands and tortured and killed those nobles who opposed him. He seized their lands and gave them to those who were loyal to him. By the end of his rule, about one-half of the Russian land actually belonged to the Tsar.

Peter the Great

Ivan IV and his successors became increasingly disturbed by Russia's backwardness in comparison to Europe as the awareness grew of how much had happened in Europe during the past four centuries. It was Peter the Great (1694-1725) who finally forced Russia to break away from her stagnant past and to strive to become a part of Europe again. This was too immense a task to be accomplished in the lifetime of one man, but Peter attempted to hurry his country along as fast as possible.

Peter was physically huge (nearly seven feet tall) and his energy and ambition for Russia were also gigantic. He influenced every aspect of Russian life, being determined that Russia should become a modern European power during his reign. Many of his subjects resisted his policies, but he treated opponents as cruelly as Ivan the Terrible had and tolerated no interference with the completion of his projects.

As a boy, Peter lived an unusual life

Peter the Great talking with Dutch shipbuilders on his trip to Holland
(Courtesy, The Bettmann Archive)

for a member of the royal family. He spent most of his time playing in the "German suburb" of Moscow with the children of merchants and craftsmen from other countries who were living in the capital. (Since many of these foreigners were from Germany and Holland, the word "German" in the Russian language came to mean *any* foreigner.) Peter was fascinated by tools and mechanical devices and is said to have learned fifteen crafts, including carpentry, ship-building, engineering, printing, and navigation. Not surprisingly, his earliest teachers were the foreigners in Moscow.

Peter's Wars of Conquest

Peter's greatest interest, however, was in the military. He was particularly determined to make Russia a full European power, respected by all other nations. During his rule, Russia was almost constantly at war, attempting to expand first in one direction, then in another (see Map 9).

Peter's principal foes were Turkey in the south and Sweden in the north. In both instances, Peter hoped to reach the sea (the Black Sea and the Baltic Sea) and thus establish Russia as a world power.

The early defeats Peter suffered at the hands of the Turks made him realize the necessity of a navy. In 1697, he sent a group of Russian craftsmen and technicians to Holland and England to learn how to build and navigate ships. He went along, disguised as a carpenter. This was the first time that any Russian ruler had left the country. Peter himself worked in the shipyards of Amsterdam and London, learning as much as he could about ship-building. He also negotiated with the king of England to buy weapons and equipment.

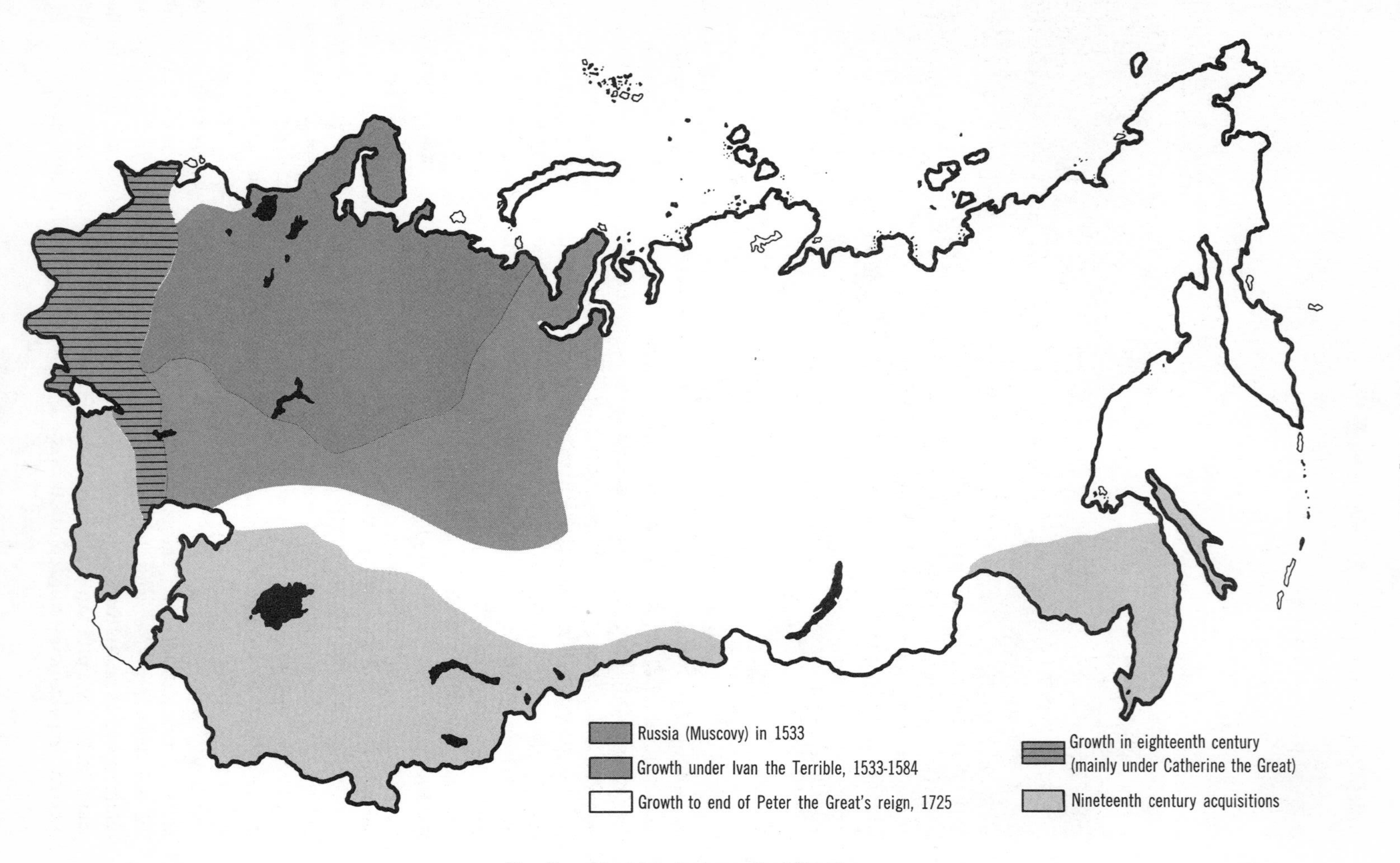

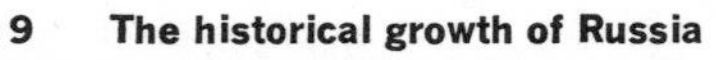

Map 9 The historical growth of Russia

Peter was tremendously impressed by Western technology, and he brought back to Russia hundreds of Dutch and English carpenters, engineers, shipbuilders, navigators, and military advisors. Within a few years the first Russian navy had been constructed and Russia entered into a twenty-one year war with Sweden.

The "Great Northern War" (1700-1721) exhausted Russia, but it achieved one of its main purposes: Russian control over a large part of the Baltic seacoast, including several ports. The defeat of Sweden also brought Russia a great deal of prestige. Sweden was one of the major European powers, whereas Russia was considered a distant and barbaric offspring of Asia. By defeating the Swedes, Russia gained recognition as one of the principle European nations.

Monument to Peter, the founder of St. Petersburg, on the banks of the Neva River

It has been famous in Russian literature since Pushkin's long poem, "The Bronze Horseman."

First Attempts at "Europeanization"

Peter realized that many changes were necessary if Russia was to become a truly modern country. One of the most important of these concerned the typical Russian attitude toward foreign ideas, especially toward technological innovations. Because of their isolation, many Russians viewed anything alien with suspicion and zealously preserved Russian traditions and dress, refusing to believe that any other way could be better.

Upon his return from Europe, Peter forced all government officials and the nobles to shave their long beards and put on modern European dress. Anyone keeping the traditional dress or beard had to pay a tax. This was only a symbol of Peter's efforts to "Europeanize" his subjects. He also sent the sons of many nobles and officials to Europe to study technology and military affairs.

Most important of all, Peter moved the capital from Moscow to the marshy shores of the Baltic. There he built a new capital he named St. Petersburg. Since the area was mainly swampland and previously uninhabited, the decision to build a great city there was both daring and costly. Many thousands of Russian peasants died from disease, hunger, and exhaustion while working on its construction. But the result was a magnificent capital, thoroughly European in architecture, which became known as Russia's "window to the West."

Organization of the State

Peter had very definite ideas about the organization of the state. Basic to his thinking was the idea of obligatory service to the state for everyone, from noble to peasant. Nobles were obliged to serve in government offices or as military officers; craftsmen and merchants were expected to contribute their skills and tax monies; peasants had to serve in the army. Under Peter, military service was extended to twenty-five years, a period which few survived.

Peter taxed the nobles heavily, and in order to meet these obligations, it was necessary for them to have sufficient labor to work on their estates. Before Peter's reign most of the peasants had already lost their freedom to move and were living in a state of serfdom. They were bound to the land, to the estate on which they were born, and were bought and sold with the estate. During Peter's reign the condition of the peasantry worsened, and they became virtual slaves. Their owners could sell them whenever they wished, and there were no restrictions on the way serfs were treated. A serf was just another piece of property.

Serfs worked not only on the land but also in the factories that were established at this time. Peter was the first Tsar to develop the rich mineral resources of the Ural mountains. Foreign engineers and technicians were brought to Russia to aid in establishing factories. A system of "industrial serfdom" was allowed to grow up. A landlord who went into industry could force his serfs to work in his factory for very little or no pay. Both agricultural and industrial serfs lived in dismal poverty and ignorance. It is interesting to note that serfdom had practically disappeared from Europe by this time, while it was still expanding in Russia.

Peter did succeed, however, in making Russia into an important industrial power, at least temporarily. By 1725, the year of his death, Russia was producing more pig iron than England. For the next two decades, Russia led all of Europe, and the world, in iron production.

Peter's Legacy

Many of Peter's accomplishments were impressive, especially in the areas of industrialization and military expansion. Some of his plans were too ambitious, however, and he created new problems for the future. The most serious was that of serfdom. Almost constantly at war, forced to pay heavy taxes and to work on such enormous projects as the construction of St. Petersburg, the Russian people were literally exhausted by the end of Peter's reign.

Not until the twentieth century and the accession of Stalin did Russia again have such an ambitious and demanding ruler. It is interesting to note that Stalin too was trying to force Russia to "catch up" with the West.

The question of the abolition of serfdom occupied Russian society for the next one hundred and forty years. The injustice and brutality of the system were becoming apparent to almost everyone. There were frequent proposals for reform and emancipation, but definite action was always delayed. Peasant unrest increased as living conditions grew more intolerable. Local serf revolts were a common phenomenon in the eighteenth and nineteenth centuries.

Catherine the Great

Ironically, serfdom reached a new peak of cruelty about the time of the American Revolution, during the reign of Catherine the Great (1762 to 1796). The irony lies in the fact that Catherine was looked upon as an enlightened ruler who would surely carry out the plans for emancipation. In 1766 she set up a Legislative Commission, consisting of several hundred Russian officials, to draw up new laws. Her instructions to the commission were very liberal, and there was great hope for wide reforms. But Catherine never followed any of the commission's suggestions, and no new laws were passed.

Catherine was impressed by the contemporary writers and philosophers of France. She corresponded with some of them and liked to use their liberal expressions in her speeches and writings. She was fond of words, but her policies were rarely influenced by them. The situation of the serfs steadily worsened. Landlords were not prevented in any way from punishing and mistreating their serfs. If a peasant was disobedient, the landlord had the right to exile him to Siberia. Under a law passed in 1767, a serf was forbidden to complain about a landlord's cruelty and was severely punished if he did.

The Pugachev Revolt

The Pugachev revolt of 1773 and 1774 was one of the largest and bloodiest of peasant revolts and should have been sufficient warning to the country's rulers. Emilian Pugachev, a Don Cossack, gathered together a band of Cossacks, Tatars, runaway serfs, industrial serfs, and religious heretics and moved along the lower Volga River. (The Cossacks were horsemen who lived in the south of Russia, on the steppes or plains. They were excellent fighters and were used by the government to repel attacks from Asiatic tribes. A Don Cossack was a Cossack from the region of the Don River.) This band grew to twenty-five thousand men, who burned and sacked many towns and large estates. There was no definite plan or goal for this rebellion. It was merely a violent attempt to repay some of the injustices of the past.

Pugachev's followers were eventually defeated by the regular Russian army but only after causing great damage. For many years after this unsuccessful revolt the landlords, with Catherine's blessing and support from the army, carried out a terrible revenge. Punishments were heavier than ever, executions were frequent, and often whole peasant villages were destroyed by vengeful landlords. One of the best stories by Alexander Pushkin, a great Russian poet and writer of the nineteenth century, concerns the Pugachev revolt. The title is "The Captain's Daughter."

Catherine's Conquests

Catherine was even more successful than Peter had been in gaining new territory for Russia. Her two major opponents were Turkey and Poland. Russian victories over Turkey gained the Crimea, the north shore of the Black Sea, and new parts of the steppe area of southern Russia. The Black Sea ports became extremely important in the next century for Russia's foreign trade.

Russia also expanded to the west, attacking Poland. Poland had been in a decline throughout the eighteenth century and actually disappeared as an independent nation as a result of the Polish Partitions of 1772, 1793, and 1795. In three stages, Russia, Austria, and Prussia simply divided Poland among themselves and incorporated her territory into their respective countries.

The French Revolution in 1789—in which the people rose up and overthrew the monarchy to set up a representative government—frightened Catherine because it raised the possibility of a similar revolution in Russia. Certainly there was sufficient unrest and discontent, as the Pugachev revolt had proved. As a countermeasure, Catherine decided against reform in favor of still stricter control and repression. When a young writer named Radishchev published a book in 1790 that realistically described the poverty of the Russian serfs, he was sentenced to death (a sentence that was later changed to permanent exile).

Critical newspapers and magazines were compelled to stop printing. Catherine began the system of censorship that developed to extraordinary extremes in the nineteenth century.

The Reign of Alexander I

Alexander I (1801 to 1825) is often called the "enigmatic Tsar" or the "Sphinx." His reign is marked by a paradoxical mixture of liberal and reactionary policies. Like Catherine, he also never fulfilled the hopes of many Russians who expected him to find a solution to the problem of serfdom.

The first few years of his rule were full of encouraging signs. Alexander talked of emancipation and of constitutional government. He even directed his ministers to draw up plans for a constitution. He relaxed the censorship controls, curbed the secret police, and allowed students to travel to Europe again. Most of these measures, however, were temporary, and Alexander soon reverted to more repressive policies. He carried out a purge of the universities, removing all students and professors suspected of being revolutionary or even liberal. Religious study was emphasized at the expense of history and philosophy.

One of Alexander's most destructive innovations was the establishment of "military colonies," or self-supporting units of farmer-soldiers. All peasants living near military outposts were forced to join them. The peasants continued to farm, providing food for the whole group, but they also participated in military training. Since the peasants had no escape from them—in fact, their service became hereditary—the colonies were essentially just another cruel variation of serfdom. Almost three quarters of a million Russian peasants were forced into this form of existence.

In 1812, the French, under Napoleon, invaded Russia. With a better trained and equipped army than the Russians could muster, Napoleon confidently marched all the way to Moscow. The outclassed Russians used their traditional tactic (to be used again against Hitler), of retreating into the vast spaces of their country. The harsh Russian winter caught Napoleon unprepared, and he lost a good part of his army.

Russia and her allies eventually defeated Napoleon, and Tsar Alexander I rode into Paris at the head of the victorious troops. Russian prestige rose to its highest level. (The defeat of Napoleon is described in many Russian works of art. Tchaikovsky's "1812 Overture" and Tolstoy's novel, *War and Peace,* are the best known.)

Russia also played an active role at the Congress of Vienna, which followed in 1815. Alexander proposed a "Holy Alliance" of great powers for the purpose of maintaining peace in Europe. This alliance, entered into by Russia, Austria, and Prussia, was originally both religious and political in character. Later it became an alliance of conservative nations against the increasing dangers of representative government, democracy, and revolution.

A Cautious Attempt at Revolution

The first vague plans for revolution in Russia began to form during Alexander's reign. Several small secret societies grew up; their members were generally the sons of rich nobles. Many were young army officers, interested also in poetry and literature. Their literary discussions gradually turned to political subjects, and their major concerns were the abolition of serfdom and the possibility of constitutional government for Russia.

The Peter-Paul Fortress on the Neva River in St. Petersburg
Inside the walls are army barracks, a church with a tall golden spire, and a famous prison where many Russian writers and revolutionaries were kept.

Paul Pestel, the son of a high government official, was one of the most extreme of the young officers. He felt that reforms were not enough and that revolution was necessary. The program he proposed included the execution of the Tsar, the liberation of the serfs, and the establishment of a representative government. Many of his fellow conspirators did not entirely share these views, and they were never able to agree on a definite program of action.

The death of Alexander in November, 1825, and the three-week crisis over which of the Tsar's two brothers would succeed him, gave the young officers an unexpected chance for action. Unfortunately, they had made only the vaguest of plans, and they were scattered around the country at the time. No definite steps were ever decided upon, but the officers in St. Petersburg agreed they had to do something. Several of them led about three thousand soldiers in a demonstration before the Winter Palace on the fourteenth of December. Nicholas, who had just assumed the throne, ordered the loyal troops to fire, killing several hundred rebelling soldiers and curious civilian bystanders. The demonstrators were quickly dispersed, and the so-called "Decembrist Revolt" was over. The leaders were rounded up, and many were exiled to Siberia. A few, including Pestel, were executed. Although they failed to accomplish anything, the Decembrists became martyrs, the first national heroes in the revolutionary struggle against the autocracy. For nearly a century they served as inspiration and example for the idealistic and revolutionary youth of Russia.

Nicholas, obviously frightened, responded in two ways to the Decembrist Revolt. On the one hand, he proceeded to increase the powers of the police and the censor. No ruler since Peter had been so authoritarian. On the other hand, he realized that the revolt was caused by the unjust and intolerable conditions in which most Russians lived. Specifically, he understood that unless something was done about serfdom, more revolts and unrest were inevitable.

The Growing Demand for Change

Nicholas was unable to find a policy that would solve Russia's problems. He hesitated to act on behalf of the serfs for fear that any change would encourage revolution. In the end his only answer was to suppress all rebellious talk and literature, hoping to keep control while waiting for conditions to improve. He realized his own dilemma and spoke of it in these terms:

> "There is no doubt that serfdom, in its present form, is a flagrant evil which everyone realizes, yet to attempt to remedy it now would be, of course, an evil even more disastrous."

Most of the nobles also recognized that serfdom was an evil which must be abolished, but they did not want to take action. They hoped somehow to solve the problem without losing anything, without giving up any of their wealth, land, or privileges. That this was impossible they knew, but still they did not act. They refused to admit that a social revolution was approaching and that the time for painless reforms was past.

The question of serfdom obsessed the writers and intellectuals of the 1840's and 1850's. The literary critic Dobroliubov put it this way: "We are seeking, thirsting, waiting. We are waiting for somebody or other to explain to us what to do." A famous novel by Chernyshevshy was titled *What Is To Be Done?* Nekrassov wrote a book of poetry under the title, *Who Is Happy In Russia?*

By this time, the emancipation of the serfs was closely connected in most people's minds with the overthrow of autocracy. New social and political ideas had been coming into Russia from Europe. The ideas of constitutional government, representative government, democracy, socialism, and communism were discussed and debated by students and intellectuals all over Russia. Small groups and circles met and discussed political and philosophic questions, arguing about the best course of action to take.

Under Nicholas any public discussion of such matters was illegal; the press, of course, was forbidden to write about them. Many famous writers, including Dostoevsky, were arrested for participating in discussion groups and were exiled to Siberia. Dostoevsky's *House of the Dead* tells of conditions in a prison camp there. Many writers became very clever at deceiving the official censors. One radical published a book about European socialist trends by disguising it as *A Dictionary of Foreign Words Used in Russia.*

The Reforms of Alexander II

When Alexander II became Tsar in 1855 it seemed that at last emancipation was near. He indicated almost immediately that the serfs would soon be liberated; the only question was how. He said, "It is better to abolish serfdom from above than to wait until the serfs begin to liberate themselves from below."

Alexander was liberal at first, and allowed quite free public discussion of the question of how to free the serfs. The basic issue was whether or not to give them land, and if so, whose land. The more liberal and radical people argued that to free the serf without land would only increase his misery. The landowning nobles agreed to give the serfs their freedom but were naturally opposed to giving up any part of their estates.

Emancipation was finally carried out in 1861. The serfs got their freedom and also some land, which they had to pay for over a number of years. In the northern regions, the serfs were given considerable land (it was poor land anyway) but were saddled with redemption payments that exceeded the value of the property. The income of many northern landlords had depended on the labor of their serfs in factories or handicraft industries rather than on the soil.

In the south, where the land was more fertile, the peasants were given only very small plots, for which, again, they had to pay more than the actual value. In many areas the free peasant ended up with less land than he had been allowed as a serf. In 1877, the total land area available to serfs was five per cent less than in 1860, despite the great rise in peasant population.

The farce of such an "emancipation" became apparent in less than a year. The unrealistically high redemption payments meant that the peasants were doomed to be in debt for twenty or thirty years. The amount of land supplied for their use was inadequate. Many peasants were forced to continue working for their former masters for very meager wages.

Alexander carried out a number of other reforms, which soon proved equally illusory. In 1864 he established local organs of government, called zemstvos. The members of the zemstvo were elected, indirectly, by the nobles, the townspeople, and the peasants. The authority of the zemstvo was not very broad, however, and in the following years it was continually narrowed. The zemstvo was intended to take care of public health, prisons, and local schools; often it did succeed in making important improvements in the standard of local health and education. The chairman, however, was appointed, not elected. The government was determined that the zemstvos should not become effective organs of opposition.

The disillusionment with Alexander's reforms grew steadily from 1861 on, and criticism in the press and journals became quite sharp. By 1866, Alexander had reimposed censorship, closed several journals, activated the secret police, and sent many young intellectuals into Siberian exile. As Alexander became more reactionary, the liberals and radicals became more bitter. Secret revolutionary groups were formed to carry out acts of terror. In 1866, a student attempted to shoot the Tsar. During the next two decades many attempts were made on his life. Assassination of government and police officials became a common form of political action.

Populism

Very few intellectuals still believed that a solution to Russia's problems would come from the Tsar. Most were convinced by now that revolution was the only way. They disagreed, however, on tactics. Most of the revolutionaries of the 1860's and 1870's were called "Populists" (or in Russian, *Narodniki*). They shared a belief in the Russian peasant as the hope of the future. The peasant was to carry out the revolution, and the traditional peasant commune was to be the basis for the future society. (The present-day collectives and state farms are theoretically rooted in this tradition. See Chapter 10.)

The peasant commune dates to the sixteenth century, but its exact origins are unknown. By tradition, the peasants did not own land privately, but in common. A village owned a certain amount of land that was distributed equally among all its families, according to their size. To make sure that no family gained more than its share of land over the years, the land was redistributed at definite intervals, for example, every five or ten years.

Although the Populists agreed that the commune was to be the basic feature of Russian society after the revolution, they split increasingly over the

Assassination of Alexander II

The Tsar was killed by a terrorist bomb while riding in his carriage in St. Petersburg, 1881. A church, "The Church on the Blood," was built on the spot. (Courtesy, The Bettmann Archive)

question of tactics. The major disagreement concerned the emphasis placed on terror and on educational propaganda. Neither tactic produced much in the way of results. Dozens of police and government officials were killed during the 1870's. The only consequence was more severe police repression and heavier punishments. The autocratic government of the Tsar remained unchanged.

Education and propaganda were equally futile. In 1873-74, hundreds of idealistic young students and nobles went to the countryside in a movement known as "going to the people." They tried to talk to the peasants, to teach them, and to preach ideas of socialism and revolution. The peasants did not understand these theories, however; they had always been suspicious of "city folk." They reacted with hostility and sometimes even turned the students over to the police.

The main Populist group, "Land and Liberty," finally split into two separate groups, the "Peoples' Will" and the "Black Partition." The members of the former group, still convinced that terror was the only solution, succeeded in killing Tsar Alexander II with a bomb in 1881. No real victory was gained by this act. Alexander III took power immediately and crushed the revolutionaries. Most members of the "Peoples' Will" were arrested and either executed or exiled. The assassination of the Tsar had proven meaningless; everything was just as it had been.

The Turn Toward Marx

Some of the members of the "Black Partition" emigrated to Europe after

1881. They were disillusioned with terrorist methods and also disappointed with the peasants as a potential revolutionary force. The peasants would rise up in revolt to destroy the estates of their landlords, as the example of Pugachev proved, but it was harder to organize them to prepare for a complete revolution. A few former Populist leaders, such as Plekhanov and Axelrod, began to study the writings of Karl Marx and shifted their attention to the industrial workers. Despite the fact that 90 per cent of all Russians were peasants, they began to put their faith in the urban working class as the core of the future revolution.

In 1883, while living in Switzerland, a handful of Russian emigrés, led by Plekhanov, formed the "Society for the Liberation of Labor," the first Russian Marxist group. The Communist Party that eventually took power in 1917 after the overthrow of the Tsar developed from this small and insignificant group. Its evolution, which took place partially under the leadership of Lenin, will be traced in detail in the following chapter.

Conditions at the Century's End

The reactionary Alexander III was followed by the equally severe and repressive Nicholas II in 1894. Many students and intellectuals who opposed him were sent to prison or into Siberian exile. Others went abroad to France, England, or Switzerland. Labor unions were not allowed to function as they had in England and the rest of Europe during the nineteenth century. They existed in

The summer palace of the Tsars, near St. Petersburg on the Gulf of Finland

Partially destroyed in World War II, this palace and its gardens have been restored and opened as a public park.

secret or were very strictly controlled by the government, which reserved its support for the most reactionary of the factory owners and rich landlords. There was also official support for the frequent *pogroms* of these years, the mob attacks on Russian Jews. Jews were harshly restricted as to where they could live, what work they could do, and the education they could have.

Industrial working conditions were similar to those in England 50 or 75 years earlier—long hours, poor pay, child labor, little or no protection against injury, and the like. A few basic laws had been passed, such as an 11½ hour work day, but they were inadequately enforced. The workers had little choice but to organize strikes and demonstrations, although they were illegal. An economic depression in 1899-1903 worsened their situation. Despite the efforts of the police and some large factory owners who had their own police forces for quelling riots, revolutionary propaganda was widely distributed and strikes became more and more frequent in the larger cities.

At this same time Russia got involved in a war with Japan by attempting to expand into Manchuria and Korea (1904-1905). This war, in which Russia was badly defeated, required great sacrifices from the people and caused widespread suffering, hunger, deprivation, and peasant unrest. There were an alarming number of local peasant revolts in which many estates were burned and their owners killed. Revolutionary agitation increased among the workers and the peasants. Frequent appeals were made to the Tsar to establish some fundamental constitution for the country and to permit the beginnings of representative government. But the Tsar and his advisors feared even the slightest reforms.

Rehearsal for Revolution

The revolution of 1905 was not a single event, but rather the sum of all the disturbances during that year. It began with a demonstration on what has since been known as "Bloody Sunday." The demonstration started peacefully on a Sunday in January 1905 as a march to the Winter Palace of the Tsar, in St. Petersburg, to present him with a petition. Leading the march was a priest, Father Gapon.

Father Gapon was not a revolutionary; in fact, he was working for the government. It was common practice for the Tsarist government to have one of its agents act as a union organizer. In this way the Tsar hoped to keep control of the workers and to direct their energies into safe channels. Such union leaders as Father Gapon were supposed to interest the workers in questions of wages and working conditions but to keep their claims moderate and prevent them from making political demands. It was a fairly clever attempt to divert the workers' attention from revolution but never too successful because of the government's refusal to grant even the most reasonable economic demands.

The purpose of this demonstration organized by Father Gapon is unclear. It seems that he had come to the conclusion that the government officials were responsible for the terrible poverty of the workers, and that if only the Tsar himself knew the truth, he would take action. A moderate and respectful petition was drawn up, and precautions were taken to ensure that no violence occurred on the march. A total of 200,000 unarmed workers, women, and children marched on the Palace from all parts of the city.

In the vast square in front of the palace, the quiet crowd was met by

One of the halls of the Winter Palace of the Tsars in St. Petersburg
(Courtesy, The Bettmann Archive)

army troops, not by the Tsar. For some unknown reason, perhaps panic, the troops opened fire on the crowd, killing and wounding hundreds. (Estimates range from 150 to 500 killed and from 200 to 3,000 wounded.) This bloody end to a peaceful protest destroyed the last hope that a solution for Russia's woes would come from the Tsar. Most intellectuals had given up this hope long before. Now the peasant and worker masses also lost faith in their ruler, their "little father" as he had been traditionally called.

Throughout 1905 there were strikes and demonstrations in all major cities, peasant uprisings in many areas, and rebellions among some military units. One famous revolt was that of the crew of the *Potemkin,* a battleship of the Black Sea fleet. (Sergei Eisenstein, the greatest Russian movie director, made a notable film about the incident, titled, simply, *Potemkin.*)

Russians of various political persuasions—liberals, moderates, even conservatives—urged the Tsar to take some steps toward representative government. He replied by offering to create a consultative assembly, one which he would consult but which would have no power of its own to make or enforce laws. As no one was satisfied with so little, the demonstrations continued. A railroad strike in October stopped all transportation, and a general strike in St. Petersburg virtually paralyzed the capital.

The Creation of the Duma

The Tsar was finally forced to make some concessions, which he announced in the "October Manifesto." The manifesto gave Russia a constitution, or at least the outward form of one. It provided for a Western-style Council of Ministers and a legislative body, the *Duma,* elected indirectly by all the people (from the Russian verb, *dumat',* "to think").

The Tsar also cancelled all redemption payments owed by the peasants for their land. Most peasants had still not succeeded in paying off the debts that had plagued them from the time of emancipation.

The October Manifesto divided the revolutionary movement. The moderates were satisfied; it marked a beginning and showed that progress was possible. The radicals feared that the Tsar was insincere and still did not intend to give up real power. They accused him of trying to deceive the people and demanded more fundamental changes. General strikes were called again in St. Petersburg and in Moscow, but this time they were crushed. In Moscow the fighting between army troops and workers lasted more than two weeks, with over one thousand workers killed before the government finally regained control.

The fears of the radicals quickly proved correct. The Tsar had acted only under threat of violence. He had no desire to see power slip from his hands. The elections to the Duma were held, and the representatives were, in fact, from all sections of Russian society, from reactionary nobles to liberals and socialists. It was apparent immediately, however, that the Duma was meant to be only a debate club, "full of sound and fury, signifying nothing." The Duma had no power to appoint or to remove Ministers or to decide any financial questions. Its proposals to the Tsar could be adopted or vetoed by him at his whim.

Many of the Duma speeches were indeed furious, criticizing the government bitterly and demanding more of a voice in public affairs. Almost from the first day the Duma met, in May 1906, the members were defiant and the Tsar began to talk of dissolving it. Many representatives were particularly critical of the measures taken by the government in the wake of the 1905 revolution. The police were more active and brutal than before. Courts were given the power to try, sentence, and execute political prisoners in a single day. Some rich nobles and priests (with government support) organized gangs of toughs, called "black hundreds." These gangs carried out "vigilante" attacks and reprisals against workers, intellectuals, liberals, and anyone suspected of being a revolutionary.

Second and Third Dumas

Cooperation between the Duma and the Tsar was obviously impossible. Within two months the Tsar dissolved the Duma and called for new elections. The composition of the second Duma was even more radical that that of the first, and the members more critical. This Duma lasted only a few weeks before it was also dissolved. New elections were called again, but this time the procedures were revised by the Tsar to give less voting power to the workers and peasants and more to the nobility.

The third Duma was quite conservative and served its full time. There was considerable cooperation between government and Duma, and this period saw some improvements of conditions in Russia. Domestic policy was based largely on the ideas of Peter Stolypin,

A nineteenth-century photograph of Russian peasants
(Courtesy, The Bettmann Archive)

Minister of the Interior and later Prime Minister. Stolypin tried to encourage the peasants to leave the traditional peasant commune and become private farmers. Laws were passed to help peasants withdraw from the commune and set up individual farms. The hope behind this policy was to create a class of rich and middle-income peasants who would support the government. This conservative class would be an ally in the struggle of the government with the poorer and more revolutionary peasants and workers.

This was a shrewd policy and might even have succeeded if more time had been available. By 1915, seven million peasants possessed their own farms, and a definite rural middle class was forming. But the majority of peasants still lived in poverty; there was not enough land for the constantly growing population. And even if the government had been able to solve the peasant question, there were many other problems which presented themselves. The situation of the industrial workers had not improved, political freedom was still limited, and Russia's international position was weak and rapidly declining. Nicholas II was not an able or even an adequate leader. He would have failed regardless of how much time he had been given.

The Failure of Autocracy

The nine year period between the October Manifesto and the start of the First World War represented a "last chance" for the Russian autocracy, a final opportunity for successful reform before the revolution. The opportunity was missed, however, just as the opportunity presented by the emancipation of the serfs in 1861 had been missed. If the serfs had been freed on more

A view of modern Leningrad (formerly St. Petersburg)
This beautiful city is criss-crossed by many canals as well as the Neva River.

generous terms, with sufficient land and lower redemption payments, the last part of the nineteenth century might have been very different. But emancipation had been half-hearted, and as a result, Russia's economic, social, and political problems grew until they reached the point of explosion.

It is interesting to speculate whether or not a revolution could have been avoided if the First World War had not broken out in 1914. If Russia had been given another twenty years of peace, could enough progress have been made to forestall revolution? No one can answer the question, but raising it may help to understand the period 1906 to 1914.

In many ways, Russian society seemed to be moving toward a more moderate, European pattern. The Russian economy was expanding faster than any other in Europe, and Russia was beginning to catch up with the industrial West. Old peasant traditions were beginning to break down. Private ownership of land and efficient methods of farming were spreading. Education was becoming more universal; in 1914, almost half of all Russian children were in school, a total of eight million. Representative government of an extremely limited nature was emerging. In continued peacetime it is possible that some degree of real power might have eventually passed to the Duma. With rising prosperity and economic growth, the workers might have been content with gradual improvements in the standard of living. The appeal of political and social revolution might have faded, as it did in Europe and the United States.

With all of these trends, revolution might have been avoided if the Tsar had followed an intelligent policy of compromise. But this never happened. Nicholas never gave serious consideration to the idea that he share government power with popularly elected representatives. He refused to allow changes that would have gained him more popular support. Instead, his obstinancy and lack of sensitivity drove almost all sections of Russian society into opposition. He actually had no policy except that of holding on to power as long as possible.

If Nicholas had allowed genuine labor unions to function freely, the workers might have become more moderate. As it turned out, they were almost forced to revolt as the only way to express their discontent and misery. The inheritance of centuries of serfdom, poverty, ignorance, and corruption presented extremely difficult problems. A strong and talented Tsar might have known how to deal with them. Nicholas was not such a ruler. When the chaos of three years of war was added to the old miseries of Russia, the country finally collapsed, more from exhaustion than from some revolutionary plot.

PROJECTS

A. Research

(1) In what areas of Central Asia did England and Russia come into conflict as both countries expanded their empires during the nineteenth century?

(2) What were the main issues behind the mutiny on the battleship *Potemkin?* A good description of the incident is given in *The Potemkin Mutiny,* by Richard Hough.

B. Activities

(1) Pretend you are a newspaper or TV reporter, assigned to interview Stenka Razin or Pugachev during the peasants' uprisings of the seventeenth and eighteenth centuries. How might they respond to your questions about their goals, about the causes of the revolts?

(2) Compare Nicholas II with political dictators of the recent past, such as Batista of Cuba, Nkrumah of Ghana, or Diem of South Vietnam. Why were they overthrown? Are there any similarities?

C. Further Reading

Adams, A. E., Mattey, I. M., and McCagg, W. O., *An Atlas of Russian and East European History* (Praeger, N.Y.).

Chevigny, Hector, *Russian Alaska* (Viking, N.Y.)—A history of Russian settlements in Alaska during the eighteenth and nineteenth centuries.

Chew, Allen F., *An Atlas of Russian History* (Yale University Press, New Haven)—Thirty-four maps, with commentary, showing the changes of Russia's boundaries.

Dostoevsky, Fyodor, *House of the Dead* (Dell, N.Y.)—A description of the author's imprisonment in a Siberian prison camp; *The Possessed* (Penguin Books, N.Y.)—A novel about revolutionaries (whom Dostoevsky hated).

Florinsky, Michael T., *Russia, A Short History* (Macmillan, N.Y.)—An excellent general history, with many good maps and photographs.

Gogol, Nikolai, *Taras Bulba* (Signet, N.Y.)—A novel about the Cossacks in the nineteenth century.

Hough, Richard, *The Potemkin Mutiny* (Spectrum, N.Y.)—A description of the famous 1905 mutiny of Black Sea fleet sailors.

Karpovich, Michael, *Imperial Russia 1801-1917* (Holt, N.Y.)—A very good, brief summary of the main events and trends.

Maynard, John, *Russia in Flux* (Collier, N.Y.)—Read Chapter 2, "The Peasant in the Nineteenth Century."

Mosse, Werner E., *Alexander II and the Modernization of Russia* (Meredith Press, Des Moines, Iowa).

Oldenbourg, Zoe, *Catherine the Great* (Bantam, N.Y.)—A good historical novel about the Russian Tsarina.

Pushkin, Alexander, *The Queen of Spades and Other Tales* (Signet Books, N.Y.)—This collection includes "The Captain's Daughter."

Risanovsky, Nicholas V., *A History of Russia* (Oxford, N.Y.)—A recent basic survey of Russian History.

Saltykov-Shchedrin, *The Golovyev Family* (New American Library, N.Y.)—A very bitter and critical novel about a corrupt noble family.

Sumner, B. H., *Peter the Great* (Collier, N.Y.)—An excellent biography.

Thompson, G. S., *Catherine the Great* (Collier, N.Y.)—An historical study of the life of Catherine.

Tolstoy, Leo, *The Cossacks* (Signet/New American Library, N.Y.)—A novel about nineteenth century Cossack life.

Turgenev, Ivan, *The Hunting Sketches* (New American Library, N.Y.)—A collection of short stories that became famous because they were the first to picture serfs as human beings, not as mere animals; *Fathers and Sons* (Bantam, N.Y.)—A novel about the new generation of radical youth that appeared in Russia around the middle of the nineteenth century.

Wallace, Sir Donald Mackenzie, *Russia—On the Eve of War and Revolution* (Random House, N.Y.)—Read Part 4, "The Peasants," and Part 6, "Industrialization and Revolution."

Chapter 5

From Marxism to Leninism

The Appeal of Marxism

Marxist ideas first became popular among Russian intellectuals and revolutionaries during the 1890's. Largely through the efforts of Plekhanov and his followers (see Chapter 4), Russian intellectuals began to study and discuss the writings of Marx and Engels. There are several reasons for their attraction to Marxism. First of all, they had given up hope that the peasants would revolt. Although living conditions were worse than ever, the typical reactions of the peasantry were apathy and despair, not revolution. Marxism offered hope that the industrial workers would create the revolution.

Secondly, Marxism claimed to be scientific. It provided a complete explanation of the past and future development of history and stated that the eventual triumph of socialism was inevitable. Such a belief was very encouraging to the Russian revolutionaries at that time. They were living under the reactionary and extremely oppressive rule of Tsars Alexander III and Nicholas II, and the future seemed gloomy indeed.

Another appeal of Marxism was its faith in the process of industrialization and modernization. In one sense, Marxism was a protest against the suffering and hardships of industrialization. But Marx believed that this process was necessary and inevitable and that in the final stage of communism, the benefits of industry would be available equally to everyone. This idea was also encouraging to the Russian intellectuals, since their country was only beginning to industrialize. A belief in Marxism allowed them to look optimistically past the existing hardships into the future.

Marx and the Russian Situation

Despite the attractiveness of Marxism, one might ask, if one thinks back to the basic ideas of Karl Marx (presented briefly in Chapter 2), just how they could be applied to a country such as Russia. Marx saw the socialist revolution coming at the end of a long period of capitalism and democratic government. During this period, industry would become fully developed and the industrial workers, the proletariat, would become a large proportion of the population. After they possessed the necessary technical skills and education, the workers would take over the economy and the government.

Russia, however, was still a relatively backward country, primarily agricultural. Industrialization had begun but was far from advanced. Only a small number of Russians were working in industry; most were peasants, poorly educated, living and farming as their ancestors had for many generations. There was very little democracy in the government on either the local or national level. The Tsar was the supreme ruler.

According to the Marxist timetable, Russia was clearly quite far from the socialist revolution. In fact, Russia was still in the stage of feudalism and had not even gone through the process of developing a merchant-industrial-business middle class. Marx and Engels themselves were aware of Russia's backwardness, and they never seriously considered the idea that the socialist revolution would occur in that country in the near future. They expected it to take place first in one of the industrially developed countries, such as Germany, England, or France.

Adapting Marxism

Many changes had to be made in the theories of Marx in order to make them fit the Russian situation. It obviously was not logical or reasonable to talk of a proletarian revolution or of socialism in a country where less than 5 per cent of the people were actually industrial workers. The work of adapting Marxism to Russia was begun by Plekhanov, but the major achievement was the responsibility of Vladimir Ilich Lenin. (Lenin's real family name was Ulyanov. He took the name Lenin when he became an underground revolutionary, and he was known by it from then on.)

It is frequently said that Lenin changed Marxism so drastically that "he stood Marx on his head." While Marx predicted socialism as the final result of industrial development under capitalism, Lenin reversed this order, placing the socialist revolution first and industrial development second. The ideas of Lenin are of great importance for understanding Russian history. The official ideology of the Soviet Union today is called "Marxism-Leninism," but, in fact, the ideas of Lenin have had much more influence than those of Marx.

Birth and Youth of Lenin

Lenin will undoubtedly be remembered as one of the most important political figures of the twentieth century, whether one regards him with admiration or extreme distaste. There was nothing unusual in his early childhood to indicate his eventual fame. He was born in 1870 in the small town of Simbirsk, a backward, isolated provincial capital on the Volga river (its present name is Ulyanovsk).

Lenin's father was a school teacher and later a district school inspector. The family lived modestly but comfortably; family relations were close and quite happy. Both Vladimir and his brother Alexander, four years older, were excellent students, always at the top of their classes. Vladimir was quiet and a little reserved; he read a great deal but was well-liked by his classmates, although he does not seem to have had any very close friends. (The best short biography of Lenin is found in *Three Who Made A Revolution,* by

Bertram Wolfe. The other two revolutionaries are Trotsky and Stalin.)

When Vladimir was 17 and in his final year of school, his older brother was arrested and executed for plotting the assassination of the Tsar. Alexander Ulyanov had gone to St. Petersburg several years before to study science at the university. Unknown to his family, he had joined a tiny group of revolutionary students. There were only seven in the group, all very young and idealistic. They had attempted to re-establish the old "People's Will" group, a band of revolutionary terrorists that was dissolved in 1881 after they succeeded in killing the previous Tsar, Alexander II (see Chapter 4). This new group, however, was totally lacking in the experience and skill of the earlier terrorists. They were soon arrested and hung. Before his execution, Alexander made an eloquent and powerful speech in defense of his actions and in protest against the cruelty of the Tsarist government.

Some people have tried to explain the fact that Lenin became a revolutionary by his desire to avenge his brother's death. This is an exaggeration. But the execution affected the boy deeply and probably helped to turn his thoughts toward the political and social problems of Russia.

Early Revolutionary Activities

After his graduation, Lenin entered the university at Kazan, another city on the Volga, and began the study of law. He was soon expelled, however, for participating in a student protest; because of his brother's notorious reputation, he was exiled to a small village. He spent several years there, reading constantly, taking notes, and thinking. Although not allowed to re-enter the university, he finally got permission to take his bar examination. Compressing four years of law studies into one, he took the exam in 1891 and received the highest possible mark.

Lenin practiced law briefly, then came into contact for the first time with the writings of Marx and of Plekhanov, the most important Russian Marxist. In 1894, Lenin moved to St. Petersburg and made contact with other young students and intellectuals who were studying the work of Marx. During the 1890's, many of the radical and revolutionary students had abandoned Populism and taken an interest in Marxism. In long discussions and in articles and essays, Lenin tried to apply the teachings of Marx to Russian conditions. He also began to make personal contact with the factory workers of the capital and to learn something of their living and working conditions.

Some of the students established so-called "Literacy Committees." These committees ran free libraries for workers, held literacy classes, and tried to give the workers a basic education. Included in this education were some Marxist and revolutionary ideas. Lenin began working with one of these committees through a young girl he knew, Krupskaya, who later became his wife. He gave lectures on Marxism, read pages of Marx aloud to groups of workers, held discussions, and constantly asked questions about factory conditions and the opinions of the workers on current issues.

In his writing, lectures, and discussions, Lenin argued primarily against the Populists, who still believed in a peasant revolt. He insisted that the industrial working class was the basis for the coming revolution. The peasants, in his opinion, were too conservative and could not be trusted to carry out the job.

In 1895, Lenin went abroad to Switzerland to meet Plekhanov and the other leaders of the Social Democratic Labor Party, as the old "Liberation of Labor" group now called itself. When he returned to Russia, he and other Social Democrats went to work organizing strikes and passing out revolutionary propaganda. Police agents had been watching him closely since his return, however, and he was arrested and exiled to Siberia.

Lenin in Exile

Lenin spent the next four years in a small Siberian village, reading, writing, and keeping up a secret correspondence with Social Democrats all over Russia. The Tsarist government had a curious policy toward political exiles. They were allowed considerable freedom. Although confined to an isolated area, usually in Siberia, they could receive books, letters, and packages and were permitted to continue their studies and writing. Except for the restriction on travel and the harsh climate, their life was almost a normal one.

Conditions in the prison camps for serious criminals and political prisoners were quite different; in fact, they were intolerably difficult and cruel. (It will be remembered that Dostoevsky described his experience in such a camp in *The House of the Dead.*)

During his Siberian exile, Lenin fought violently, in articles and letters, against the increasingly cautious tone of the revolutionary movement. In the last years of the 1890's there was a trend away from revolution toward reform. German, French, English, and Russian Marxists began to consider the possibility that the workers might benefit more by gradual reforms than by revolution. More emphasis was placed on the work of trade unions, on cooperation with the government, on attempts to change the system peaceably.

The Struggle Against Moderation

Lenin and those who agreed with him were upset by the new moderate attitude. They insisted that complete political and economic revolution was still necessary and particularly opposed those leaders who were content to replace political goals with economic ones. In other words, they opposed the tendency to settle for higher pay instead of struggling for more political power or for the socialist revolution whereby the workers would "own" and control everything for the benefit of all.

In most of Europe and in the United States, this moderate policy was generally successful. Trade unions were able to bring about reforms that yielded higher wages and better working conditions for the workers. The standard of living rose, the workers were satisfied, and as a result, revolution lost its appeal. That is one of the reasons so few people in the West today are attracted to Communism; there are other ways, other possibilities for making improvements and carrying out reforms. It must be said in Lenin's favor that this did not seem true in Russia around 1900. The Tsar opposed the creation of trade unions and they were allowed very little power or influence. Reforms seemed almost impossible, and revolution seemed to be the only solution. Almost every attempt at reform was stifled, or ruthlessly crushed, as with "Bloody Sunday" in 1905.

When he was released from exile in 1900, Lenin went again to Switzerland. (From then until 1917, he spent most of his time abroad, returning to Russia only briefly in 1905-1906.) There he argued and discussed issues with Plekhanov and other Social Democrats.

Lenin continually stressed the danger of moderation, of giving up the political struggle against the Tsar to concentrate on economic reforms. To him, this was a betrayal of Marxism.

Lenin's Revisions of Marx

Lenin himself, however, was already revising some aspects of Marx's writings. Marx had shown complete faith in the inevitable triumph of socialism and believed that the proletariat—the industrial workers—would bring this about. Lenin began to have doubts, even about the proletariat. He eventually came to the conclusion that the workers, like the peasants, would not by themselves be capable of bringing about the revolution and would not even be interested in doing so.

He realized that most workers would be satisfied to get a pay raise or an extra holiday and would easily lose their revolutionary zeal. Therefore, strong leadership was essential; the workers had to be led to the revolution that Marx had said would occur spontaneously. In Lenin's opinion, this leadership must come from the Social Democratic Party.

Lenin's idea of the role of the party was very different from that of his fellow Social Democrats. Most of them felt that the party should have a mass membership, in other words, all workers, students, intellectuals, and the like who supported Marxist ideas. This was the typical European and American idea of a political party. Most European parties, including the socialists, had millions of members. The same is true of the Republican and Democratic parties in this country. But Lenin wanted to limit the membership very strictly. In his view, the party should be composed exclusively of "professional revolutionaries," totally dedicated men and women who worked for the revolution full time. They should make up an elite vanguard whose responsibility would be to direct and lead the workers. Therefore, there must be severe tests of loyalty for anyone allowed to join the party. Lenin wrote, "We must train people who will dedicate to the revolution not a free evening but the whole of their lives."

Lenin also emphasized the need for strong central control within the party and for unified action. There were to be no local groups or members who acted independently. All members were to follow and support a single policy. Members who disagreed were to be expelled. It was better to have a very small party of completely devoted members than a large party in which there were various factions. Only by being united could the party act quickly and strongly.

Bolsheviks and Mensheviks

Lenin's views aroused a controversy within the Social Democratic Party. He convinced a few members, but many others were violently opposed. His ideas were debated at the Second Congress of the Social Democratic Party, held in 1903 in London, and attended by 43 delegates. (All party gatherings, or congresses, were held in Europe, since the Tsar would not allow political opposition within Russia.) The debate was bitter and led to a split within the party between those favoring moderation and those favoring violent action. Over the next decade this split grew more serious.

A vote was taken on Lenin's proposals concerning the nature of the party and its membership. Lenin was defeated on his motion to limit membership to full-time revolutionaries. He won the vote on central control within the party, mainly because several of his opponents were absent when the vote was taken! From this victory, Lenin and his supporters took the name "Bolsheviks," which in Russian means "those in the majority." They called their opponents the "Mensheviks," or "those in the minority." These titles stuck with the two groups, although Lenin and his followers were often in the minority. Eventually, *Bolshevik* came to mean "extremist," *Menshevik* to mean "moderate." (After the 1917 revolution, the Bolsheviks changed their title to the Communist Party.)

For almost ten years after the first split, the Bolsheviks and Mensheviks remained within the Social Democratic Party. Several attempts were made to unify the two groups, but Lenin refused to compromise, and the differences grew, becoming more and more bitter. Two separate parties actually came into existence. In 1912, the final break occurred, and Lenin declared that the Bolsheviks were the only true Social Democratic Party (Socialists).

Crystallization of Lenin's Theories

Lenin's ideas continued to develop, as he sought to apply Marx to Russia. The failure of the 1905 revolution had an important influence on the development of his theories. According to Marx, the socialist revolution had to be preceded by a bourgeois revolution, that is, one carried through by the middle class. Many Russian Marxists thought that the events of 1905 would produce this bourgeois revolution. But events did not conform with their theories and expectations. The Russian liberals and middle class did not finish the struggle to overthrow the Tsar and establish a democracy. They accepted the Tsar's "October Manifesto" and his obviously insincere promises and gave up the fight.

Lenin decided that the Russian middle class could not be trusted. They were weak, few in number, and unwilling to fight against the Tsarist government. They did not seem capable of carrying out the bourgeois revolution that was theoretically the necessary preparation for the socialist one to follow. Lenin could not accept this "inevitability," because it meant that the socialist revolution might be delayed for decades or even centuries. So he revised Marx further. If the bourgeoisie was too weak, the proletariat would have to replace them. Lenin urged the Russian proletariat to prepare to seize power as soon as possible, without waiting for Russia to go through the stage of bourgeois capitalism. This might have sounded nonsensical to Marx, but it seemed realistic in the Russian situation. Lenin is often called an "opportunist," because he believed in taking advantage of an opportunity, even if this conflicted with Marx's theories or his own.

The Mensheviks disagreed with Lenin and the Bolsheviks on this issue of speeding up history, as might be expected. They were more moderate, less impatient, and closer to traditional Marxism. It was Lenin who was the "realist," and he was able and willing to act when the time came.

Lenin's Opportunism

Lenin's opportunism is illustrated by several other aspects of his program. Marx, as mentioned earlier, rejected the peasant as a force for revolution, placing his faith in the proletariat. Lenin also accepted this idea, at first. Gradually, however, he realized that this traditional viewpoint was unrealistic in a country with only three million industrial workers out of a population of a hundred and twenty million. Lenin urged that the workers cooperate with the peasants to bring about the socialist revolution. This was not good Marxism, but again, it was realistic. The Bolsheviks gained much popular support among the peasants by promising to turn over to them the estates of the nobles and the Church.

The Bolsheviks also promised national independence for the non-Russian peoples, such as the Ukrainians, the Georgians, the Uzbeks, and the like. This was another deviation from traditional Marxism, which stressed the international unity of all workers and condemned nationalistic pride. According to Marx, the strongest loyalty was to one's class, not to one's nation. Lenin realized that this was a naive viewpoint. (He was proven correct by the First World War, when French, German, and English workers did not hesitate to kill each other.) Nationalist feelings were especially strong in Russia, where over half of the people were non-Russian. By promising national independence after the socialist revolution, Lenin and the Bolsheviks gained much support from the national minority groups, especially those in the Caucasus.

A final example of Lenin's opportunism was his willingness to seize power in a backward nation, before a revolution had taken place in a more industrialized country. The usual Marxist view was that the revolution would start in an advanced country, such as Germany, and spread to other less advanced countries. Lenin argued the exact opposite. The revolution would occur in a backward country and then spread to more developed countries. The advanced countries would then aid the backward ones in their industrialization and modernization. Even Lenin did not believe that the revolution could succeed in Russia unless it also took place elsewhere, but he felt that it could be brought about in Russia first and that it would later spread to other nations.

Lenin in Red Square, 1919
(Courtesy, Sovfoto)

Lenin's Influence

The ideas in Lenin's book, *Imperialism, the Highest Stage of Capitalism*, written in 1916, have been extremely important, especially among intellectuals in Africa, Asia, and Latin America. Lenin revised and added to Marx's original theories. According to Lenin, capitalism's final development—its last breath—was imperialism, the building up of empires. By rushing to Africa and Asia in the nineteenth century and seizing colonies, the capitalist European nations had temporarily delayed the socialist revolution. But the exploitation of these colonies (the underdeveloped nations of today) could help only temporarily.

Lenin predicted that eventually the class struggle described by Marx would become international and that the struggle would be between the rich and the poor nations, just as the struggle within any one country was between the rich and the wealthy bourgeoisie and the proletariat. In the end, the colonies of Asia and Africa would defeat the imperial powers.

From Lenin's time, and especially in recent years, the Communists have tried to associate their name and ideas with the movement in Asia and Africa toward national independence. One of the significant trends of the last twenty years is the break-up of the colonial empires of the European powers. The number of independent nations in the United Nations, for example, has more than doubled. Many leaders and students in these new nations call themselves "Marxists" or express sympathy with Marxism, socialism, or Communism. Traditional Marxist ideas have very little relation to underdeveloped, agricultural countries such as Guinea or Ceylon, where there are almost no industrial workers. But Communism, in many minds, has come to stand for anticolonialism, for ending foreign rule and achieving national independence.

More will be said in the final chapter about the appeal of Communism in the underdeveloped countries of the world today. Keep in mind, however, that there are two basic elements to this appeal: the link with anticolonialism, and the attractiveness of the Soviet experience as a model for rapid modernization.

Summary

Lenin is the most important figure in recent Russian history and one of the outstanding political leaders of the twentieth century. He is constantly referred to and quoted by Soviet leaders today. His picture and his writings are everywhere. He revised Marx to suit Russian conditions and his name is always linked with that of Marx. They are Communism's two great political and economic thinkers. The official ideology of the Communist Party of the Soviet Union is called Marxism-Leninism.

Lenin's accomplishment in leading a small party of Bolsheviks to power in Russia in 1917 was a remarkable feat, as the next chapter will describe. His ideas influenced the development of all aspects of Soviet society, but his most important contribution was the organizing of the Bolshevik-Communist Party. He insisted on a small, elite, disciplined, tightly controlled Party. When the opportunity came to seize power in 1917, the Bolsheviks were able to move quickly. The function of the Party, then and today, is to lead, to educate, to control. This will be discussed more fully in Chapter 8.

Lenin was ahead of his time in at least one important respect. He was one of the first world political leaders to recognize the tremendous significance of the areas that we now call the underdeveloped world: Asia, Africa, and Latin America. By connecting Communism with the emerging struggle for national independence, he gave the Soviet Union an edge over other world powers who were either colonial powers themselves or as yet unaware of the direction of future world developments. One of the major tasks facing the United States today is to show to the underdeveloped world that we are as anticolonialist as the Soviets say they themselves are. A second great task, mentioned earlier, is to offer a better and faster method of modernization than the Soviet example provides.

PROJECTS

A. Research

(1) Is there a Socialist Party (or parties) in the United States? Have Socialists ever been elected to local or national offices? When and where?

(2) When was the Labor Party founded in England? To what extent is its program based on traditional Marxism? In what major ways does it differ from Lenin's version of Marxism?

B. Activities

(1) Debate whether Lenin would have been a successful political leader if he had been born in the United States instead of in Russia.

(2) Write an article by Lenin attacking the Populists and their belief in a peasant revolt. Support your contention that the peasants will not revolt with historical examples. Write an article by a Populist answering Lenin's attack. (Chapter 4 may be useful.)

(3) Stage a debate between Lenin and a moderate European socialist about whether change can come peacefully, that is, through economic reforms without political revolution.

C. Further Reading

Daniels, Robert, *The Nature of Communism* (Random House, N.Y.)—Read especially the chapters on Lenin's contributions to Communist theory.

Fischer, Louis, *The Life of Lenin* (Harper and Row, N.Y.)—A long, difficult biography but the best available.

Shub, David, *Lenin* (New American Library, N.Y.)—A brief biography.

von Laue, Theodore, *Why Lenin? Why Stalin?* (Lippincott, Philadelphia)—An interesting discussion of the question of whether or not leaders such as Lenin and Stalin were "inevitable" in Russia.

Wolfe, Bertram, *Three Who Made a Revolution* (Dell, N.Y.)—An excellent account of the early lives of Lenin, Trotsky, and Stalin.

Chapter 6

War, Revolution, and Recovery (1914 to 1928)

Because of her alliance with the small Balkan nation of Serbia, Russia entered World War I a few days after it began. For many years Russia had declared herself the protector of the related Slavic peoples in the Balkan Peninsula, especially of the Bulgarians and the Serbs. (Serbia is a large part of present-day Yugoslavia.) When a Serbian nationalist assassinated the Austrian Archduke and Austria declared war on Serbia, Russia was obliged to support her smaller ally. Complicated systems of alliances eventually involved almost every European nation in a long and unimaginably destructive war for which no country was really prepared. Russia ended up fighting against both Austria and Germany.

Of all countries, Russia was perhaps the least able to support the effort of an all-out, lengthy (1914-1918) campaign. Her army was poorly equipped and supplied, her industry just beginning to grow, her domestic social problems explosive, and her political leadership totally inadequate, even in peacetime. It seems surprising not that the government of the Tsar was overthrown by a social and political revolution, but that this revolution did not occur before February, 1917.

As already mentioned (Chapter 4), Nicholas II was a weak and untalented head of state. He had no great awareness of conditions in Russia and dealt with most problems by ignoring them. His main policy was to drift along, having faith that things would turn out all right in the end. Actually, during the last few years of his reign, effective control of the government was frequently exercised by his wife and by an extraordinary character named Rasputin.

The Spell of Rasputin

Rasputin was a Russian monk, a mystical and superstitious holy man. The Tsar's wife, also superstitious, fell under the influence of this strange and perhaps even mad creature. Part of his

Russian soldiers marching to the front during World War I
(Courtesy, The Bettmann Archive)

influence over the Tsarina resulted from the fact that she believed he had the power to cure her son of hemophilia, a rare blood disease.

(The name Rasputin comes from a Russian word meaning "dissolute," or "debauched," which describes the man quite accurately. His religious faith was based on the idea that salvation came only through repentance, and that to repent one first had to sin. The more sin, the more repentance, and the better the chances for salvation. Rasputin concentrated his efforts on the first part of this process.)

Rasputin's advice was taken more and more seriously, not only on matters of health and religion, but also of politics. Especially during 1915 and 1916, he and the Tsarina virtually ran the Russian Empire. Rasputin exercised his influence to dismiss and appoint government ministers and officials. Since he knew nothing of political affairs, these decisions were purely personal. A number of excellent ministers were arbitrarily discharged. The government administration became increasingly disorganized. The situation became so desperate by late 1916 that a group of nobles finally conspired to murder Rasputin. Even then he had to be poisoned, shot, and drowned before he finally died.

Breakdown of the War Effort

Such leadership, plus the tremendous strain of the war losses, brought Russia to the point of collapse. Nearly all of the other European armies were equipped with better and more modern weapons and machinery. Russia relied on numbers, not on technology. The manufacture and distribution of equip-

Rasputin, the Russian monk who dominated the Tsar's family and government
(Courtesy, The Bettmann Archive)

ment and supplies began to break down by 1915. Shortages of food, supplies, and consumer goods appeared at home also. The domestic economy declined steadily. In the cities, factory strikes and bread riots occurred frequently. In the countryside, peasants revolted and seized the land and estates of many nobles.

Discipline in the army began to break down. Russian casualties were greater than those of any other nation; over nine million Russians were killed or wounded. By the end of 1917, it is estimated that two million men had deserted from the front. The war dragged on into a third year, with no end in sight. The government seemed unable to cope with the domestic problems of agriculture and industry, much less with the war. Conditions finally reached a crisis in February 1917.

Abdication of the Tsar

In that fateful month food riots and strikes occurred throughout the capital, Petrograd. (The capital's name had been changed from the German-sounding St. Petersburg to its own Russian equivalent, Petrograd, shortly after the onset of the war. *Grad* means "city" in Russian just as *burg* does in German. The name of this city was soon changed once again.) The police and some army units refused to fire on the demonstrators and joined them instead. The Tsar, not in the capital at the time, dissolved the Duma, or parliament. The Duma refused to disperse and in return sent the Tsar a telegram demanding that he abdicate his throne. Nicholas II abdicated on March 2, 1917 and offered the throne to his brother, Michael. Michael, however, refused. On March 3, 1917, three centuries of rule by the Romanov dynasty ended. The Tsar fell not by any revolutionary plot but by his own inability to control events in Russia and to solve the coun-

The Russian Royal Family, before the Revolution
Nicholas II, his wife, and children were put to death by the Bolsheviks.

try's pressing social problems. The strikes and demonstrations that contributed to the downfall of his government were largely spontaneous, not organized by any particular group or political party.

The Provisional Government

Governmental power was picked up on March 3, 1917 by the Duma, which appointed a Provisional Government made up mainly of former Duma members. The head of this temporary government was Prince Lvov, and most of the other leaders were nobles or members of moderate and conservative political parties. They planned to carry out political changes that would probably have given Russia a parliamentary system somewhat similar to that in England, where the leader of the Majority Party becomes Premier or Prime Minister. Elections were scheduled for sometime in the late fall, and consideration of basic social reforms, such as land redistribution, was delayed until after the elections.

Such a slow, deliberate, and moderate approach would probably have been successful some years earlier. Russia might have developed a political system similar to those in most European republics. But the disruption and chaos of war had intensified Russia's social unrest. Immediate reforms were desperately needed. The Provisional Government never realized the seriousness of the situation and hesitated too long. The first stage of the Russian Revolution of 1917 was the overthrow of the autocratic (one-man) rule of the Tsar. But this step alone provided no relief for the masses of people. When the new government failed to act quickly, the second stage of the revolution began. It is at this point that Lenin and the Bolsheviks resumed their activities.

Re-establishment of the Soviets

The Bolsheviks had almost nothing to do with the February revolution and the abdication of the Tsar. Most were in prison or in European exile. The demonstrations and strikes were spontaneously organized and directed by "workers' councils," or *soviets,* in factories and army units in most Russian cities and towns. The Russian word *soviet,* meaning "council," was first used in its modern sense to refer to the workers' councils set up in 1905 to direct the numerous strikes of that year (see Chapter 4).

The worker's councils were repressed in 1906 but emerged again in 1917 as local strike organizing committees. Their political leadership usually came from the Menshevik (moderate Marxist) Party or from the large peasant party, the Socialist Revolutionaries. Few Bolsheviks (extremists) had influence in the soviets in early 1917.

Three critical problems faced the Provisional Government: (1) popular opposition to continuing the war (most Russians wanted out) ; (2) the need for immediate land reform (too few owned too much) ; and (3) the desperate shortage of food and material goods, especially in the cities.

As the Provisional Government still hesitated to act, many people began to look for some alternative. The suggestion was heard increasingly that the soviets should play a political role or even that they should take over as a new government. In fact, the months from February to October 1917 are sometimes referred to as a period of "two governments." The legal and official power lay with the Provisional Government, but the soviets held more and more public support as well as practical control over many cities and towns.

Activities of the Bolsheviks

With the overthrow of the Tsar, political exiles and prisoners, including Bolsheviks, returned to action in Russia, particularly in the capital, Petrograd. Stalin came back from Siberian exile, Trotsky from the United States, and Lenin from Switzerland. Stalin, a Georgian and a former student at a seminary, was insignificant at this time but eventually succeeded Lenin and ruled for twenty-five years. Trotsky was a brilliant orator and leader, second only to Lenin, and played a key role in the revolution and subsequent civil war.

The story of Lenin's return has become almost a legend. In order to travel from Switzerland to Petrograd, Lenin had to cross Germany, with whom Russia was still at war. Lenin was granted permission to make this journey by the German government. They were glad to help Lenin to return because they were certain that he would oppose the Provisional Government's attempt to continue the war. Lenin had already indicated that if he were in power, he would take Russia out of the war immediately. (Although the German government did not know that Lenin would soon be in power, they hoped that he might have some influence on Russian policy.)

In April, Lenin arrived by train at the "Finland Station" in Petrograd to direct the Bolshevik effort to overthrow the Provisional Government. His strategy was to gain control of the "Soviets of Workers' and Soldiers' Deputies" for the Bolshevik Party, to encourage the swing of popular support from the Provisional Government to the soviets, and eventually to replace the Provisional Government with a government based on the soviets. He set forth his program in a famous short document, called his "April Theses."

The "April Theses"

Among the policies Lenin advocated were: (1) Immediate withdrawal of Russia from the war; (2) distribution of nobles' land to poor peasants; (3) nationalization (government control) of banks; (4) control of industry by the workers; (5) shift of all government power to the soviets.

These "April Theses" were not adopted immediately by the other members of the Bolshevik Party. Lenin had to spend weeks debating with and convincing his followers that such a program could be successfully carried out. Several Bolshevik leaders argued, as did the Mensheviks, that Lenin was moving too fast. According to the Marxist viewpoint (see Chapter 2), the February revolution had been a bourgeois one, moving Russia from the historical stage of feudalism to that of bourgeois capitalism. Now, Lenin's opponents within the party argued, a long period of development must take place before the final socialist revolution.

Lenin was unwilling to wait for this to come about. He urged the Bolsheviks to prepare for further revolution in the near future. He saw clearly the weaknesses of the Provisional Government and felt that in the general political confusion in Russia at that time, a tightly organized group like the Bolsheviks might be able to seize power.

Eventually Lenin persuaded most of his fellow Bolsheviks to support this program of action. When Trotsky returned to Russia in May, he too encouraged the attempt to carry out the second stage of the revolution as quickly as possible. Many of the "April Theses" were turned into simple and appealing slogans that became popular in Petrograd, Moscow, and the smaller cities and towns. Such slogans as "Bread,

Workers and soldiers demonstrating in June, 1917, in Petrograd (now Leningrad)

The banners call for land, peace, freedom, bread, and the transfer of all power to the soviets. (Courtesy, Sovfoto)

peace, land!" and "All power to the soviets!" had far greater public appeal than the long deliberations of the Provisional Government or its promises of parliamentary elections in the fall. It is easy to understand why hungry workers and landless peasants, sick of the war and a life of hopeless poverty, began to support the Bolsheviks.

Contesting for Power

Bolshevik prestige and support grew rapidly throughout the summer. The party grew from approximately twenty-five or thirty-five thousand in February to over two hundred thousand in August. Still, the Bolsheviks were only a minority; there were several larger political parties, including:

(1) *Kadets*—This was a middle-class group, moderate but anti-Tsar. Many Kadets were in the Provisional Government.

(2) *Mensheviks*—These were Marxists, but Marxists entirely separate from and more moderate than the Bolsheviks. They supported the Provisional Government.

(3) *Socialist Revolutionaries* (SR's)—This was the peasant party and the largest by far in the whole nation. Its main concern was land reform.

Compared with any of these three large parties, the small Bolshevik Party would seem to have had little or no chance of power. But two factors were of crucial importance. First, the Bolsheviks were by far the best organized

Leon Trotsky, a leader of the October Revolution
(Courtesy, Sovfoto)

party in Russia and able to act with ruthless speed and determination. Second, the Bolshevik program was closer to popular sentiments than that of any other party. They promised land to the peasants, more food for the cities, workers' control of factories, independence for Russia's national minorities (see Chapter 3), and most vital, an immediate peace. Whether or not these promises were sincere is irrelevant. The Bolsheviks said what the people wanted to hear, and they therefore won popular support, at least temporarily.

By July, the Bolsheviks had gained a majority in most of the local soviets, including the two of greatest importance, in Petrograd and Moscow. At this time the composition of the Provisional Government also changed somewhat, with conservatives and moderates replaced by members who were more liberal or radical. The new Prime Minister was Alexander Kerensky, a leading Socialist Revolutionary who was, ironically, from the same town as Lenin. (Kerensky's father was director of the high school that Lenin had attended in Simbirsk.)

For a brief period in July and August the Provisional Government suppressed the Bolshevik Party. Lenin and other leaders were forced temporarily into hiding. But, like Prince Lvov, the new Prime Minister proved unable to solve Russia's desperate problems. Kerensky still refused to take Russia out of the war and put off land reform until after the fall elections. The prestige of the government sank lower and lower. Living conditions continued to deteriorate. Public criticism grew, as did strikes, demonstrations and desertions from the army.

The October Revolution

In October, Leon Trotsky formed a Military Revolutionary Committee, which was associated with the Petrograd soviet. This military arm of the soviet, with help from Bolsheviks in the regular army and navy units stationed around the capital, was to execute Lenin's plan for seizing control of the government. The date decided upon was October 25, the day before the

Some of the Red Guards organized by Trotsky in October 1917

During the night of October 25-26, these men occupied all the strategic positions in Petrograd and ensured the success of the Bolshevik seizure of power. (Courtesy, Sovfoto)

Exterior of the Winter Palace of the Tsars

Its seizure by the Bolsheviks climaxed the October Revolution and is the subject of many Soviet paintings.

The Smolny Institute

This private girl's school was used as Bolshevik headquarters during the October Revolution. A statue of Lenin stands before it today, and Lenin's office is preserved as it was in 1917.

second Congress of Soviets was to assemble in Petrograd. (Until after the Communist revolution the Russians used a calendar which was twelve days behind that used in the West. The new government switched over to the Western calendar. Thus, the anniversary of the "October" revolution is now celebrated on November 7.) Lenin planned to announce at this meeting that government power had been transferred to the soviets. Because of careful planning and organization the Bolshevik strategy worked almost without incident, and Lenin was able to make exactly that announcement.

During the night of October 25, armed guards of Trotsky's Military Revolutionary Committee moved quckly to occupy all important points in Petrograd: bridges; railroad stations; post, telegraph, and phone offices; armories; and the Winter Palace, seat of the Provisional Government. Some members of the government, including Kerensky, fled. (Kerensky came to the United States, where he now lives.) Others were arrested. There was virtually no opposition to the Bolshevik coup. No more than half a dozen lives were lost in this swift and almost bloodless takeover. At the Congress of Soviets the next day, Lenin was elected head of the new Russian government.

Although the Bolsheviks had come to power with relative ease by capitalizing on the chaotic social conditions in Russia, it was not at all certain that they could hold on to their position. They were still very much of a minority, and even if they had had no political opponents, there were serious problems to solve, the same problems which had helped to bring down both the Tsar and the Provisional Government. In order to retain the political support of the people, the Bolsheviks had to make good their promises of "Bread, peace, and land!" Civil war seemed to be a definite possibility; in fact, it broke out after only a few months.

Invitation to Civil War

One of the things that contributed to the outbreak of the civil war in 1918 was the Bolshevik handling of the elections to the Constituent Assembly. The Provisional Government had promised elections in the fall of 1917 for a national assembly to decide the form of Russia's future government. The Bolsheviks went ahead with these elections as planned but were disappointed by the results. They received only nine million of thirty-six million votes. The largest share of votes, twenty-one million, went

Lenin addressing a crowd in Red Square
(Courtesy, Sovfoto)

to the Socialist Revolutionaries (SR's). In the new assembly the Bolsheviks had only 175 out of 707 seats.

The Constituent Assembly met for exactly one day. The Bolsheviks were out-voted and walked out of the hall, accompanied by a few left-wing SR's who had split from the main party. The next morning, Bolshevik armed guards locked the doors of the hall, declared the assembly dissolved, and announced that governmental power was permanently transferred to the soviets.

The Russian civil war lasted for more than three years and involved a bewildering variety of groups. The Bolsheviks captured the major cities in European Russia and the central part of the country. But large areas of the Russian Empire, especially in Siberia and the south, were still controlled by various opponents. When one looks at the list of anti-Bolshevik forces, it is hard to believe that Lenin's party had the slightest chance of surviving.

The Anti-Bolshevik Forces

First of all there were the political opponents, ranging from conservative to liberal; each group had an army or military force. There were several "White" armies, made up largely of representatives of the conservative wealthier classes. (The color white has traditionally been associated with groups that support a king or emperor.

This use of white to indicate opposition to revolution probably goes back to the white flag of eighteenth-century French kings. By contrast, red has come to be the color of revolutionaries, especially extreme groups such as the Communists.) The Whites wished to return to the old system, restoring power to the nobility. Many even wished to restore the Tsar to his throne. The SR's formed several opposition armies and were sometimes joined by Mensheviks and moderate democrats.

Perhaps the most violent anti-Bolshevik forces were to be found among the non-Russian nationalities. Having accepted Lenin's promise of national self-determination, they were angered to find that it had not been sincere. One way of looking at the civil war is to view it as the Bolshevik struggle to regain control of the old Russian Empire. The peoples of the Caucasus, the Moslem peoples of Central Asia, and especially the Ukrainians fought hard but generally unsuccessfully to free themselves from Russian rule. Only the Baltic peoples gained independence. After World War II, they were again incorporated in the Soviet Union.

Another group that dreamed of independence was the Cossacks of the steppe region. One of the finest modern Soviet novels, *The Quiet Don,* by Mikhail Sholokov, paints a vivid and objective picture of the Cossack struggle during the civil war.

Foreign Intervention

In addition to domestic foes, the Bolsheviks also faced foreign intervention. At various times and places during the civil war, small numbers of British, French, Czech, Japanese, and American troops either fought against the Bolsheviks or supported their Russian opponents. This intervention was never on a large scale and was not well-planned or coordinated. In some cases, foreign involvement was almost accidental. The main causes of intervention were concern over Russia's withdrawal from the war with Germany and opposition to the Marxism of Lenin's government.

When Lenin took Russia out of the war, he upset Russia's former allies, particularly England. The Allies were worried that the Germans would seize war supplies that they had sent to the Russians; they also hoped that if Lenin were ousted, his successor would reopen the eastern front against Germany. Some British troops were already in Russia, delivering food and military supplies through the Arctic ports of Archangel and Murmansk. The British persuaded President Woodrow Wilson, against his better judgment, to send several thousand American troops to help protect these supplies from the Germans. The British also hoped to influence events by supporting those Russians who wanted to continue the war with Germany.

At this time, early 1918, the civil war was just starting and the Bolsheviks did not yet have control of many parts of the country, including Archangel and Murmansk. Almost inevitably, the British and American troops were drawn into cooperation with the local authorities, anti-Bolsheviks, and they were soon involved in political confusion that they did not fully understand. As it turned out, by the time the American troops arrived, most of the military supplies had been removed by various Russian groups. A few months later the war ended. There was now no reason for their presence in Russia, but they stayed on for nearly a year and became involved in the civil war.

Actually, the British and American troops did relatively little fighting against the Bolsheviks, either in the Far North or in Siberia where they also intervened. They participated in several battles with Red Army forces around Archangel and Murmansk, and they gave material support to the "Whites" and other anti-Bolsheviks. But they made no concerted military effort, and they were withdrawn in 1919. The damage to Soviet-American relations, however, was serious. The presence of foreign troops aroused resentment among many Russians and increased Bolshevik hostility to the West. In addition, the anti-Bolshevik forces were compromised by their ties with the foreign troops and lost support among the Russian people. The intervention was probably more harmful than helpful to their cause.

The intervention was a poor beginning for Soviet-American relations and is still a source of some bitterness. It was not, however, as sinister as the Russians maintain. It was largely the result of a series of misjudgments and partially thought-out actions, based on misinformation (such as the rumor of an imminent German attack on Archangel and Murmansk) and almost total ignorance of political realities in Russia in 1917 and 1918. Once the Allies got involved, it was difficult to get out, although it was soon realized that the whole affair had been a mistake.

Soviet-American relations continued on an unfriendly basis for a number of years, even though there were extensive American efforts to distribute food in Russia during the famine of 1921-1922. The United States expressed its disapproval of the new Soviet government by refusing to grant it diplomatic recognition until 1933. (England had granted recognition in 1924, and France soon afterwards.) This belated gesture only added to the mutual hostility.

One of the cavalry units of the Red Army
Consisting of workers and peasants, such units played an important role during the Civil War, 1918-21. (Courtesy, Sovfoto)

The Bolshevik Victory

With all of this opposition, how did the Bolsheviks manage to stay in power? The answer lies in the fact that there was an almost total lack of cooperation among their opponents. Everyone was fighting the Bolsheviks for his own reasons. The various groups could agree on one thing and on one thing only: they wanted to defeat Lenin. But on the question of what would replace the Bolshevik government there was chaotic disagreement.

Some, such as the national minorities, fought the Bolsheviks simply because they were Russians; the national minorities hated all Russians, whether Red or White. Some wanted to bring back the Tsar, some wanted a military dictator, and still others wanted the Duma to govern in the way that the British Parliament governs. Not only did the various anti-Bolshevik forces refuse to cooperate, they often hated each other more than they hated the Bolsheviks. And they lost their advantage of being a majority by being spread out all over the country as well as by not joining their energies.

The result was a long, confusing, bitter, and destructive war, which the Bolsheviks won only gradually. The Ukraine was an area of particularly hard fighting. The capital city, Kiev, changed governments nine times during the war. But the Red Army, under the leadership of Trotsky, slowly extended its control from the center. The Red Army was tightly organized and had a definite purpose: to hold onto power and to regain all formerly Russian territory. By 1921, the Bolsheviks had defeated both foreign and domestic opponents and controlled nearly all non-Russian areas of the old Tsarist empire. (The sole exception was the Baltic territories of Latvia, Lithuania, and Estonia.)

The Bolsheviks not only had to win a civil war, they also had to do something about social conditions in Russia. Since their program had included promises of radical changes, after October 26, 1917 they were forced to carry out this program. The period 1917-1921 is usually called the period of "War Communism" not only because of the civil war going on, but also because of the extreme measures taken. Many Bolsheviks wanted to achieve communism, or at least socialism, immediately. They expected to see the world Marx had predicted come into existence overnight. Therefore some of the experiments and policies of the period were quite extreme.

The first two decrees of Lenin's government, issued October 26, 1917, called for immediate land reform and for peace with Germany. By approving land reform, the Bolsheviks merely recognized what was in fact already happening. The peasants were seizing the land of the nobles, and the government could not have stopped them had it wished to do so.

The Treaty of Brest-Litovsk

Negotiations were begun with the Germans to end the fighting. The Germans demanded large areas of Russian territory that the Bolsheviks were reluctant to give up. But the German army continued to advance, and the Russian army rapidly disintegrated. Peace was finally arranged and a treaty signed at Brest-Litovsk in March 1918. The terms of the Brest-Litovsk Treaty were harsh and increased anti-Bolshevik feelings among Russians. The only allies of the Bolsheviks, the left SR's, quit the government and turned against Lenin.

By this treaty Russia lost more than a quarter of her territory. This area, which included much of western Russia and parts of the Ukraine, was of great economic significance. It contained not only a fourth of Russia's railroads and agricultural production but also three-fourths of her coal and iron deposits.

How could Lenin afford to give up so much? The answer is twofold. First of all, Lenin's main concern was to maintain power. So much of the Bolshevik appeal had been based on the promise to end the war that Lenin knew he had to make good on that, regardless of the price. The Bolsheviks also agreed to give up this amount of territory because they felt that world revolution was only a few weeks or months away. Lenin's revision of Marxism (see Chapter 5) assumed that a revolution in Russia would touch off revolution in the rest of Europe. Handing over Russian territory and natural resources to Germany was viewed as only temporary. The German workers would soon revolt, and then Germany, Russia, and all of Europe would cooperate.

This faith in world revolution seems naive today, but it was undoubtedly sincere, and in 1917-1918 it was not entirely foolish. Revolts did occur in Germany and Hungary in 1918 and 1919. For brief periods Hungary and parts of Germany were actually ruled by soviets, but these revolts were eventually crushed. By 1921, the idea of world revolution had become unrealistic, even to the minds of the Bolsheviks. In any case, Russia regained the territory lost by the Brest-Litovsk Treaty because Germany was eventually totally defeated in World War I, not because of a world-wide proletarian revolution.

A Policy of Extremes

In attempting to put Marx's ideas into action, the Communists adopted some extreme policies. (In 1918, the Bolsheviks changed their name to Communists largely to emphasize the difference between them and the European socialists of more moderate and revisionist tendencies.) In June 1918, all large industry and banks were taken over by the government. Before the October Revolution, Lenin had spoken of the control of industry by the workers. The actual result was government control of both industry *and* the workers. This was not only a betrayal of the ideals of Marx, it also proved to be hopelessly inefficient.

The new government could not hope to administer Russian industry effectively because the Communists had little or no previous industrial experience. When they took over the factories, many of the directors, engineers, and skilled technicians left the country. It was impossible to run these complex industries without the technical knowledge of such men. In addition, much of the Communists' energy was devoted to the civil war at this time. Industrial production continued to decline; more and more factories shut down. Raw materials became scarce, as did skilled administrators. By 1920, industrial production had fallen to sixteen per cent of what it had been in 1912. The European war, the Communist revolution, and the civil war all contributed to the disorder.

The drop in industrial production also had a disastrous effect on agriculture. Ordinarily the peasants raised more food than they needed themselves and traded or sold the surplus in the cities. Since the factories in the cities were producing less and less, and many workers were unemployed, there was no way to pay the peasants for their grain and vegetables. Yet the urban population had to be fed. If there was nothing to offer to the peasants, then their produce would have to be taken by force.

By late 1918, the Communist government had to rely increasingly upon forced requisitioning of grain in order to feed the Red Army and the city workers. The peasants naturally resented this and fought back. Some joined anti-Bolshevik forces in the civil war; others simply stopped growing more than enough to feed their own families. The government reacted by using more and more military and police force.

Although Lenin's party won a military victory in the civil war and held uncontested power by 1921, it was losing popular support. War losses and hasty, unrealistic "Marxist" policies had made a mess of the economy. Consumer goods and food were scarce. Famine swept over many regions of Russia in 1921-1922, killing hundreds of thousands. Public opposition was increasing not only among the middle class, but even among the original supporters of Lenin, the workers and poor peasants.

The NEP

In March 1921, the sailors at the Kronstadt naval base near Petrograd revolted and nearly succeeded in overthrowing Lenin. This was interpreted as a serious danger sign by the Communists, since the Kronstadt sailors had played a major role in the October Revolution. Changes in policy were desperately needed if the Communists were to stay in power.

During the same month, March 1921, Lenin announced the New Economic Policy, or NEP as it was known. The NEP represented a drastic shift from the policies of "war communism." It was not intended, however, as a permanent shift, but as a strategic retreat, a series of temporary concessions to anti-Communists, a breathing spell in the revolution.

Basically, the NEP was a return to many of the features of capitalism after the failure of the economic program of "War Communism." This program naturally had favored the workers at the expense of the middle classes and the peasants. It was the middle class, however, that possessed the technical knowledge needed to run modern industry and the peasantry that grew the food to feed the cities. After October, 1917, some of these men had fled abroad and others refused to work for the government. To attract these people back with their skills and money, the NEP turned many factories back into private hands. Trade was also left largely to private individuals. The government continued to control only the most important industries and transportation.

The NEP took a new attitude toward the peasants, too. Instead of forcing them to give up their grain in return for future goods, the NEP tried to encourage them to produce more by giving them real cash incentives. The state would stop commandeering the grain and start buying it at fair prices. The more the peasants grew, the richer they could become. This policy, of course, was a return to capitalism and resulted in some peasants becoming much wealthier than others. Although these concessions refuted socialist ideals of economic equality, Lenin felt them necessary in order to get the economy moving again. Once production was back to a pre-war level, socialist policies could be introduced again.

The NEP worked. By 1926 production was equal to that of 1913. The famine was ended, and factories were operating normally. The economy was a mixture of private and government control. Major industries such as coal, steel, machinery, transportation, and electrical power were run by the government. Many less important industries were left in private ownership. In a sense, capitalism had saved communism. Today, (see Chapter 10) the Soviet leaders are again trying to solve their economic problems by borrowing capitalistic techniques.

While the Communists tolerated some variety in the economy, all political opposition was crushed. Most nobles and members of the wealthier classes left Russia by the end of the civil war. Democratic or socialist opponents, such as the Mensheviks or SR's, were suppressed by the secret police. Finally, in 1927, all political parties except the Communist Party were declared illegal in Russia.

The Death of Lenin

While Russia was gradually rebuilding after the civil war, Lenin died. He had been wounded in the head by a would-be assassin in 1920. In 1921 and again in

A view of Kurejka

In this tiny village in eastern Siberia, Stalin was exiled by the Tsarist government from 1913 to 1917. (Courtesy, Sovfoto)

1922 he suffered strokes that temporarily paraylzed him, and his health declined steadily until he died in January, 1924. Lenin's death created a great vacuum. The Communist Party had been molded by Lenin more than by any other individual. His will and leadership had brought the Bolsheviks from obscurity to control of potentially the richest nation in the world. He had guided the Party and the government through a dangerous civil war and had introduced the successful NEP and thus prevented a possible counter-revolution. The question of who was to follow Lenin was of profound importance.

Most people assumed that the next head of the Party and the government would be Leon Trotsky. Of all the Bolsheviks only Trotsky's mind equalled that of Lenin in brilliance and imagination. His role in the October Revolution, directing the Military Revolutionary Committee, was as important as that of Lenin. He used his genius with similar success during the civil war, molding and directing the young Red Army to victory against its numerous enemies. Trotsky was a man of great intelligence and wide learning, a theorist and writer on many subjects. It is no wonder he was considered the most likely successor to Lenin.

Emergence of Stalin

The man who emerged as Lenin's successor, however, and who dominated Russia during the next quarter century, was a relatively obscure Georgian named Joseph Stalin. Stalin had been an early member of the Bolshevik Party's underground at home. Loyal and hard-working, shrewd but unoriginal, and by no means the intellectual equal of Lenin or Trotsky, he spent much of his time working with the national minorities. By also concerning himself with internal Party affairs and organization, he rose to the position of Party Secretary by 1924. He was not an exciting figure, and few people expected him to challenge Trotsky.

Stalin's work within the Party organization, although undramatic, had been important. He had used his powers to appoint his supporters to high positions within the Party. This careful planning produced rewards in the four years of debate and maneuvering that followed Lenin's death. Stalin cleverly played off various groups within the Party against each other, aligning himself first with one side, then with the other. Stalin succeeded in dividing his opponents and defeating them one by one, finally expelling them from the Party. Trotsky was expelled in 1927 and left Russia in 1929 for exile in Europe. (He later lived in Mexico City, where an alleged secret agent of Stalin murdered him in 1940.) During the early years, 1924-1928, Stalin did not have the power to imprison or kill his opponents. Later, however, when he assumed complete control of the Party, most of his rivals, as well as many other people, were murdered (see Chapter 7).

By 1928, Stalin's control of the Party and the government was complete, far more complete than Lenin's had been. There was no effective political opposition outside the Communist Party and practically none within it. Using his dictatorial powers, Stalin now struck out on a new path, ending the experiment of the NEP. The two major policies adopted after 1928, the Five-Year Plan for industry and the collectivization of agriculture, caused far-reaching dislocations in Russian life.

If 1917 was the year of political revolution, destroying the old regime of the Tsar and the nobility, 1928 marked an even more significant social revolution. This year saw the beginning of an intense, often violent, campaign to make Russia into a modern industrial and military power. To accomplish this, immense changes were necessary. Stalin demanded that the whole process be completed as rapidly as possible; the human sacrifices required were not important to him. His success in raising Russia to the status of a full world power came only with a terrific cost in suffering.

PROJECTS

A. Research

(1) How extensive was the Western intervention in the Russian Civil War? Where did the major campaigns take place? What was the United States' role in the intervention? (Chapters 5 through 8 in George Kennan's book, *Russia and the West Under Lenin and Stalin,* will be helpful.)

(2) Despite its intervention in the Civil War and refusal to recognize the Soviet government, the United States did not turn its back on Russia during the famine of 1921-1922. Herbert Hoover, who later became President, was in charge of this relief program, part of the American

Relief Administration. What difficulties did the program encounter? How successful was it?

(3) What were the basic issues behind the Kronstadt Revolt of 1921? Who was involved? How close to success did they come?

B. Activities

(1) Debate whether or not the revolutions of 1917 were "inevitable." Could the Bolshevik takeover have been prevented?

(2) Write an article by Kerensky explaining why he was unable to keep his provisional government in power and justifying his own role.

(3) If there had been no censorship in Tsarist Russia, there undoubtedly would have been many political cartoons about Rasputin. Draw one criticizing his relationship to the royal family or his role in the government.

C. Further Reading

Chamberlin, William, *The Russian Revolution* (Grosset and Dunlap, N.Y.) —A long but revealing book by a journalist who was in Russia in 1917.

Furmanov, Dmitri, *Chapayev* (Foreign Language Publishing House, Moscow)—An exciting novel about a Red Army hero of the Civil War.

Sholokov, Mikhail, *And Quiet Flows The Don* and *The Don Flows Home to the Sea* (New American Library, N.Y.)—A long two-volume novel about the Civil War and the Cossacks, known in its entirety as *The Quiet Don.* The best work of Mikhail Sholokov, who received the Nobel Prize for Literature in 1965.

Taylor, A. J. P., *Illustrated History of World War I* (Berkeley Publishing Corp., N.Y.)—An excellent brief history with many good photographs.

Trotsky, Leon, *The Russian Revolution* (Doubleday, N.Y.)—A long and detailed book by one of the major leaders of the revolution. You might want to read parts of it to get an idea of the atmosphere of the times.

von Laue, Theodore, *Why Lenin? Why Stalin?* (Lippincott, Philadelphia) —A discussion of Soviet history that tries to explain why these two men gained power.

Zamiatin, Eugene, *We* (E. P. Dutton, N.Y.)—A novel about totalitarian society by a Russian writer who criticized the new Communist government. It was written before *1984* and *Brave New World,* which are similar and better known.

The Russian Revolution and the Bolshevik Victory, "Problems in European Civilization" (series by D. C. Heath)—This is a collection of short articles about the revolution, giving different interpretations of what happened and why. Particularly interesting ones are: Bernard Pares, on Rasputin; William Chamberlin, on the March Revolution; Richard Pipes, on the non-Russian peoples; Merle Fainsod, on Bolshevik strategy.

Chapter 7

The Creation of a Modern Power

Stalin often referred to the changes begun in 1928 as "the revolution from above." And indeed the changes resulting from rapid industrialization and collectivization represent a revolution of greater significance than those of 1917. The appeal of the Soviet system in the underdeveloped world today is based on the revolution of 1928-1933, not on the political coup of October, 1917.

Brezhnev and Kosygin point out the Soviet accomplishments of the past forty years to the peoples of Asia, Africa, and Latin America, and say: "Look what we have done. In a few decades we have taken a backward peasant country and made it into a world industrial, scientific, and military power. This is why socialism is better than capitalism." Tremendous changes have taken place since 1928, as Americans realized in 1957 when the Russians shocked us by developing long-range missiles and launching the first sputnik. The first part of this chapter will look at how these changes were brought about.

The political ancestor of Stalin is Peter the Great. Both Stalin and Peter were energetic and brutal in their attempts to force Russia to modernize, and to catch up with the West (see Chapter 4). They used terror and compulsion to step up the pace of Russian technical development and to drastically change the old Russian way of life. One sample statistic gives an idea of the immense changes that Stalin initiated. In 1926, 82 per cent of the Russian population lived in rural areas, only 18 per cent in cities. In 1933, 67 per cent lived in rural areas, 33 per cent in cities. This rapid shift to urban areas had many consequences.

Stalin and Marx

In the first chapter, the problem of modernization was discussed briefly in general terms. The Soviet Union offers a specific example of the process of modernization carried out under new and special circumstances. The Soviet leaders claim that their success has been due to the theories of Marxism-Leninism (see Chapters 2 and 5).

Training a young peasant girl to take over a factory job

This was a common scene during the industrialization speed-up after 1928. (Courtesy, Sovfoto)

Actually, there is little relation between what Marx predicted and what Stalin did. Marx foresaw the working class in advanced industrialized countries revolting and taking over the factories and mines for their own benefit. Russia in 1928 was still quite backward; the working class had first of all to industrialize the country, a task which Marx assumed would have already been completed by the capitalists. The measures that Stalin took to accomplish this task have no basis in Marx's works, since Marx could not imagine socialism coming *before* industrialization. Stalin's crash program was based on such "principles" as terror, coercion, and total control of society.

Choosing an Economic Policy

While economic conditions were improving under the NEP (1921-1928), a vigorous debate took place within the Communist Party over future economic policy. There are several possible ways to industrialize, as mentioned in Chapter 1; not all of these ways were open to the Soviet government. For example, many of the richest Russians had left the country after the Bolshevik Revolution, taking much of their wealth with them. Another possible source of needed capital, foreign aid and loans, was not readily available because of the hostile relations between the capitalist Western nations and the new socialist government of Russia. The United States, for example, did not officially recognize the Soviet government until 1933.

Foreign trade is another way to finance industrialization. One of Russia's largest export items before the First World War had been grain. But since the war there had seldom been enough for domestic consumption, much less surpluses for export.

The conclusion was that Soviet industrialization had to be paid for largely by savings within the country. Since the Soviet Union in 1928 was still quite poor, this meant that someone had to make sacrifices for the future. The debate centered around which people were to sacrifice how much and for how long a period. The decision would determine the speed and success of Soviet industrialization. Another point of debate was whether to convince people to make sacrifices voluntarily or to use force.

The "Hard" and "Soft" Positions

During the debate over industrialization in the 1920's, two general positions emerged, a "hard" and a "soft" position. The hard position, favoring coercion and speed, could be summarized roughly as follows: The majority of Russians, the peasants, would have to make the major sacrifices. Grain, collected by force if necessary, would be exported in return for factory and construction equipment. All available resources would be put into heavy industry, not into the production of consumer goods. There would be a shift of labor from agriculture to industry. Admittedly, this policy would hurt and people would oppose it, but it had to be carried out in order to get the economy moving at a rapid rate. Change is painful however you do it, so do it fast, start immediately, and get it over with as soon as possible.

The "soft" position was based on persuasion and an emphasis on the production of consumer goods. The argument went approximately as follows: The hard policy of coercion would antagonize the peasants and lead to a new civil war. In the long run it would be better to begin by producing more consumer goods, which could then be offered to the peasants as an incentive to raise agricultural production. Agricultural surpluses could be traded for European heavy machinery. The wealthier peasants should be encouraged to produce more grain by lower taxes, not by force. The poorer peasants should

Adults being taught to read and write in the crash program to eliminate illiteracy
At the time of the Bolshevik takeover the illiteracy figure for the population as a whole was 80 percent and as high as 95 percent in some areas. (Courtesy, Sovfoto)

be attracted to cities and factories by higher wages and good living conditions. This gradual policy would require many years, but it would be more efficient in the end and would have the genuine support of the people.

To oversimplify, the choice was between doing it fast and by compulsion or taking it easy and getting the cooperation of the people. Stalin took first one side and then the other, using the issue to defeat his rivals for power. At one point he sided with the "softs" against the hard position, which was strongly defended by Trotsky. After eliminating his chief opponent, Stalin turned around and took the hard position: rapid, forced industrialization.

The First Five Year Plan

In preparation for industrialization, a Five Year Plan for the entire economy was drawn up in 1928. The NEP was ended and the government again took over control of all industry and trade. As early as 1921 a government agency called GOSPLAN (abbreviation of the Russian for State Planning Committee) had been set up to plan for and regulate large-scale industry.

This agency now drew up the plans for all industrial production in the entire country. Certain goals were set for each factory, mine, and agricultural area. Such direction of an entire country's economy by one agency is called central planning. (For more details, see Chapter 10.)

The first Five Year Plan placed great stress on heavy industry, specifically coal, oil, steel, and electric power. Very little attention was given to consumer goods. The steel produced went into railroad tracks, military equipment, trucks, or construction materials for more factories, not into private automobiles or apartment houses. Only a minimum amount of resources went into such things as clothing, furniture, housing, and recreation. These things had to wait until basic industries had been built. This policy of favoring heavy industry over consumer industry has continued to the present, although Khrushchev and his successors began to strike a more even balance between the two.

As the threat of the Second World War grew, priority was given increasingly to the production of military equipment, while consumer needs were largely ignored. Since the war, much emphasis has been given to the construction of new apartment buildings, but a very large percentage of Soviet resources still goes into military equipment and space projects, not to mention heavy industry.

Implementation of the Five Year Plans

The mood of the period of the Five Year Plans was like that of a military campaign. The government spoke of production goals as if they were military objectives to be taken by storm. Bold and vigorous plans were announced for doubling the production of oil or tripling the production of steel in a few years. A famous and often repeated saying of Stalin's was: "There are no fortresses that Bolsheviks cannot storm!" Another slogan heard constantly at this time urged the workers to fulfill "The Five Year Plan in Four Years!"

Typical of the energetic industrial plans was the tendency to set production quotas for each individual worker and to encourage competition. When a miner in the Donets Basin, Alexei Stakhanov, mined thirteen times his daily quota of coal, his name became famous throughout the country. From then on, workers in all fields were urged to follow his example. Workers who performed such production feats were referred to as "Stakhanovites" and 1936 was declared to be a "Stakhanov Year."

Many Soviet novels of the 1930's describe the sense of enthusiasm and energy of the Five Year Plan period. A good example, by Fyodor Gladkov, has the romantic title, *Cement*. Another typical novel of the period is *Time, Forward!*, by Valentin Katayev. An interesting description of the huge construction projects by an American who spent several years in the Soviet Union during the 1930's is *Behind the Urals*, by John Scott.

Along with genuine enthusiasm there was growing resistance. Many of the workers in the new factories had only recently come from the countryside and were not used to industrial work. They had to adjust to strict daily work schedules and submit to regulation and control. Industrial labor was very different from the traditional agricultural work of the Russian countryside. On a farm, people are generally independent. They do not have to begin work at a certain time or work a specific number of hours. Wages were also a source of discontent. Since the government wanted to put as much of the country's resources into expansion as possible, consumption was cut to the bare minimum. During the 1930's wages rose, but prices rose much more, so that the worker was actually worse off in the end.

Labor discipline was enforced by the government in various ways. Labor unions existed but were denied the right to strike. Collective bargaining did not exist; wages were set by the government. Very severe penalties were imposed on workers who were late to work or skipped days or were sloppy and careless on the job. Control became tighter in 1932, when passports for travel within the country were introduced. A few years later, labor books were required for all workers. In these books were recorded all the jobs held by the man, with a statement by his boss about his performance on the job. By 1940, it was prohibited by law to change one's job without official permission. The worker in the proletarian state of socialist Russia had come to have considerably less freedom than the worker in capitalist England or America.

Collectivization of Agriculture

There were both practical and ideological reasons for the collectivization of agriculture. In the theories of Marx and Lenin, private property, including the private farm, was considered to be the source of all evil because it made people think only of their own profit and encouraged them to be selfish. Just as industry should be controlled by the whole people, or by the government, so agriculture should be operated on a collective basis, not on an individual basis. The Communists believed that it would be more efficient and more just to abolish private farms and to combine them into collective farms. In these collective farms, all land and livestock would be owned and shared in common.

But it was the practical reasons rather than the ideological ones that compelled Stalin to begin the campaign for collectivization in 1928 and 1929. In order to keep industry expanding rapidly, large agricultural surpluses were needed, both for export (to get money to buy industrial materials) and for feeding the growing city population.

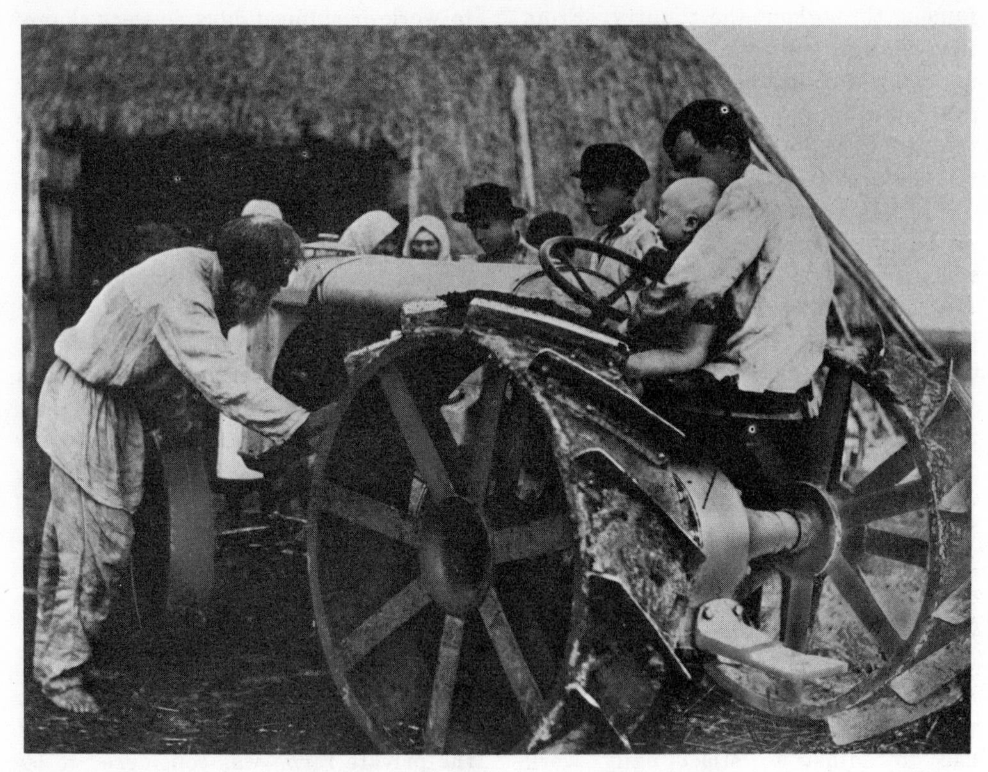

Arrival of the first tractor on a soviet collective
(Courtesy, Sovfoto)

The economic policy, however, called for emphasis on heavy industry and the lowest possible prices to the peasants for their agricultural produce. The peasants, naturally enough, reacted negatively to this policy, as the "softs" had warned in the industrialization debate of the 1920's. They protested as they had under similar conditions in the period of "War Communism" (see Chapter 6) and refused to produce more than they needed for themselves and their families.

Stalin declared that the serious grain shortage in 1928 was caused by the sabotage of the *kulaks* (a Russian word meaning both "fist" and "rich peasant") and their unwillingness to produce grain for the workers in the cities. The grain, therefore, would have to be seized by the government and plans for collectivization would have to be speeded up as a gradual policy was no longer tolerable. Force was used more and more frequently to make the peasants join the collective farms and to supply the cities with food. The police and even the army were employed when peasants resisted. The word *kulak* came to be a general term, applied to any peasant, rich or poor, who opposed Stalin's policies.

Defiance and Reprisal

Collectivization was pushed through rapidly, but with great losses and suffering. Over 20 million individual farms were taken over and combined into collective farms. As a last desperate and senseless act of defiance, many peasants slaughtered their livestock rather than turn them over to the new collectives. In 1933, there were 14 million fewer horses than there had been in 1929, 30 million fewer cattle, and 100 million fewer sheep. Not until the early 1960's did Soviet meat production recover from this destruction, and again reach the level of 1933.

Even more destructive was the government's revenge on those who resisted. Many peasants were sent to labor camps in the far north or in Siberia, where the terrible climate took many lives. By forcibly seizing grain from the peasants in order to feed the city workers, Stalin deliberately caused famines in many rural areas. In 1931-1933, about five million Russians died of starvation, or to be more exact, were allowed to die by Stalin. (He rejected all offers of aid from the U.S. and other nations.)

By 1933, the *kulaks* had been eliminated and most of the land collectivized. As a concession to the peasants, they were permitted to keep a small private plot of land, less than an acre, and a certain limited number of livestock. (See Chapter 10 for some details on the present importance of these private plots.) *Harvest on the Don,* by Mikhail

Siberian peasant listening to an early radio

The Soviet goal of electrification of the countryside brought many changes to towns and isolated rural areas. Note the traditional Russian samovar on the left. (Courtesy, Sovfoto)

Sholokov, is an interesting novel about the period of collectivization. It deals with a Commuist Party official from the city who is sent to the countryside to persuade the peasants to join a collective farm.

The Extension of Terror

The elements of terror and compulsion so evident in the collectivization drive became central concerns and increasingly necessary to the Soviet system of government under Stalin. Terror came to be directed not just at political opponents, such as Trotsky, and peasants who resisted collectivization, but against anyone whom Stalin distrusted. As Stalin's dictatorial powers grew, so did his fears of being betrayed or overthrown. Some people argue that Stalin grew increasingly insane; others feel that he was merely carrying his policies to their logical conclusion. In the late 1930's, these fears lead to the "purges" of all Party members whom Stalin suspected. The secret police became the most powerful organization in the country, permeating the entire society with fear. Such was the hysteria that one Party member, a writer, was expelled when it was discovered that many years before he had written a review of a book by another writer who was later accused of being a "traitor."

According to various estimates, between eight and twenty million Soviet citizens were killed during the period of the purges. People from all occupations, inside and outside of the Communist Party, were victims of Stalin's directives. Labor camps were full of *kulaks*, workers who had broken minor work rules, writers who refused to write the correct kind of literature, and Party members who were accused of plotting against Stalin. People were arrested on the unlikely charges of being spies, German agents, or secret supporters of Trotsky, who had fled to exile in Mexico. A reasonable guess is that at the start of the Second World War in 1941, about ten million Soviet citizens were in prison or labor camps. The only thing comparable to Stalin's purges in size and madness was Hitler's attempt to annihilate the Jewish people.

Some evidence of the insanity of the purges was given by Khrushchev in a "secret speech" in 1956 (see the latter part of this chapter for more details on the circumstances of this speech). Khrushchev stated that within three years of the 1934 elections of the Communist Party Central Committee, 125 of the 140 members had been arrested by the Secret police, of whom 98 were shot. Of the 1,966 delegates to the 1934 Party Congress, 1,108 were also arrested. These were not ordinary citizens but the highest Party officials. Many of them had belonged to the Party before the 1917 revolution, had worked closely with Lenin, and had held important government posts. But Stalin was willing to sacrifice all of this ability and service to his obsession for absolute power.

The purges extended even into the armed forces, despite the rising danger of attack from Nazi Germany. In 1937 and 1938, thirteen of the top fifteen generals were arrested, and 65 per cent of all higher officers were purged. The charges, when the Stalin government bothered to make any formal charges, were unfounded ones of plotting with foreign powers to take over the Soviet Union or of acting as agents of England or Hitler or Trotsky. There was no logic, reason, or limit to these purges. As Trotsky, writing from exile, put it: "Stalin is like a man who wants to quench his thirst with salt water."

Preparations for World War II

The purges finally began to die down somewhat after 1938. Hitler was obviously preparing for war, taking over Austria, Czechoslovakia, and finally Poland, on September 1, 1939. Stalin realized that an attack on Russia was inevitable, that it might be delayed, but not avoided. In preparation for such an attack, during the last half of the 1930's over one-fourth of the Soviet budget had gone into defense. One last and surprising delaying tactic on the part of Stalin was to negotiate a nonaggression pact with Hitler in August 1939. Neither country was sincere in signing this agreement but both hoped to profit from it, in different ways. Hitler sought to avoid fighting in the east against Russia until after he had defeated France and England in the west. Stalin was mainly playing for time, while building up his armed forces. In addition, both sides cynically agreed to divide the territory lying between them. In 1939 and 1940 Hitler took over most of Poland, while Stalin attacked Finland and recaptured the three Baltic states, Latvia, Lithuania, and Estonia, which had become independent from Russia after the First World War.

Today Stalin is the object of much criticism in the Soviet Union, his excesses are frequently denounced, and he is no longer regarded as a great leader equal to Lenin. Even so, he is recognized as having made a major contribution to the growth of the Soviet Union, especially in the early part of his rule. There is no doubt that the Soviet Union was many times stronger in 1941 than it was fifteen or twenty years earlier. By the time of Hitler's attack, the Soviet Union was one of the top industrial and military powers in Europe. The sacrifices had been terrible—forced collectivization, mass terror, labor camps, consumer needs ignored for heavy industry, purges, millions of lives lost and a society built on fear and obedience. But weak, backward Russia had been built into a modern country which could stand up against Hitler's Germany, endure four years of war, and finally emerge as master of Eastern Europe. Were the sacrifices worth it? Could any other methods have been as successful in such a short time? These questions are impossible to answer, but in some form they face the newly independent nations today. Given their desire to modernize rapidly, do the methods used by Stalin, including terror, offer the quickest solution, or are there less painful ways?

The German Onslaught

For the first years of World War II, the Soviet Union faced Germany almost alone. The United States and England sent aid, eleven billion dollars worth, including 400,000 trucks, 13,000 tanks, and nearly 2,000 steam locomotives. But United States and British troops did not land in Europe until 1944. For three years, Hitler was able to concentrate much of his army against the Soviet Union. The suffering and the tremendous endurance and courage of the Russians during the Second World War are very difficult for Americans to grasp. The stories of two cities, Leningrad and Stalingrad, are representative of the will to survive that kept Russia going throughout the war.

Despite its growing military strength, the Soviet army was no match for the well-trained German army, which launched a surprise attack in June, 1941. The best tactic for the Russians was the traditional one: retreat. In this way they could take advantage of Russia's immense size and bitter weather and make the enemy follow after until his supply lines were stretched across thousands of miles. By the end of 1941, the Russians had lost an area which included 40 per cent of the population, 40 per cent of the grain-producing land, and 60 per cent of the coal, iron, and steel reserves. The large industrial cities of Leningrad, Moscow, and Stalingrad were all threatened. Factories were moved in their entirety from western areas to the east, beyond the Volga River to the Ural Mountains, and even farther (see the maps in Chapter 3). About 2,500 plants were relocated to keep them out of German hands. The Russians also followed a "scorched-earth" policy; that is, what they could not move, they burned or destroyed.

The Germans never succeeded in taking Leningrad, Moscow, or Stalingrad, although they came extremely close. Russian military heroism is always associated with these names, especially with Leningrad and Stalingrad. The seige of Leningrad is one of the great stories of wartime courage and endurance. For 900 days (almost 2½ years) the city was surrounded by German troops and under bombardment. Supplies had to be flown in or, during the winter only, brought in over the ice on a nearby lake. People were forced to eat anything alive, including pet dogs and cats and rats, and finally food substitutes such as sawdust, leather, or tree bark. The most important people, workers in weapons factories and soldiers, received daily rations of two or three ounces of bread. Disease and starvation became common. Nearly 600,000 Leningraders starved to death during the 900 day seige, and hundreds of thousands more died of various diseases. But the Germans were never allowed to take this important industrial center and it remained as an inspiring symbol of resistance throughout the difficult early years of the war.

Stalingrad, the Turning Point

Hitler was perhaps even more determined to capture Stalingrad, which was not only an important industrial center and a vital trade mart on the Volga River, but also bore the hated name of Stalin. Hitler was so confident of his power that he launched drives toward Stalingrad and the oil fields of Baku at the same time, in the late summer of 1942, expecting quick victories. But Stalingrad was not easily taken; the early Russian winter found Hitler's 600,000 troops still struggling from street to street in the totally destroyed city. The battle of Stalingrad lasted all fall and winter, with the Russians refusing to give up a single building without a fight. Hitler would not permit retreat, despite the unpreparedness of his army for winter fighting.

By February, 1943, the Siberian troops of the Soviet Army had finally retaken the city and captured the entire German Sixth Army, one of Hitler's best. Not a building was left standing, but the battle of Stalingrad marked the psychological and military turning point of the war. Stalingrad was the furthest point of German penetration, and after the battle the tide of fighting began to roll westward. Throughout the winter of 1942-1943 the attention of the entire world was focused on the stubborn defense of Stalingrad. The Russian victory renewed the hopes of anti-Hitler forces in Europe. The importance of the battle is reflected by the fact that many cities of Europe have streets and squares named after Stalingrad.

Hitler's Mistakes

Although it is always easy to second-guess a quarterback or a general, it is useful to look at Hitler's mistakes in order to point up some important Soviet attitudes. In addition to military mistakes, Hitler made several political mistakes which cost him the support of many Soviet citizens who were anti-Communist and who might have aided the Germans in defeating Stalin. In general, the Russians fought the Nazis with great determination; but in the first year of the war there were a number who welcomed the Germans and fought alongside of them. Had Hitler been more perceptive and less blinded by the myth of German superiority, he might have used the discontent within the Soviet Union to conquer the country quickly. The 1930's had been a period of great suffering and fear for the Russians. Many peasants still opposed collectivization, and the general population was weary of sacrificing improvements in housing and consumer goods for the production of steel and oil. This dissatisfaction plus the desire for independence of national minorities like those in the Caucasus and the Ukraine, could have been turned against the Soviet government with relative ease.

In fact, when German troops marched into the western sections of the Soviet Union, they were sometimes greeted as liberators and some Ukrainians and Russians joined the German army. Hitler did nothing to keep this support, however, and quickly lost it forever. The Nazis viewed the Slavic peoples as "subhuman," only slightly above the Jews, and far below the Germanic peoples. They were good for working in factories, but that was all. As Hitler conquered Eastern Europe and parts of the Soviet Union, millions of Poles, Czechs, Slovaks, Ukrainians, and Russians were shipped back to Germany to work in factories, essentially as slave labor.

Hitler missed an excellent chance to gain Ukrainian and Russian support when he failed to abolish the system of collective farms. This act would have won over many peasants to the German side. Since one major goal of the Germans, however, was the seizure of the rich grain areas of southern Ukraine and Russia, Hitler decided to keep the collective farm system as a good method of collecting grain. Contrary to their hopes, nothing changed for the peasants; grain was merely taken from them and shipped in a different direction, westward to Germany.

The Soviet people living in areas of the USSR occupied by the Germans not only lost their illusions about German "liberation," but they became a significant military factor, carrying out guerrilla warfare behind the German army. From Berlin to Moscow is about 2,000 miles and German supplies had to travel that distance. These extended lines presented a good target to Russian partisans, who caused considerable trouble and contributed much to Hitler's eventual defeat.

It is virtually impossible for Americans to understand what the Second World War was like for the Russians. There was no fighting on American soil and less than a half million Americans were killed. In contrast, a large part of European Russia was occupied (see Map 10), and many cities and towns were partially or wholly destroyed. It is estimated that ten million Russian soldiers and fifteen million civilians died. Hardly a family escaped without the loss of some member. Such facts should be kept in mind when trying to understand Russian opposition to the

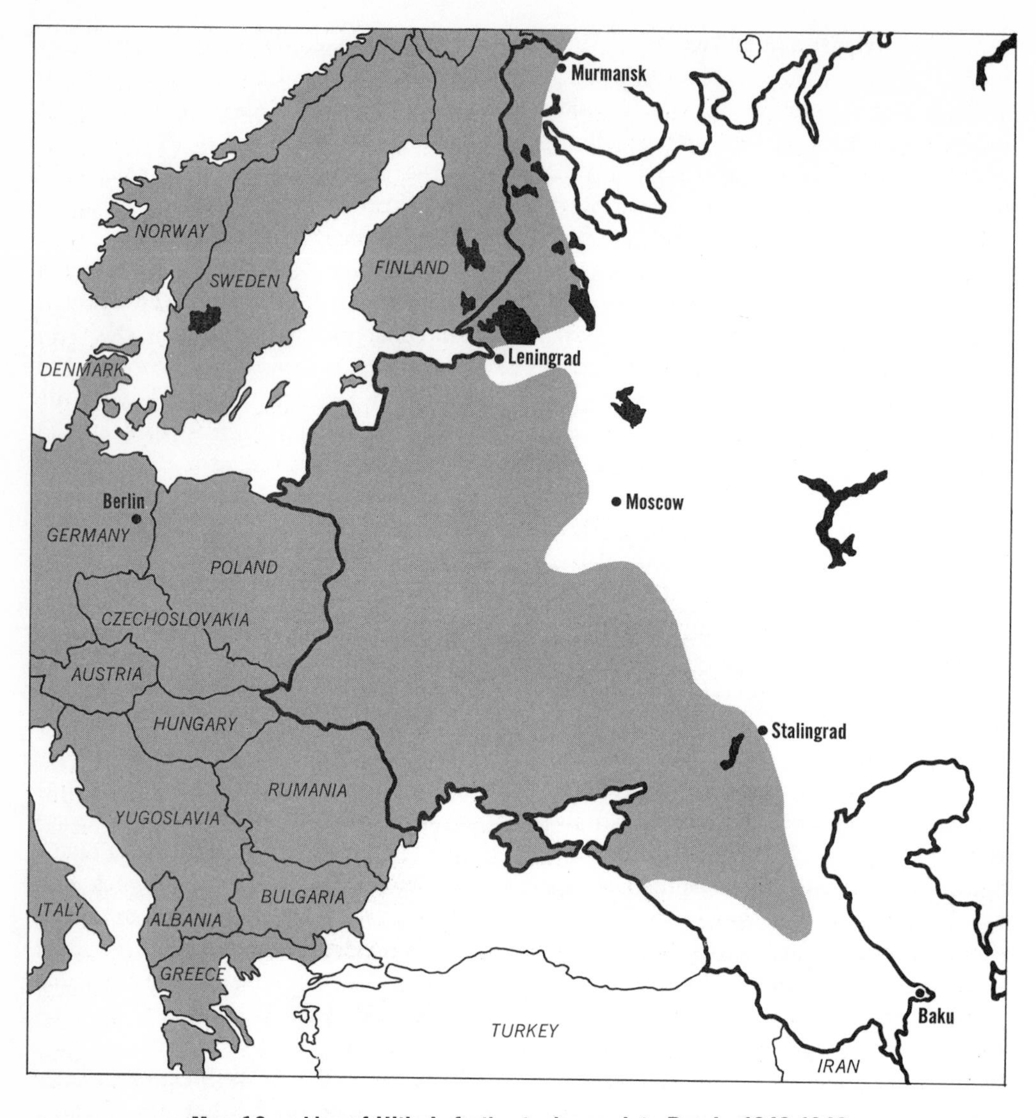

Map 10 Line of Hitler's farthest advance into Russia, 1942–1943
The Germans never succeeded in capturing any of their major objectives: the oil fields at Baku or the cities of Stalingrad, Moscow, or Leningrad.

reunification and rearmament of Germany today. Some of this opposition is naturally propagandistic, but a very genuine fear and hatred of the Germans will exist in the Soviet Union for many years. Many Soviet citizens are sincerely upset that the U.S. is considering giving West Germany control over nuclear weapons.

The End of Hostilities

By 1944 and 1945, Nazi Germany was gradually being squeezed between the British and Americans on the west and the Russians on the east. After driving the Germans from Soviet territory, the Russians moved on into Eastern Europe, first into Bulgaria and Rumania, then into Poland, Hungary, and Czechoslovakia. The western allies landed in France and in Italy. The three major powers were already looking ahead to the situation in Europe after the war, although it seems now that the Russians had a clearer idea of the future than had the British or Americans.

Several meetings of the "Big Three" —President Roosevelt, Prime Minister Churchill of England, and Premier Stalin—were held in 1944 to 1945 at Tehran, Yalta, and Potsdam to discuss the future of eastern and central Europe. (President Roosevelt died in early 1945, and the Potsdam meeting was attended by Harry S. Truman, who had succeeded him.) Tentative agreements were made about dividing central Europe into "spheres of influence," areas in which Russian or British or American influence would be dominant. What precisely was meant by a "sphere of influence" was never decided. It turned out that the Soviet interpretation of this term was rather different from the understanding of it held by Roosevelt and Churchill. By the last of the "Big Three" meetings in July, 1945, there was not really anything left to discuss. The Russians had pushed the Germans back into their own country and had occupied all of central and eastern Europe. There was no way to avoid recognizing these Soviet gains, except by military attack, which no one wanted after four years of war.

Beginnings of the "Cold War"

Most Americans have forgotten how warm our relations with Russia were during World War II. American and Russian cooperation against Hitler was the high point in our relationship, which has always contained elements of conflict and friendship. The early hostility between the two countries gradually diminished in the 1930's, and when Hitler attacked Russia in 1941, England and the United States immediately sent large amounts of aid. Russian and American newspapers and books from this period stress how much the two peoples have in common, how similar they are. Even today these years of cooperation are warmly remembered by many older Russians and Americans.

The wartime cooperation between the Western allies and the Russians proved to be temporary, however, a policy which had been necessary because Hitler's Germany represented a menace to all nations. Even before the actual end of the war, tensions began to emerge between the allies, particularly over the fate of eastern Europe. Western suspicions of Soviet motives grew as it became clear that the Soviets interpreted "sphere of influence" to mean complete control over the areas involved. Using various tactics, the Russians gradually took over the governments of Poland, Czechoslovakia, Hungary, Rumania, and Bulgaria in the period 1945 to 1948. In some cases they used false elections; in others, "popular front" governments, which involved a variety of parties including Communists, were gradually changed into Communist governments. In some countries the local Communist parties were quite strong, in others very weak. Whether the takeover was gradual and seemingly legal, or by means of a violent coup d'état (a sudden military take-over), its success depended ultimately on the presence of the occupying Red army.

By 1948, all countries in eastern Europe were ruled by Communist parties which were obedient to the Soviet Communist Party. Germany was divided into zones, four at first: American,

British, French, and Russian. It was later divided into only two: East and West. Berlin, cut-off in the Eastern Zone, was similarly divided. It was Churchill who coined the phrase "Iron Curtain" to describe the new situation. An "iron curtain" surrounded the territory now held by the Russians. Very few westerners were allowed to visit behind it, and barbed wire and gun towers ensured that eastern Europeans would not go through the curtain to the West. Europe, and to some degree the whole world, was now seen to be divided into two parts, east and west, Communist and anti-Communist. The "cold war," which is still with us today, began in those early post-war years.

The Break with Yugoslavia

In 1948 an event took place in eastern Europe the significance of which became fully apparent only much later. It was the break in relations between Yugoslavia and the Soviet Union. At the end of the war, Yugoslavia was also taken over by the Communists, and it was considered to be just another of Russia's "satellites," which obeyed every command from Moscow. There were differences in Yugoslavia, however, and they explain the Yugoslav actions in 1948 and later. The Yugoslav Communist Party, led by Tito, had come to power after the war without Russian support, unlike the governments in Poland, Czechoslovakia, and the other east European countries. (In Albania also, the Communists came to power without Russian support; this helps to explain why tiny Albania has remained largely independent of Russia. See Chapter 13 for Albania's role in the Russian-Chinese dispute.)

When the Russians began to treat the Yugoslavs as they treated their other satellites, ordering them to carry out this or that policy, Tito refused. One important issue was economic policy. Stalin expected all the countries of eastern Europe to adjust their economies to fit in with and to benefit that of the Soviet Union. The Yugoslavs resented this attitude and refused to cooperate. When Russian agents tried to overthrow Tito, Yugoslavia split away from what had been called the "Communist bloc." Not only did Tito break with Russia, but he got away with it.

This was the first successful break in world Communism. From the point of view of today this split seems far more important than it did in 1948. It is seen now as the beginning of a process which has been picking up speed in the last decade. After 1948, and especially in the past few years, it has not been possible to speak of a single Communism. Rather, we see a variety, an increasing variety, of Communisms —Russian, Chinese, Yugoslav, Polish, and the like—each one claiming to be the *true* one (see Chapter 13).

Developments in China and Korea

Of even greater importance than Tito's breakaway, however, was the triumph of the Chinese Communists in 1949. The civil war between the Communists and the Nationalists of Chiang Kai-Shek, who were supported by the United States, had begun even before the Second World War. Despite tremendous American financial and military aid, the corrupt Nationalist government was gradually pushed entirely out of China. Chiang and his troops fled to the island of Formosa (or Taiwan), where they have been now for a generation, claiming to be the real Chinese government, waiting to return to the mainland. The United States still refuses to recognize the Chinese Communist government, just as we refused to recognize the Soviet Union until 1933.

In 1950, the year after the Communists came to power in China, the Korean War began. Korea had been divided in 1945 somewhat as Germany had; North Korea was regarded as a Soviet sphere of influence, South Korea as an American one. Stalin apparently gambled on taking over the whole country by a surprise attack, counting on American reluctance to get involved in a war 10,000 miles away. He miscalculated, and three years of bitter fighting followed. The United States took the matter to the United Nations and got a resolution passed condemning the North Korean aggression. A United Nations army, mainly composed of American troops, took over most of Korea by 1951. Then the Chinese Communists entered the war and recaptured most of North Korea. After another year of fighting and negotiations, a truce was arranged and the boundary between North and South Korea was fixed at approximately the 1950 location.

The events in China and Korea represent a significant shift of world attention from Europe to Asia (and Africa) in the two decades since 1945. With the exception of the bloody, unsuccessful Hungarian revolt of 1956 (see below), post-war Europe has been relatively stable. By comparison, vast changes have been taking place in the non-European parts of the world, most notably the collapse of colonial empires. The Russians realized the importance of the "East" earlier than the Americans. Stalin, and even more so, Khrushchev, looked to Asia and Africa as key areas of the "cold war." Their success in closely relating Communism to the struggle for independence from colonial rule has increased Soviet prestige while United States prestige has declined in many parts of the non-European world. (See Chapter 13.)

Stalin's Death and the Repudiation of Terror

The death of Stalin in 1953 marked the beginning of what one Russian writer, Ilya Ehrenburg, called "the thaw," the breaking up of the Stalinist system of wide-scale terror. The changes in the Soviet Union since 1953 are numerous and important; the things that remain the same are also numerous and perhaps just as important. There are many opinions as to whether or not the Soviet system has really changed in the post-Stalin years, and the debate continues among politicians, journalists, and scholars.

Two major reforms in the post-Stalin period have been the decentralization of the economy and the substitution of persuasion for terror in the Soviet system as a whole. These reforms came not only because of the change of rulers, but also because of basic developments in the Soviet Union over many years. The Soviet economy had grown tremendously since 1928, and the old methods of central control began to fail as the economy became larger and more complex. By the 1950's it was clearly impossible to direct every factory and farm from one place, Moscow. The economic reforms of the post-Stalin period are described in more detail in Chapter 10.

The end of the system of terror was also a product of changing situations and demands. Terror and compulsion can be fairly effective in forcing social change if all one wants is passive and fearful obedience. Fear, however, works in several ways. People can be forced to obey out of fear, but the same fear often kills initiative and the willingness to take chances. People are not likely to risk expressing a new idea if they are afraid that the disagreement of a superior will totally undermine their own position. It is safer to do nothing except what one is told to do and to repeat only the ideas of higher-ups in the government or the economy.

Obviously, terror is not a very efficient way to run a highly complicated modern country. No government or economy will work smoothly if everyone below the top officials is afraid to make decisions because a wrong one could mean ten years in a labor camp. The Soviet system in 1953 was exhausted by fear. Stalin's successors, first Malenkov and later Khrushchev, began to abolish terror as the basis for Soviet rule, hoping to increase the efficiency and productivity of the system. Most of the labor camps were closed, and many political prisoners were released. The famous writer, Solzhenitsyn (author of *One Day In The Life of Ivan Denisovich*), was one of these prisoners. He had been a German prisoner of war during the Second World War and when he returned to the Soviet Union in 1945 he was arrested on suspicion of collaborating with the Germans. Millions of other innocent Soviet citizens were in labor camps in 1953 for similar "crimes."

Effects of "The Thaw"

The effects of the "thaw" have been felt in all aspects of Soviet life; only a brief description is possible in this limited space. The harsh labor laws of the 1930's and 1940's have been abolished. Workers are now permitted to change jobs or apartments and are no longer imprisoned for being late or missing a day of work.

The "iron curtain" has lifted to an increasing degree. Very few Americans traveled to the Soviet Union in the first decade after the Second World War. After 1955, more and more tourists, students, scientists, musicians, and exhibitions have been exchanged. Freedom of movement is not complete. Only a few hundred Soviet tourists are permitted to visit the United States annually compared to the 15,000 American tourists who visit the Soviet Union. Few Western newspapers and magazines are sold in the Soviet Union. Nevertheless, there is far more contact between the West and the Soviet Union than there had been under Stalin.

Art and literature were greatly affected by the "thaw." Under Stalin, the arts had grown increasingly political; that is, every novel, story, play, picture, movie, and the like, had to be about some important current political or economic problem. If there was a big campaign on to build new factories in the Ural Mountains, then many books would be about heroic Party officials and "Stakhanovite" construction workers in the Urals. The tone of all art and literature was optimistic and heroic. Pessimism and criticism were not permitted, and positive characters always triumphed over negative ones. A writer was expected to describe the present in terms of the future communist ideal, not as he himself might actually see it. This kind of art and literature, the only officially approved kind, was called "Socialist Realism." Its function was to present heroic models for the Soviet citizen to imitate in his daily life. In real life, however, boredom was probably the most common reaction to most Soviet novels, plays, and films.

After 1953 this situation gradually changed. Writers began to criticize more widely; new subjects were mentioned; characters were described in more complicated ways; sometimes no mention was made at all of politics or work. The range of subjects about

Soviet Leader Josef Stalin in 1936, one of the peak purge years

Behind him is Nikita Khrushchev, a rising figure in the Communist Party hierarchy. (Courtesy, Sovfoto)

which artists can write or paint has been steadily widening. There are still limitations, however. For example, the novel, *Dr. Zhivago*, by the great Russian poet Boris Pasternak, was published in the West in 1958 but could not be published in the Soviet Union because of the negative attitude toward the Russian Revolution which the novel expressed. But the changes are very great. For some of the most critical writings of the early "thaw" period, see the paperback collection, *1956: Year of Protest*. (See Chapter 12 for more about Soviet art and literature.)

The Anti-Stalin Campaign

The major turning point in the "thaw" was Khrushchev's "secret speech" denouncing Stalin at the Twentieth Communist Party Congress in February, 1956. In this speech, which later became public in the West but not in the Soviet Union, Khrushchev attacked many of the myths surrounding Stalin and exposed some of his crimes of the purge period. A campaign began to discredit Stalin's policies in many fields and to condemn his mistakes. Many political opponents and innocent victims of Stalin were "rehabilitated," that is, released from prison if they were still alive or their names cleared if they had died or been killed.

The second important point in Khrushchev's anti-Stalin campaign came in 1961 when the Twenty-Second Communist Party Congress voted to remove Stalin's body from the Lenin-Stalin mausoleum on Red Square and to rename all cities, factories, and farms named after him. Stalingrad was changed to Volgograd, for example.

One motivation behind Khrushchev's anti-Stalin campaign was the desire to win the confidence and support of the people, to show them that he would govern more by persuasion and less by terror and that he would permit more criticism and tolerate greater differences of opinion than Stalin had. Some Communist leaders did not share Khrushchev's views on this method of governing. When Poland was upset by demonstrations and Hungary by a bloody but unsuccessful revolution in 1956, these leaders argued that Khrushchev's policy was the cause and that it was too risky to allow even limited criticism.

Another intention of Khrushchev's speech was to discredit his main rivals for power, Malenkov and Molotov. Khrushchev, of course, had been a leading Party figure during the Stalin period and had participated in carrying out his policies. But in his speech he cleverly gave the impression that he had not known until recently of Stalin's crimes, while hinting that his rivals had been deeply involved.

Domestic "Hard" and "Soft" Lines

Khrushchev also realized the dangers of this policy, and after 1956 he shifted frequently between a "hard" or orthodox line and a "soft" or liberal line. The general trend, however, was toward a more liberal policy, allowing criticism and some diversity, and clamping down only when it appeared that the criticism might become a danger to the state. Even then, the "hard line" of Khrushchev was not like that of Stalin, which usually meant prison or execution for offenders. If, for example, a Soviet magazine had a policy of printing the critical work of younger writers, the Soviet government clamped down by replacing the editor with a very conservative Party official. A writer who went too far was prohibited from traveling or even from publishing but was seldom imprisoned as he would have been under Stalin.

This liberalizing trend has continued under Brezhnev and Kosygin. A significant example of a shift to a hard line, however, was the 1966 trial and imprisonment of two Soviet writers, Yuli Daniel and Andrei Sinyavsky. They were convicted of smuggling their writing out of the Soviet Union to have it published abroad. Such actions would hardly be considered a crime in most of the world. They received sentences of three and five years, respectively. (Sinyavsky is perhaps better known by his pseudonym, Abram Tertz.)

Another indication of the difference between the 1930's and the 1960's is the difference in the fate of Stalin's political opponents and the fate of Khrushchev and his. Both of these men rose to power through the Communist Party. After Lenin's death, Stalin gradually eliminated his rivals, Trotsky, Bukharin, Zinoviev, Kamenev, and others by the simple expedient of having them murdered.

By comparison, Khrushchev, Brezhnev, and Kosygin have been far more humane. In the first four years after Stalin's death in 1953, Khrushchev rose to the head of the Party and of the government. He defeated such important leaders as Malenkov, Molotov, Beria, Kaganovich, and Bulganin. Of these, only Beria, former head of the secret police, was executed. All the others were either retired or sent to run factories or hydroelectric plants in Central Asia and Siberia. An irony of recent history is that in 1965 Khrushchev was reported living in retirement in the same apartment building with Molotov and several other political opponents whom Khrushchev had earlier "retired." Both Khrushchev and Molotov were seen in public in June, 1966, when they voted in the elections for the Supreme Soviet, and Khrushchev was nearly mobbed by well-wishers when he appeared to vote in early 1967.

International "Hard" and "Soft" Lines

Khrushchev's policy towards the West was also marked by shifts between "hard" and "soft" lines. At the 1956 Twentieth Party Congress, Khrushchev, in addition to denouncing Stalin, also made some significant revisions in Marxist-Leninist thinking. Both Marx and Lenin generally believed that capitalist and socialist nations would not be able to live together without war. As the capitalists saw the socialist countries becoming stronger, they would eventually resort to war, out of fear.

Khrushchev maintained that war was no longer inevitable. He believed that both sides now recognized the awful power of nuclear weapons (which neither Marx nor Lenin had foreseen) and would avoid a nuclear war, since it would destroy both sides. Therefore, "peaceful coexistence," competition between the two systems by all means except war, was possible. Khrushchev carried the policy of peaceful coexistence to the point of a good will visit to the United States in 1959. On this trip he emphasized the possibilities of increasing Soviet-American cooperation.

Khrushchev also revised the traditional Marxist-Leninist view of the violent class struggle leading to the socialist revolution. Khrushchev stated that violent revolution might not always be necessary, that there might be peaceful ways of establishing socialism. He even spoke of a situation where socialism might be voted into existence by a majority of the people. Kosygin and Brezhnev seem to have accepted these views and support peaceful coexistence and the possibility of the peaceful triumph of socialism.

These two revisions, which allowed the possibility of a peaceful change to socialism and the avoidance of war between east and west, provoked some significant criticism. The Chinese Communists pointed to these new ideas as evidence of Khrushchev's betrayal of Marx and Lenin. The Chinese refusal to accept these revisions is one basis for the Soviet-Chinese split (see Chapter 13 for a discussion of this subject). It is more than an ideological disagreement; it is a serious difference in everyday tactics. The Russians see a long period of nonmilitary struggle from which the Communist world will emerge as victors. The Chinese contend that this is a dream and urge a more militant policy, using guerrilla warfare and the taking of some risks. They want quick results, whereas the Russians are more concerned to avoid war.

Khrushchev and After

Khrushchev's Russia, to use the title of an interesting book by Edward Crankshaw, was a very different place from Stalin's Russia. How significant is the difference and what it means for the future are questions we cannot yet answer for sure. Most journalists, scholars, diplomats, and travelers who lived in Russia fifteen or twenty years ago and have returned to visit there recently report that it is a vastly different country. Some experts believe that the Soviet Union and the United States are gradually becoming more like each other. Others feel that while the Soviet Union may become more like the West in some ways, there will always be very basic differences. Most observers, however, are hesitant to predict the future. The unexpected fall of Khrushchev illustrates the wisdom of their hesitation.

Khrushchev was removed from office in the fall of 1964 for a variety of reasons. We do not yet know exactly how it happened or what was the most important cause of his ouster. Two failures, in agriculture and in relations with China, undoubtedly contributed to his downfall. The fact that Russia was forced to buy wheat from the United States in 1963 was a shocking admission of the failure of Soviet agriculture. The growing disorder within the socialist bloc, especially the increasingly hostile relations with China, was probably considered even more serious.

The Soviet press frequently cited Khrushchev's "hare-brained schemes" as a reason for his removal. Khrushchev loved grand experiments and adventures, such as the "virgin lands" program, or the short-lived attempt to grow corn in cold parts of the Soviet Union, or the 1962 Cuban missile adventure. Khrushchev lost considerable prestige and the confidence of some of his colleagues when the secret Soviet attempt to place missiles in Cuba in 1962 was discovered and the United States forced their withdrawal.

More uncertain than the causes of Khrushchev's fall are the mechanics: how it actually happened, who planned it, how much support Khrushchev had at the end. It seems that the decision to remove Khrushchev was taken at a meeting of the Central Committee of the Communist Party of the Soviet Union on October 14, 1964. Several party leaders made speeches denouncing Khrushchev personally as well as his political and economic failures. Khrushchev angrily attempted to defend himself, but the decision appears to have been made beforehand. The vote to remove him from office was reported to have been unanimous, as most votes in the Soviet Union have been since the early 1920's. But what actually occurred, whether Brezhnev and Kosygin or others actually did the planning for Khrushchev's overthrow, all this is still a matter of speculation.

After Lenin died in 1924, and again after Stalin's death in 1953, several years passed before it became clear who was in charge and what were to be his new policies. Trotsky, the obvious successor to Lenin, was defeated by Stalin, a rather obscure Party official. After Stalin, Malenkov seemed most likely to assume power, but Khrushchev gradually gained control. At present Brezhnev, as General Secretary of the Communist Party, seems to be the top man, but in several years some less well-known figure may emerge as the real power.

The basic features of Khrushchev's rule have been retained by Brezhnev and Kosygin. The new leaders have made it clear that no return to Stalinist policies is planned. The economic reforms of Khrushchev are being continued and expanded, but in a more sensible and practical manner.

A larger investment in agriculture is recognized as of crucial importance. Consumer goods are to be given increasing emphasis in response to public demands. The new Five Year Plan (1966 through 1970) is more realistic than previous ones and takes into account problems that Khrushchev ignored. Neither Brezhnev nor Kosygin is the unpredictable personality that Khrushchev was. Both are bureaucrats, concerned with making the Soviet system work better. (Kosygin has spent most of his life as an industrial manager and economic planner. He was once head of Gosplan.) They are not afraid to try new ideas, but they are not as adventurous as Khrushchev.

The increasing dissolution of the "socialist bloc" seems to be something beyond Soviet control, regardless of who the Russian leader is. Relations with China and the countries of Eastern Europe have continued to deteriorate (in fact, a formal break in relations with China is now more than a distinct possibility) despite the efforts of Brezhnev and Kosygin. The unknown future of the war in Vietnam makes it impossible to predict Soviet relations with America during the next few years. Most indications are, however, that Brezhnev and Kosygin want to continue recent policies of "peaceful coexistence" with the West.

Profound changes have taken place since 1928 when Stalin determined to pull the Soviet Union up by its bootstraps. The Soviet people have survived, at great cost, a major war and wracking internal disorders; a military and industrial power has been created; Soviet influence and prestige are far greater than those of Tsarist Russia.

But the thirty years of Stalin's brutal dictatorial rule created serious problems, which are only beginning to be dealt with. The complete suppression of political opponents and of all social protest created a society of silent and fearful automatons. Khrushchev opened a dangerous window in 1956 by denouncing Stalin. He raised a number of important questions about the Soviet system and about recent Soviet history, but neither Khrushchev nor his successors have provided honest answers to these questions. Since 1953 Soviet policies have swung back and forth between hard and soft positions. This inability either to throw off entirely the methods of the Stalinist past or to return wholeheartedly to them has led to particular unrest among Soviet youth. A constant concern of many students today, and a subject of some of their favorite writers, is the Stalinist past; how to evaluate it, how to understand it, and how to keep it from being repeated.

PROJECTS

A. Research

(1) Why was the Battle of Stalingrad of such great significance? What was the general situation of the war when this battle took place?

(2) Describe the methods used by the Russians to take over Eastern Europe after World War II. (Chapter 3 in *Soviet Russian Imperialism,* by Victor S. Mamatey, is particularly good on this subject.)

(3) The resistance of the Russians during the siege of Leningrad is one of the great stories of World War II. What made it possible? (The books by Goure and Pavlov—see Further Reading—are good sources of material.)

(4) What were some of the obstacles to United States-Soviet cooperation against Hitler in World War II? How successfully did the alliance work? (See Chapter 23 in George Kennan's *Russia and the West Under Lenin and Stalin.*)

B. Activities

(1) Debate whether the Soviet Union can ever return to the policies of the Stalin regime. What is to prevent the re-establishment of the absolute power of the secret police and the massive use of prison camps? How much has the Soviet Union actually changed since Stalin's death in 1953?

(2) Suggest how some underdeveloped nation today, for example, Peru or Kenya, should go about industrializing. Use the Soviet "industrialization debate" of the 1920's as a starting point. What policies would you follow if you were the leader of one of those countries?

(3) Debate whether or not the U.S. should recognize Communist China. What do we have to gain or lose? What did we accomplish by withholding recognition of the Soviet Union for 15 years?

C. Further Reading

Chuikov, V. I., *The Battle for Stalingrad* (Holt, N.Y.)—A description of the famous battle by a Soviet military leader.

Crankshaw, Edward, *Khrushchev's Russia* (Penguin Books, London)—A description of the main aspects of life under Khrushchev. Also, *Khrushchev* (Viking, N.Y.)—A brief biography.

Dallin, D. J., *Forced Labor in Soviet Russia* (Yale University Press, New Haven)—The best book on the labor camps of the Stalin Period.

Daniels, Robert V., editor, *Stalin Revolution: Fulfillment or Betrayal of Communism?* (D. C. Heath, N.Y.)—A collection of short articles discussing the reign of Stalin from various viewpoints.

Gladkov, F. V., *Cement* (Frederick Ungar, N.Y.)—A novel about Soviet industrialization during the 1930's.

Goure, Leon, *The Siege of Leningrad* (McGraw-Hill, N.Y.)—A good description of the 900-day siege.

Ilf and Petrov, *Twelve Chairs* and *The Little Golden Calf* (Vintage Books, N.Y.)—Two very humorous satirical novels about Soviet life in the 1920's and 1930's.

Kochan, Lionel, *The Making of Modern Russia* (Penguin, N.Y.)—Easy-to-read survey, emphasizing nineteenth and twentieth centuries.

Koestler, Arthur, *Darkness at Noon* (New American Library, N.Y.)—A fictional description of the experiences of the "purges."

Leonard, Wolfgang, *The Kremlin Since Stalin* (Praeger, N.Y.)—An excellent analysis of the period 1953-1963.

Mamatey, Victor S., *Soviet Russian Imperialism* (Van Nostrand, Princeton, N.J.)

Pavlov, Dmitri V., *Leningrad 1941: the Blockade* (Univ. of Chicago Press) —A description of the siege of Leningrad by the man who was in charge of food supplies for the city.

Scott, John, *Beyond the Urals* (Houghton Mifflin, N.Y.)—A description of the 1930's, the period of the first Five Year Plan, by an American engineer who worked in the Urals.

Sholokhov, Mikhail, *Harvest on the Don* (New American Library, N.Y.)—A novel about the collectivization period.

Solzhenitzen, Alexander, *One Day in the Life of Ivan Denisovich* (Frederick A. Praeger, N.Y.)—Recent novel about life in one of Stalin's prison camps by a man who unjustly spent many years in one after World War II.

Treadgold, Donald, *Twentieth Century Russia* (Rand McNally, Chicago)—Basic history of modern period.

Von Rauch, Georg, *History of Soviet Russia* (Frederick A. Praeger, N.Y.) —Good, up-to-date history of modern period.

Chapter 8

THE COMMUNIST PARTY

The Communist Party is the only political party in the Soviet Union. It has about 12 million members, including candidate members, far fewer than either of the major American political parties. Not only is it much smaller, but its purpose is quite different. It is primarily a mechanism for the guidance and control of the entire society. Communist Party members are found in every type of organization: in the army, in trade unions, in collective farms, in student groups, in local government, in writers and artists groups. Their function is to guide the development of these activities, to prevent any group or organization from gaining power as a "special interest."

The United States, in contrast, is made up of countless special interests: dairy farmers, laundry workers, wealthy oil men, lawyers, railroad owners, school teachers, and so forth. Each interest works for its own benefit, often in conflict with other interest groups, and each individual is likely to support and gain support from several organized groups or "special interests." In the Soviet Union there is said to be only one interest, that of the whole society. The Communist Party is the protector of this interest.

The Arguments for a Single Party

The official explanation of why there is only one party is simple and goes back to Marxist-Leninist ideology. Marx stated that political parties represented social and economic classes. One party might represent the working class, another the middle class, a third the nobility. The logical conclusion to this thinking is that after the socialist revolution, when there would no longer be classes, there would be no need for more than one party. So the Soviet Union, which claims to be a "classless society," has a single political party.

As discussed in Chapter 5, tight central control—control of the party, the government, and the society—was a primary concern of Lenin. Lenin's tolerance of opposing viewpoints was never very great, as illustrated by the Bolshevik-Menshevik split. Soviet leaders since Lenin have justified the lack of other political parties by arguing that all citizens of the classless Soviet society are in complete agreement on the goals of the society and disagree only over methods of reaching these goals. Such minor differences can be worked out within one party and do not require separate parties.

Advantages of Party Membership

To reach the top in most occupations in the USSR it is almost essential to belong to the Communist Party. Although much larger than Lenin's original party of a few thousand members, the present Communist Party includes only five per cent of the population of the Soviet Union and still reflects Lenin's idea of the party as an elite vanguard of social leaders. All government ministers are Party members, as are 98 per cent of all factory managers. In lower levels of government, the percentage of Party members is much lower (less than fifty per cent in local organizations). Many engineers, technicians, factory foremen, and the like are Party members, but by no means all.

The Communist Party, then, is quite different from American political parties. Belonging to it means something very different from belonging to the Democratic or Republican Party. To understand the Communist Party in the Soviet Union better and to compare it to our own political parties, it is necessary to look at its historical development, its membership, the way it is organized, and the powers that it exercises.

Origins of the Party

The modern Communist Party developed from one wing of the small, secret Social Democratic Labor Party of late nineteenth-century Russia. The Social Democratic Party was one of several only semilegal, and therefore partially "underground," political parties that opposed the autocratic rule of the Tsar. It was not as large as other parties, but it had some outstanding leaders. In previous chapters (5 and 6) the Bolshevik-Menshevik split in the Social Democratic Party has been described, as has Lenin's leadership of the new Bolshevik Party. From the Bolshevik wing, Lenin built a strong, tightly organized revolutionary party that took control of Russia during the chaotic months of 1917 and has remained in power ever since. The change in name from Bolsheviks to Communists occurred in 1918. The new name was more descriptive of the Party's goals; the old name referred only to the past split in the original Social Democratic Party.

The nature of the Communist Party has changed tremendously since its early days, but it is important to remember its background. Since anti-Tsarist political parties were either forbidden or their activities severely limited in prerevolutionary Russia, much of the early Bolshevik activity was secretive. It consisted of propagandizing workers in the larger Russian towns, leading strikes and anti-government demonstrations, and distributing small anti-Tsarist newspapers and magazines, which were printed abroad and then smuggled into Russia. In fact, many of the leaders of the Bolshevik-Communist Party spent most of the decade before 1917 in western Europe (Lenin from 1906 to 1917) or in Russian prisons.

Because it had to operate under police surveillance, and because Lenin believed strongly in a small, centralized, highly disciplined party, the Bolshevik Party never had more than 20,000 members until 1917. It was above all a conspiratorial group, planning for the overthrow of an autocracy.

For a brief period immediately following the October Revolution, the Bolsheviks ruled Soviet Russia in cooperation with the left wing of the Socialist Revolutionary (SR) Party. This partnership was felt to be necessary during the confusion of the first year of the new government, especially since the Socialist Revolutionaries had far greater popular support than did the Bolsheviks. The cooperation with the SR's continued until 1921-1922 in some local soviets. Soon after the civil war, however, all non-Communist political activity was forbidden and in 1927 all parties except the Communist Party were officially declared illegal.

Organization

The Communist Party is organized on many levels: local, regional, republic, and national. The structure forms a pyramid. At the base are approximately 300,000 local primary Party units or cells. They are usually organized at places of work, factories, offices, or collective farms. The smallest primary units consist of at least three Party members and may have several hundred. At the top of the pyramid is the Central Committee and its Politburo. The members of the Politburo, known as Secretaries, are the most powerful figures in the Soviet Union.

Most of the nearly 12 million Party members do not work full-time for the Communist Party. Usually the ordinary members and even the local and regional officials have regular jobs and work for the Party only in their free time. Only between 150,000 and 200,000 Party members are full-time *apparatchiks* (literally, "part of the apparatus," that is, bureaucrats).

Party officials at each level are responsible to Party leaders at the next higher level. At the highest level is the national Party Congress, attended by delegates from Party organizations from the entire country. It is supposed to be held at least once every four years, but, in fact, the congresses have been held irregularly, especially during Stalin's rule. At the most recent, the 23rd Congress, in March, 1966, there were nearly 5,000 delegates. The delegates at the congress elect a Central Committee which is given the responsibility for running the Party between congresses. The Central Committee, which at present has 195 members and 165 alternates, is supposed to meet once every six months.

The Central Committee, in turn, elects a Politburo, which manages Party affairs on a daily basis. There are now eleven Politburo members, or Secretaries, as they are called, and eight alternates. Khrushchev was, and Brezhnev now is, General Secretary. Each of the Secretaries is in charge of a particular department or section: agriculture, education, heavy and light industry, armed forces, international relations, police, ideology, and the like. (During the rule of Khrushchev, the Politburo was known as the Presidium and the General Secretary was known as the First Secretary. The decision to return to the old titles was announced at the 23rd Party Congress.)

Most basic policy decisions are made by the Politburo or the Central Committee and passed down to the republic, regional, and local Party secretaries. The Party Secretary of the Georgian Republic, for example, checks to see that current policies are being carried out by the regional secretaries in his republic. Each regional secretary, in turn, checks on the local Party secretaries in his region. Although, on paper, the Politburo and the Central Committee derive their power from the organizations below them, in actual fact, authority flows in only one direction, from top to bottom.

"Democratic Centralism"

The Party is organized on the principle of "democratic centralism," which was initiated by Lenin. The definition of this term has varied over the years, but the emphasis has always been on the "centralism," not on the "democratic." The most significant aspect of the principle, as it appears in the Party rules, speaks of "the absolutely binding character of the decisions of higher bodies upon lower bodies." In other words, the regional Party leaders do not question the orders they receive from the republic Party Secretary, who in turn is simply passing on the decisions of the Central Committee.

In fact, the Central Committee seldom questions the decisions of the Politburo. In the 1930's and 1940's it was not even the Politburo, but Stalin alone, who established policies. One of the important changes in the post-Stalin years was that Khrushchev's policies had to win the approval of the Politburo and of the Central Committee. He ruled with their cooperation, not as an absolute dictator. Eventually his policies and his manner of governing were rejected by the majority of these bodies and he was removed from office.

The democratic aspect of the principle of democratic centralism is supposed to come from the fact that leaders are always elected by the Party organization one step lower on the ladder. Actually there is only one candidate for each position; he has been chosen beforehand by Party leaders on the next higher level. For example, a candidate for the Moscow Party Central Committee may be chosen by the First Secretary of the Party in Moscow but "elected" by the Party members in one district of the city. The "democratic" election is simply a vote of approval for a decision already made.

Membership

Who belongs to the Party? Since the Communist Party represents, in theory, the working class, one would expect workers to form the majority of the membership. In the early years of the Soviet period this was usually true. Over the years, however, a shift in membership has developed, from workers and nonagricultural laborers to engineers, factory managers, and intellectuals. In 1962, nearly half the members did not work with their hands and over 18 per cent had a university education. In the past decade, over two-thirds of all members have come from the scientific and technical elite.

Oddly enough, the peasants, who until very recently made up the vast majority of the population, have never been well represented in the Party. Because of their stubborn opposition to collectivization, the peasants have never been fully trusted. In addition, Marx and Lenin always preferred the working class to the peasantry, believing industrial life to be superior to agricultural life, more advanced technically and therefore of greater value.

The Party draws its members from every part of society but increasingly from the newly important group of "technocrats"—the engineers, factory managers, and scientists. The Party tries to bring into its membership everyone who has authority and prestige in

A Party member addressing a meeting of workers

The scene is a farm machinery plant in the city of Rostov. (Courtesy, Sovfoto)

order to increase its own prestige and to make certain that no competing centers of influence can arise. Membership is often conferred as an honor for some achievement. For example, the cosmonauts were made Party members. Membership is generally beneficial for both the individual and the Party. However, because of the amount of work involved in Party membership (described below), some people prefer not to join and do not seek membership. Most people are eager for the chances of advancement that membership brings, and to refuse memship when it is offered would be a great insult.

Admittance to the Party is strictly controlled. A prospective member must be over twenty-one and usually over twenty-five. His application is processed by the local Party unit. He must be recommended by three Party members of five-years standing and by the Communist youth group, the *Komsomol* (discussed later in this chapter). If his application is approved, the new member is admitted to candidate status for one year. He may then be admitted to full membership after successfully completing this year of probation. If a member does not perform his Party duties regularly over the years, his membership can be reviewed and he may be expelled.

Training of Party Candidates

The function of the Party has been described by *Pravda* in the following way: "Party work should be aimed at organizing and teaching the masses, at improving management of the economy, at constant growth of the socialist economy, at improving the living standard of the Soviet people, and raising their cultural level."

During the year of candidacy, the prospective Party member is expected to prove his worth by full participation in the daily work of the Party. To understand the Party's role in Soviet society, let us look at the work of a typical candidate member who is a foreman in a steel plant. A Party member in a school, a government office, or a collective farm would have essentially the same duties.

The main responsibilities of the foreman, as a candidate member, would be to see that Party economic policies are observed in his factory and to carry on propaganda activities and agitation among his fellow workers. An important function of Party members is to ensure the observance of the correct Party policies. In a steel plant these would have to do mainly with questions of production: priority for certain items, fulfillment of production goals, quality control, and so on. Such questions are really the business of the managers and engineers of the plant. The Party members in the plant act as a further check, making certain that the Party's directions are being followed.

The second function, the carrying on of propaganda activities and agitation, is the primary duty of all Party members. In a sense the Party members act as a transmission belt between the Party leaders and the people. The task of this transmission belt is to educate and inform.

All varieties of policies and decisions make up this so-called "agit-prop" work. The people may need to be educated about the new policy of higher meat prices or changes in work rules; or about the dangers of spending time with foreign tourists; or about a new campaign against drunkeness; or about the removal of Khrushchev.

Agit-Prop Activities

The duty of the foreman-candidate member is to organize and lead discussions or lectures on these and other topics of current importance. He is responsible for the workers in his section of the steel plant. Party members in other jobs have similar responsibilities where they work. One basis on which the candidate is accepted as a full Party member is his performance in this agit-prop work. His enthusiastic and energetic propagandizing is an important recommendation.

Sometimes this enthusiasm and the desire to prove worthy get a bit out of hand. A few years ago, during a campaign against "Western influences" such as jazz and loud sport shirts, the following item was reported in the Soviet press. One Party member, who was involved in youth work in a small city on the Black Sea, took this campaign more seriously than was intended. In his zeal to prove himself, he organized groups of teen-age boys to roam around the streets and rip off any loud shirts they saw. When this activity, and the fights

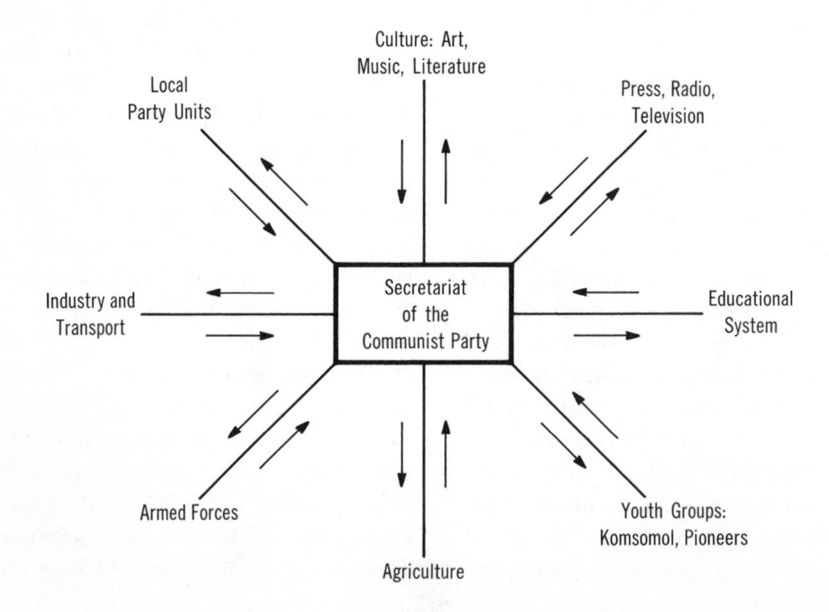

that resulted, became known, the Party member was reprimanded for his excessive enthusiasm.

If such cases are serious enough, a member may be put on probation or even expelled from the Party. Some members are dropped for lack of enthusiasm, others for "anti-Soviet" activities. For example, there are occasional newspaper articles describing a Party member who was discovered attending church regularly or having his children baptized. The most extreme example of such a "cleaning out" of the party was the period of the Stalinist purges, 1934-1939. The same process goes on continually, but without the loss of life, torture, and hysteria of those years.

Union Activities

The typical foreman-candidate Party member we are discussing might also have certain responsibilities connected with the trade union in the steel plant. (See Chapter 12 for a discussion of unions.) A major concern of the Party is that no special interest groups should arise that are independent of its own self-interest. The Party members in a trade union should make sure that the union also follows the policy decisions of the Party. The union must not make demands for higher wages or different working conditions unless the Party has already approved. Often the duty of the Party members is to organize the union members to do "volunteer" work, to work without pay one Sunday a month or an extra hour a day constructing a football stadium or a recreation center. The Party members "educate" and persuade everyone to volunteer this free labor.

Party Schools

At some point in their careers, and perhaps more than once, many Party members attend special schools established to give extra training to Party workers. The schools have two and four year courses of study that prepare Party members for the tasks of leadership and supervision. There are two main areas of study: political history and ideology (Marxism-Leninism) and practical subjects such as industrial management, agricultural technology, trade, and finance. The future Party leaders are trained to apply the theories of Marx and Lenin to all basic economic and social aspects of Soviet life.

Despite the extra work involved in Party membership, many Soviet citizens feel that the advantages outweigh the inconveniences. In almost any field, Party membership is an aid. If two workers or journalists or scientists or teachers have equal qualifications, the Party member would probably be promoted. Members often get preference in assignment of new housing, vacation trips, permission to travel abroad, admission to the university for their children, and the like. Party members generally have what Americans would call "pull." (The picturesque Russian word is *blat.*)

Relationship Between Party and Government

The relationship between the Party and the Soviet government is not easy to understand. It must be remembered at all times that the Party is the center of authority, not the government. As you will see in the next chapter, the government has institutions which are similar to those in the United States, for example, a national legislature divided into two parts. But these forms are largely meaningless. Like all economic and social organizations in the Soviet Union, the government also is guided and controlled by the Party. The basic governmental policies are estab-

The present two top Soviet leaders

Prime Minister Alexei Kosygin on the left and Leonid Brezhnev, General Secretary of the Communist Party, on the right. (Courtesy, Wide World Photos)

lished by the leading Party officials and then executed by the government officials.

In some cases the highest Party officials are also the government leaders, but this is not necessary. Khrushchev held the highest positions in both the Party and government, General Secretary of the Party and Prime Minister of the government. His power came from his position in the Party. Kosygin, the successor to Khrushchev as Prime Minister, is a less powerful figure than Khrushchev's successor as General Secretary, Brezhnev. The leading government figures are given the task of running the Soviet system on a daily basis. In doing this, they follow the guidelines laid down by the top Party officials. Their titles may sound impressive, but the real power remains in the Party.

It is interesting to note that when Mao Tse-tung retired from part of his job of leading Communist China, he dropped his role as Premier but retained his position as head of the Party. He therefore gave up some of the work and daily responsibilities, but none of the power.

The Komsomol

The Komsomol, or Communist Youth League, is a very important organization that sponsors a variety of activities for its twenty-three million members. A majority, but by no means all, of Soviet youth, ages fourteen to twenty-eight, are Komsomol members, organized in nearly 350,000 local units or clubs. In his speech to the Fifteenth Komsomol Congress in 1966, the First Secretary, S. P. Pavlov, outlined the main tasks of the Komsomol: (1) Edu-

A reading room in a Pioneer palace

These palaces also provide recreational activities and music and arts and crafts programs. (Courtesy, Sovfoto)

cation of the youth in Marxism-Leninism; (2) encouragement of social and political activity and participation in major national economic campaigns; (3) inculcation of patriotism and feeling of solidarity with all workers of the world.

As mentioned earlier, the Komsomol is in one sense a "training ground" for future Party members. Those young people who aspire to Party membership often take an active role in the political activities of the Komsomol: lectures, discussions, demonstrations. They also lead the government's economic campaigns among the young workers. Under Khrushchev, thousands of young men and women were organized to move to the "virgin lands" of Kazakhstan or to construction projects in Siberia. A large city on the Amur River in eastern Siberia was built largely by Komsomol members during the 1930's and is named Komsomolsk.

The Komsomol also concerns itself with cultural and athletic activities. It sponsors dances, sports events, recreation clubs, concerts, and publishes youth magazines and newspapers. Most young people join for these social activities but a few join as a way of starting their Party or government careers.

There is also a youth group for children from ten to fourteen years of age, the Pioneers. Almost all youth of this age belong to the Pioneers. Their activities are similar to those of our Boy Scouts and Girl Scouts, YMCA, YWCA, and other recreational groups. Some time is devoted to political education but most of the activities are such things as nature study, camping, sports, art and music lessons, folk dancing, crafts and hobbies, chess, and the like. Pioneers also do some useful work such as gardening and cleaning up parks. The slogan of the Pioneers is almost the same as that of the Boy Scouts: "Always Prepared!" Pioneers wear white blouses and bright red scarves.

PROJECTS

A. Research

(1) Lenin took some of his attitudes toward the organization of his party from the ideas of two nineteenth-century revolutionaries, Nechaev and Tkachev. Find out more about these figures; the books by Reshetar and Schapiro have some material. Dostoevsky's novel *The Possessed* (sometimes translated as *The Devils*) is partially based on Nechaev and his followers.

(2) The Soviet philosophy of raising children, on which many Komsomol and Pioneer activities are based, owes a great deal to an early Soviet educator, Anton Makarenko. Some of his work is now available in English, in a recent paperback, *The Collective Family: A Handbook for Russian Parents.* In Makarenko's approach, the emphasis is placed on raising children in the "collective" spirit rather than one of individualism. How might this approach differ from the methods used in American schools?

B. Activities

(1) Compare the Soviet Communist Party with our Democratic or Republican Parties. What are some differences in the way they are organized? In their activities and functions?

(2) Discuss whether a one-party system is always "undemocratic." Can a one-party system give people a chance to express their views and influence their government? Can one party, for example, the Democratic Party in the U.S., include a wide variety of viewpoints? Did the opinions expressed in the "industrialization debate" within the Communist Party during the 1920's differ as much as those expressed by the Democratic and Republican Parties today? What role does the ordinary American citizen play in choosing a President or Senator?

C. Further Reading

Kassof, Allen, *Soviet Youth Program* (Harvard University Press, Cambridge, Mass.)—A description of the Komsomol and Pioneer programs.

Makarenko, Anton S., *The Collective Family: A Handbook for Russian Parents* (Anchor, N.Y.).

Miller, Wright, *Russians as People* (E. P. Dutton, N.Y.)—Read Chapter 8, "Russians and their government."

Reshetar, John S., *A Concise History of the Communist Party of the Soviet Union* (Frederick A. Praeger, N.Y.)—A good short history of the party from its nineteenth century beginnings.

Schapiro, Leonard, *The Communist Party of the Soviet Union* (Vintage Books, N.Y.)—A longer, more detailed history than Reshetar's.

Chapter 9

THE SOVIET GOVERNMENT

To understand how the Soviet Union is ruled, one must look at the Communist Party, not at the formal government structure. The government is subordinate to the Party since it has no actual power to make policies. The influence of the Party in all aspects of Soviet life was described briefly in the preceding chapter.

The different branches of the Soviet government do not act independently as do those of the American government. One principle of the United States government is a balance of powers between the executive, legislative, and judicial branches. When the President sends a bill to Congress, for example, there is no guarantee that Congress will pass it. All branches of the Soviet government are "executive" in that they execute or carry out policies decided upon by the Communist Party leadership. Government officials function as bureaucrats; that is, they follow orders and put into action policies that are determined by someone else. The role of the Soviet government is thus a passive rather than an active one. Real power is concentrated in the Communist Party Politburo and Central Committee (see diagram).

There is much overlapping of government and Party membership. Many, though by no means all, government officials are also Party members. This situation is especially true at the highest levels of government. Thus, all members of the Council of Ministers belong to the Communist Party. (These would be men such as the Minister of Defense, the Minister of Foreign Affairs, and the like. The corresponding group in the United States would be the President's Cabinet.)

In the Supreme Soviet, the highest legislative body in the nation, similar in form to our Congress, 76 per cent of the delegates are members of the Party. Each republic has a *soviet,* or council, and on the lowest level are city and district soviets. In the local soviets, about half of the officials are Party members.

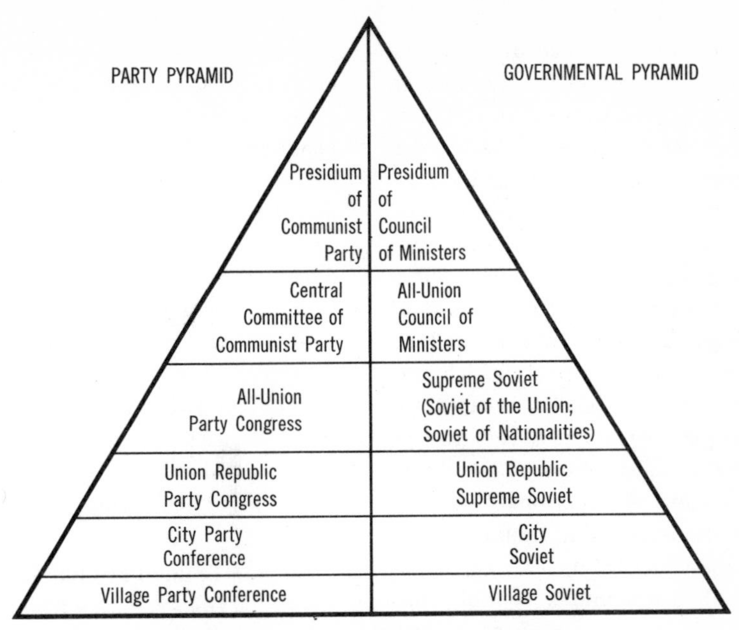

Relationship between Party and government

The entire pyramid of government and public organs shown at right is in fact controlled by a corresponding pyramid of Party organizations shown at left. Party leaders determine basic policies; government leaders carry them out. Often the members of the two groups overlap.

It is assured, then, that although many non-Party people are involved in government organizations, especially on the local level, Party policy will be carried out. Even at the lowest level, in a small village, for example, there will be some Party members whose job it is to see that Party directives are followed.

Development of the Soviet

The basic unit of government in Russia is thus seen to be the soviet. As we learned in Chapter 6, the history of the soviet goes back to the beginning of this century. Soviets were organized by factory workers in Moscow and St. Petersburg to direct strikes and to give voice to their complaints and demands for higher wages. Later, in 1917, these soviets began to make political demands. Trotsky headed the soviet in Petrograd, and the Bolsheviks demanded that all government power be turned over to the soviets of workers' and peasants' deputies.

After October, 1917, the system of soviets became the new government of Russia. In theory, and for several years in practice also, soviets were democratically elected on various levels —district, town, city, province, republic, and national. This system still exists today, but the soviets no longer have the power they once had. For a few years after 1917, representatives of several parties besides the Bolsheviks participated in the work of the soviets. Gradually, however, the Bolsheviks assumed absolute power, and the Party took over the former power of the soviets.

The Supreme Soviet (The Legislative Branch)

A good illustration of the emptiness of the formal structure of government is the Supreme Soviet, according to the Constitution the highest law-making body in the Soviet Union. In outward appearances, the Supreme Soviet can be compared to our Congress, with its House of Representatives and Senate. The Supreme Soviet also has two houses, a Soviet of the Union and a Soviet of Nationalities. To the first of these houses, delegates are elected on a straight population basis, with one representative for each district of 300,000 people. (Compare this to our House of Representatives.) Delegates to the Soviet of Nationalities are elected on the basis of national quotas: each Republic has thirty-two representatives, each autonomous republic has eleven, each autonomous region five, and each national district one. (Autonomous republics, regions, and national districts are separate governmental units representing minority peoples within the framework of the fifteen major republics.) The system ensures each national group in the country at least some representation. Even a Siberian tribe or a small ethnic group in the Caucasus will have one representative.

This impressive democratic appearance, however, is soon seen to be purely formal. The Soviet of the Union has 767 members; the Soviet of Nationalities has 750. The two Soviets generally meet together, twice a year, each time for four or five days. It is difficult to believe that real and significant debate can take place in a body of some 1,500 delegates who meet for less than two weeks during the year. Obviously, there is very little a group of that size can accomplish in such a short period except to vote their approval of decisions already made elsewhere.

A number of facts support the view that the Supreme Soviet is not an active legislative force. Votes are always unanimous. The delegates hold a variety of full-time jobs and could not be expected to know much about the government. (They represent many fields and always include well-known writers, athletes, cosmonauts, productive workers, and the like.) It is not a coincidence that meetings of the Central Committee of the Party are frequently held shortly before the sessions of the Supreme Soviet. Major policies are debated and decided upon by the Central Committee, and these decisions are then turned over to the Supreme Soviet for its "rubber stamp" approval.

Council of Ministers (The Executive Branch)

The actual administrative or executive duties of the government are delegated to the Council of Ministers, a group of over fifty men, headed by a chairman and several deputy chairmen. The Council of Ministers is appointed by the Party. Although the Party decides policy and the Supreme Soviet passes laws based on that policy, the Council of Ministers is responsible for the daily implementation of the laws and decrees. Khrushchev's official government title was Chairman of the Council of Ministers, or Prime Minister. His real power, however, came from his position as General Secretary of the Party. When Khrushchev was forced from power, he was replaced as Chairman of the Council of Ministers by A. N. Kosygin and as General Secretary of the Party by L. I. Brezhnev. Many observers concluded from this division of powers that Brezhnev is the more important of the two.

Among the members of the Council of Ministers are the heads of ministries such as Defense, Transportation, Education, Trade, Agriculture, Electric

The auditorium of the new Congress Hall

This modern structure built in 1961 inside the old Kremlin walls houses the Supreme Soviet and the Party Congresses and is also used for ballet performances and concerts. (Courtesy, Sovfoto)

Power, Health, and the like. Also included are the chairmen of committees on automation, atomic energy, and other specialized subjects, and the heads of agencies such as police, scientific research, development of natural resources, and the like. The number of Council members has varied greatly over the years, but the Council has always been much larger than our Cabinet.

Local Authority

According to the Constitution, the Soviet Union is a federation of fifteen independent republics, voluntarily joined together but with the right to conduct their own affairs and even to secede from the Union. Each republic, therefore, has its own Supreme Soviet and Council of Ministers. The laws passed in the Supreme Soviet of the Ukrainian Republic are usually identical to those passed by the Armenian Supreme Soviet or the national Supreme Soviet. There has never been an attempt by any republic to test its rights to secede from the Union; the government would consider such an effort "counterrevolutionary" and would suppress it.

The individual republics and provinces do have a certain amount of control over their own affairs. This is due to the different types of ministries. Some ministries are tightly centralized and act for the nation at large. That means, for example, that the Ministry of Foreign Trade is run directly from Moscow. All trade with other nations is handled in Moscow, not by individual republics, or local groups, or factory managers in various parts of the country. In less important ministries, however, control is shared by Moscow and the republics. For example, general educational standards are set and developed by Moscow, but each republic has its own ministry of education that adapts the national policies and standards to local conditions. Instruction in most republics is in the native language, as well as in Russian, at least in the schools, and sometimes in the universities also.

Other less significant matters may be handled entirely on the local level, for example, recreation, city transportation, housing, or light industry. Especially since 1953, there has been a trend toward decentralization. Stalin tried to keep as much power and control in Moscow as possible. Obviously, to refer every problem or decision to Moscow, however, involves such delays that chaos often results. Recent Soviet leaders have been trying to strike a balance between central control and local initiative. (For more details, specifically in the economic sphere, see Chapter 10.) Standards set up by some government official in a Moscow office cannot be expected to fit every local situation. Local soviets in cities or districts (similar to our counties) generally follow central guidelines but with some adjustments for specific local conditions.

There is no real danger that local actions will be taken that are in conflict with the basic policies of the Party. Remember that even in a village soviet some of the officials will be Party members whose first concern is that Party objectives be fulfilled. It is difficult, if not next to impossible, for special interests to win out over those of the national government and the Communist Party.

Elections

Elections to the national Supreme Soviet are held every four years and to the republic Supreme Soviets and to local soviets, every two years. Candidates may be nominated by various groups: trade unions, youth organizations, and most importantly, local Communist Party organizations. Only a single candidate is selected to run for each position so that the voters are presented with only one slate of candidates. Their choice is simply to approve or reject the names on this single slate.

In the 1966 elections, 99.94 per cent of all eligible voters cast their ballots. The candidates for the Soviet of the Union received 99.76 per cent favorable votes. The candidates for the Soviet of Nationalities received an even greater majority, 99.80 per cent.

This remarkable percentage is often much lower in republic or local elections. There is still no choice, only a single candidate for each position, but in recent years it is no longer unusual for a particularly unpopular local official to receive less than 50 per cent of the votes. In such cases, another candidate is offered to the voters, again only for their *yes* or *no* vote. A recent report stated that 208 local candidates were rejected in various 1965 local elections. Most of these elections were held in villages.

Until recent years, the method of voting in Soviet elections discouraged people from marking their ballots *no*. The voter received his ballot at the polling place. To vote *yes* all he had to do was fold the ballot, without marking it in any way, and drop it in a box that was usually placed in the center of the room. To vote *no*, however, he had to enter a curtained booth and mark the ballot with a pencil before dropping it in the box. Obviously, if someone went into the booth he was going to vote *no*. He would naturally be noticed doing this and perhaps asked why he had done so. This situation could hardly be described as a "secret ballot," one of the rights guaranteed by the Soviet Constitution.

Since Stalin, however, there has been a trend toward a genuine secret ballot, even if there is only a single name or slate on it. It does offer the voters an opportunity to express their disapproval

Anniversary parade of October Revolution across the main square of Volgograd
Top city and Party officials sit in the reviewing boxes in front of portraits of major national leaders. Such parades are held in all Soviet cities.

of local officials, since it is now considered acceptable to enter the booth.

There have been some suggestions recently about placing several candidates on the ballot for each position. The head of the Armenian Supreme Soviet has acknowledged that although everyone is agreed on basic questions, there are still some differences of opinion. So far, no action has been taken on such proposals.

Election Campaigns

Although there is only a single slate of candidates, Soviet election campaigns are vigorous and noisy. It is not a campaign in the usual sense, with two or more candidates arguing and debating issues, attacking each other, and making promises. The purpose of Soviet elections is educational. During the weeks preceding the elections, newspapers, radio, and television are full of articles and commentary about the latest policies of the Party. Speeches and propaganda meetings are frequent. Candidates hold campaign meetings with various groups to discuss and explain certain issues. Party agitators visit homes and talk to voters about the candidates. Elections provide an opportunity for the government to explain its new policies to the people, not a chance for the people to choose between several different policies.

Soviet elections are also supposed to demonstrate that the government is supported by the entire Soviet people and that there is no disagreement among Soviet citizens. Only the most naive person, however, would accept the nearly unanimous election results as proof that the Soviet people are in complete agreement on all questions.

Soviet Courts (The Judicial Branch)

In the American system of checks and balances, each branch of the government, executive, legislative, and judicial, acts as a check on the others. There is a different kind of relationship in the Soviet system: the party controls and dominates all branches of government. This includes the Soviet judiciary, that is, the courts. In both the United States and the Soviet Union, there is a Supreme Court and a system of lower courts on the republic, county, city, and precinct levels. The role of the courts in the two countries is different, however.

The United States Supreme Court often has to decide whether or not a law passed by Congress or by a state is constitutional. (For example, when the 1964 Civil Rights Bill was passed, it was immediately challenged in the courts by segregationists.) The Supreme Court serves as a check on other powers, interpreting the Constitution so as to prevent lower courts, the states, the Congress, or the President from passing or enforcing laws that contradict it. In a sense, the Supreme Court and the rest of the American judiciary stand above the rest of the government, maintaining an objective view and guarding the basic principles of the Constitution.

The Soviet courts are more involved in daily political life. They are influenced by the Communist Party, which sets general policy for the courts as it does for all government and non-government organizations. A clear statement of the role of the courts in the Soviet Union is given in this quotation from a Soviet law book, cited in George Feifer's recent book, *Justice in Moscow* (see Further Reading):

> "The court does not and cannot stand beyond politics, beyond the solution of the tasks that face the state, beyond the direction of the Party. The court is an active, effective conductor of the policies of the state, a participant in the construction of Communism."

The traditional Marxist-Leninist view of law is that law, like all aspects of a society, is a product of the class struggle. Law is the instrument of the ruling class. In the United States, law is "capitalist"; in the Soviet Union, "socialist." There are no absolute or universal laws. Every ruling group uses laws to keep itself in power.

This attitude, combined with a general view that the end justifies the means, helped to make possible the period of Stalinist terror in the 1930's. During this period, it was impossible to get a fair trial. Many accused persons had no defense lawyer; trials were usually held in secret; there were no guarantees of appeal, or even a real chance to defend oneself. Sentences were often unbelievably harsh.

How Soviet Courts Function

As in other areas, the Soviet Union has moved away from these excesses of the Stalin period toward a more objective legal system. Most trials are public; the accused is guaranteed a lawyer; judges generally stay within standard limits in issuing sentences. Still, there are some basic differences between Soviet and Western law, and there are still tendencies in the direction of Stalinist practices.

The typical Soviet court, called a People's Court, has a judge and two "lay assessors." The judge is "elected" for five years by the people. The "lay assessors" are men or women chosen by their trade unions in the factory or office where they work. They serve for two weeks a year for two years. Two-thirds of the judges are Communist Party members; the lay assessors may or may not be Party members. These three people hear the case and decide it by majority vote. Usually the lay assessors follow the judge, but sometimes they out-vote him.

There is no jury in a Soviet court, but this is not as strange as it might seem to Americans. In most European legal systems there is no jury. Jury trial is largely an English tradition, which the U.S. adopted.

Another difference is the importance of the pre-trial investigation in the Soviet legal system. (Again, this Soviet practice is very close to European, but not to English, traditions.) The investigation is very thorough. Testimony is taken from all people involved, including the accused and witnesses. Much of the actual trial consists simply in going over this material. The idea behind this system is that if a person is innocent, he will probably demonstrate this during the investigation. He would then be released, and no trial would be necessary. In theory, only the guilty are actually brought to trial. This system avoids the long delays between arrest and trial that are common in American courts. It also has some advantages for poor people accused of crimes. Since the State conducts the investigation and assigns the lawyers, a rich person cannot take advantage of his wealth by hiring a better lawyer. The great disadvantage in this system is that everyone brought to trial is generally assumed to be guilty.

Conduct of the Trial

During the trial the court interests itself not just in the actual crime but in the whole character and life of the accused. It hears many opinions about the man from his friends, neighbors, fellow-workers, and others who know him. One of the unique Soviet legal practices is the "social representative."

Suppose a factory worker is caught stealing money from another worker's locker. Before the trial, his fellow workers at the factory will meet and select a representative to testify at the trial on the accused's character. The representative may plead in his favor, saying that the man is a hard worker, never drinks or gets in trouble, and that he should be treated leniently. Or he may testify that the man is often late for work, gets into fights, and is generally a "bad egg."

The attempt to draw society into the legal system is also made by having the courts travel to the people. For example, in the case cited above, the trial might have taken place after work at the factory itself, with the workers assembled to observe.

In general, Soviet courts are more informal than ours, partially because the verdict is usually known in advance. A primary aim then becomes the education of the accused and the observers. Thus the emphasis on examining the whole man and his life, the attempt to find out how he went wrong. There is little argument over the facts of the case, since they were usually established in the pre-trial investigation. The defense will, however, try to show why the accused should be given a light sentence.

Punishment

Very few convicted criminals are sent to prison in the Soviet Union. Most are sent to some type of labor colony in a rural area, the type depending on the severity of the sentence. Generally the convicts live in barracks and work in forests or on construction projects. If the crime and the criminal's record warrant, he may be sent to isolated areas of the Far North and Siberia. Overnight visits by the convict's wife are usually permitted. The life in Soviet labor colonies today is less like that described in *A Day in the Life of Ivan Denisovitch* (written about Stalin's labor camps) than it is like the rough life of any frontier. In many labor colonies the life of a convicted man is a much more normal and healthy one than that of a convict in most Western prisons.

In some ways Soviet treatment of criminals is more advanced than its Western counterpart. The legal system, however, still lacks a solid foundation of independence and freedom from political excesses. The court is still influenced by whatever political or social campaign has been initiated by the Party. In 1961, for example, the Party began a tremendous offensive against economic crimes. The death penalty was instituted for persons convicted of large-scale embezzlement, misuse of state funds, or speculation in foreign currency. Very heavy penalties were handed out for what would be minor crimes in other countries.

The danger remains that the Party will use the courts, as well as other organizations, to attack what it considers the worst evil of the moment. A return to Stalinist tactics is probably impossible, but something of that spirit lingers. Many Soviet lawyers and jurists are struggling against this past. They wish to see Soviet law reach a stable position, beyond politics, a position somewhat like the one law holds in Western countries. Great progress toward that goal has occurred since 1953, although some distance still remains.

Summary

It is tempting, but not entirely accurate, to conclude smugly that the whole elaborate Communist system of national, republic, and local soviets is a sham, that the Soviet constitution is a farce, and that the people have no voice in their government. Certainly the Soviet government is not a representative democracy as Americans think of one. Elections are essentially meaningless, and the ordinary citizen cannot express his discontent by replacing his mayor with one of his own choice.

The hierarchy of the government, running from the Supreme Soviet and its Council of Ministers down to the village soviet, is designed, as Stalin expressed it, as "a transmission belt between the party and the masses." A few men at the top decide questions of policy and their orders eventually filter down to the lowest levels.

But the "transmission belt" works both ways. Reactions, complaints, protests, filter up from the masses of ordinary citizens. They may be, and frequently are, completely ignored. There are no built-in means by which the views of the people can influence government decisions. No one has to listen to the demand of many citizens for more housing construction. Nevertheless, since the end of the Stalin terror, the government leaders have begun to realize that at least a minimum of attention must be paid to public opinion.

A government can be responsive to the demands of its citizens, it can govern by force, or it can use both tactics. The Soviet Union under Khrushchev began to move in the direction of winning the public's loyalty by satisfying some of their demands. The new government seems to be moving further in that direction.

PROJECTS

A. Research

(1) Compare the personal backgrounds of some American and Soviet political leaders such as Johnson, Kennedy, Brezhnev, Kosygin, and Khrushchev. Outline their rise to political power.

(2) Why do the Soviet Union, the Ukrainian Republic, and the Belorussian Republic have three separate representatives at the United Nations?

(3) Why did Franklin Roosevelt attempt to "pack" the Supreme Court with judges who agreed with his policies? If he had been successful, what effect would this have had on the system of checks and balances?

B. Activities

(1) The Soviet system has no checks and balances such as ours. The legislative, executive, and judicial branches all act according to one policy. Compare to the United States system. Give an example (1) of a law that a President recommended but that Congress rejected; (2) of a law that Congress passed but the President vetoed; (3) of a law that Congress passed but the Supreme Court ruled unconstitutional.

(2) In the United States there is often tension between national and local government. The Southern defense of "states rights" is a dramatic current example. Is this also true in the Soviet system? Discuss the amount of local governmental power in the Soviet Union as compared to that in the United States.

C. Further Reading

Armstrong, John A., *Ideology, Politics, and Government in the Soviet Union* (Praeger, N.Y.)—A brief introduction to Soviet government.

Brezezinski, Z., and Huntington, S., *Political Power; USA/USSR* (Viking Press, N.Y.)—A comparison of some aspects of the two political systems and how they solve common problems.

Fainsod, Merle, *How Russia is Ruled* (Harvard University Press, Cambridge, Mass.)—The best single work on the Soviet system although detailed and difficult.

Feifer, George, *Justice in Moscow* (Dell Publishing Co., N.Y.)—A good description of how Soviet courts work by an American who spent a year studying law in Moscow.

Hazard, John N., *The Soviet System of Government* (Univ. of Chicago Press)—Basic textbook on Soviet Government.

Mote, Max E., *Soviet Local and Republic Elections* (Hoover Institution Studies No. 10, Stanford, Calif., 1965)—A brief description of the Soviet election process.

Chapter 10

The Soviet Economy

Running the Soviet economy is an extremely complex task. In theory it is a collectivist economy, which means that all enterprises belong to the people. Actually, the government owns and manages all factories, stores, mines, railroads, electric power plants, and communication facilities; it also exerts a large measure of control over farms. No factories or stores are privately owned. Management of such a vast economy requires an immense amount of planning. The most important organization in the Soviet economic system, therefore, is *Gosplan,* the State Planning Committee.

Planning Through Gosplan

Gosplan must make many kinds of planning decisions for the whole economy. What sectors of the economy will be developed most rapidly, what items will be produced and in what quantities, how natural resources will be used, how supplies will be delivered to factories, how manufactured goods will be moved around the country—these are only a few of the questions that occupy the planners in the Moscow Gosplan office.

Early each spring, Gosplan receives certain general instructions from the Politburo of the Communist Party, the real center of governmental power (see Chapter 8). These instructions reflect basic policy decisions about the nature of economic development during the next year. The decisions are made for political as well as economic reasons. For example, the Soviet Union produces all the sugar it needs but buys Cuban sugar in order to support the Castro government. The Party leaders establish a list of priorities for major kinds of production: military equipment, housing construction, new factories and mines, transportation facilities, farm machinery, and consumer goods. They decide which projects are the most important and will therefore have a priority on natural resources and the best workers.

Gosplan must now get to work to translate this list of priorities into specific production goals for every sector of the economy: 5 per cent more clothing, 20 per cent more kilowatts of electric power, 10 per cent more mining equipment, 25 per cent more drills. There will be thousands of such specific production targets, each based on what was produced the previous year and reflecting the highest hopes for a great increase in the next year. Often the targets are set at extremely optimistic levels in order to stimulate Soviet workers to greater and greater efforts.

These production goals are then passed down to the Gosplan bureaus in each republic, who will turn them into specific instructions for every enterprise in their republic. For example, the Ukrainian Republic may be assigned a goal of 10,000 pieces of farm machinery. The Ukrainian Gosplan distributes this total among all the machine building factories in the republic. One factory may be ordered to concentrate on producing harvesters, another on combines and tractors.

Meeting Quotas

The factory directors receive their orders, and they must figure out how to meet their quotas. They send back to the republic Gosplan a list of the raw materials, supplies, and money for wages they need in order to fulfill the quotas. The common reaction of directors is to protest the high production quota assigned to their factories. The manager of a Latvian shoe factory assigned to produce 200,000 pairs of men's shoes may report that he cannot raise his output to more than 185,000 pairs. He will also request delivery of more leather and extra money to purchase new machines and to hire more workers.

In almost every case the original production goal is set at the absolute maximum, or even higher. There is constant pressure to increase production at ever faster rates. Factory managers naturally resist this pressure and ask for the lowest quotas they can get. They often succeed in winning some revisions, but many quotas are still quite unrealistic. Everywhere one looks in the Soviet Union one sees posters of smiling workers struggling to meet their quotas. Such slogans as "Fulfill and overfulfill!" are posted everywhere.

The republic Gosplan collects all the requests for materials and for quota revisions from the individual enterprises. It coordinates all this information and sends a report back to Moscow. To take one example, the Ukrainian Gosplan may report that Ukrainian factories can increase production of farm machinery next year by 10 per cent, not by 12 per cent as ordered. To accomplish this, Ukrainian enterprises must be supplied with x tons of steel, x tons of coal, x additional kilowatts of electric power, x thousands of extra parts, x million rubles for wages, and numerous other materials. This process is repeated for hundreds of items and thousands of enterprises. (There are now over 250,000 state industrial enterprises, plus state farms, trading organizations, and retail stores.) The central Gosplan must collect and collate the data for all these enterprises and issue a revised plan.

By the end of the year the revised plan is ready and is sent to the republic Gosplan agencies. Again they work out specific schedules for all enterprises and send instructions to the directors. Monthly production quotas are established for most factories. Plans cannot cover every detail, however, and unexpected occurrences cannot be foreseen. A drop in steel production, a delayed delivery of machine parts, or a

Part of a work-team in a Moscow factory

Workers are often organized into brigades which then compete with each other. The banner, typical of many hanging in factories and public places, urges workers to increase production in honor of the Twenty-Third Party Congress. (Courtesy, Sovfoto)

poor cotton harvest can disrupt the schedules of many factories using these materials.

A great amount of time is spent during the year revising plans and changing priorities. If a clothing mill receives only 70 per cent of the cotton expected because of a poor harvest, how should its quotas be revised? Should the original number of army uniforms be made and fewer women's coats? Or should fewer of each be made? Because of the failure of the cement manufacturers to meet their production quotas, should less housing be built, or fewer roads, or fewer recreation facilities? Questions such as these come up constantly and must be referred back to the central or the republic Gosplan for answers, a procedure that creates a great deal of inefficiency and delays.

Advantages of Central Planning

These examples only begin to give an impression of the problems involved in planning the Soviet economy. There are advantages to this system of centralized planning, however, especially from the point of view of the government leaders. Since they control the use of all the resources of the country, they are able to decide how the country is to develop. Especially under Stalin, top priority was given to heavy industry and defense. Stalin's goal was the construction of a modern military and industrial machine. To accomplish this, strict limits had to be put on the production of consumer goods. Only the absolute minimum of resources went into housing, food, clothing, appliances, and cars. An abundance of consumer goods was promised in the future, but steel and electric power were the immediate necessities.

Under Khrushchev, more resources were devoted to consumer goods. Television sets, refrigerators, good clothing, and new housing became available in large quantities, although they are still expensive. The Soviet economy is now advanced enough to allow for the development of both heavy and consumer industries. Nevertheless, the majority of Soviet resources still go into heavy industry. Although the standard of living seems low to a Western visitor, the Soviet citizen has seen a steady improvement since 1950, and especially since 1953.

Administration

The Soviet leaders have swung back and forth between two conflicting approaches to the problem of administering the Soviet economic system. One approach is to centralize all procedures, with all decisions made by the highest authorities in Moscow and then handed down to local factory managers. This approach attempts to forestall any deviations from the plan chosen. The opposite approach allows each factory manager considerable freedom in making day-to-day decisions on how to carry out the plan. Its aim is to eliminate the delay and "red tape" (excessive government forms and regulations) of extreme centralization and to encourage local initiative. Since 1917, emphasis has been placed first on central control and then on local control, and then back again on central control. The proper balance that will permit the Soviet system to function smoothly has not yet been found.

Even at those times when many decisions are left to local Soviet industrial managers, there are still very large differences between the Soviet and American systems. The manager of an American automobile plant makes all the decisions about his product. He decides from whom to buy steel and metal parts, what price to charge for the car, whether to make more convertibles or compacts, what kind of advertising to do, and hundreds of other similar questions. It is up to him to decide how many cars to produce, when to raise prices, where to get the raw materials needed. In the Soviet system, most of these questions are decided for the factory directors by the central planners.

Under Stalin, the administration of the economy was divided into separate Ministries. There were Ministries of Heavy Industry, Construction, Electrical Power, Agriculture, Foreign Trade, Lumber Industry, Light Industry, and many others. As the economy grew in complexity, the number of Ministries increased from eleven to thirty-one.

Each Ministry was responsible for all enterprises of that kind in the country. For such relatively unimportant items as athletic equipment or silverware, there was little central control; matters were left to local authorities. But for items of major concern, such as machine-building, there was extremely tight control. All problems and questions were referred back to the Moscow office of the Ministry of Machine-Building. If the director of a factory in Tashkent wanted to replace some old worn-out machinery, his request was sent to Moscow, and a reply might return only after months of waiting.

Establishment of Economic Areas

In an effort to combat the growing red tape, Khrushchev ordered a complete reform in 1957. He abolished the

Ministries and divided the countries into 104 economic areas, called *sovnarkhozy*. Each *sovnarkhoz* (the singular form of the word) assumed the responsibility (previously divided among many different Ministries) for all economic activity in its area. Now if a director wanted permission to buy new equipment, he asked the local sovnarkhoz, not Moscow. Under the new system there was a great improvement in the cooperation between local enterprises. They formed a natural unit; they were no longer simply links in several enormous chains stretching back to Moscow.

The Khrushchev reforms did not work perfectly. The decentralization gave local authorities too much power to suit Moscow. Although the central planning authority was still retained by Gosplan, in practice its instructions were often ignored. Many enterprises tended to think and act on a local level only. There were many instances in which steel plants, for example, first filled all orders from factories in their own area and then delivered what was left to the factories located in other regions. Some individual enterprises functioned more efficiently, since their managers had more initiative, but the coordination of separate sovnarkhozy was unsatisfactory.

In the early 1960's a compromise was attempted. The 104 sovnarkhozy were combined into seventeen major regional groups. It was hoped that this arrangement would combine the advantages of local management and more centralized control. This system had hardly been tested, however, when Khrushchev was ousted, and his successors returned to the old system of central ministries' controlling all factories and plants of one type. Experimentation and shifts from one system to another will almost certainly continue.

Extra-Legal Activities

The Soviet economic system has been described in the past few pages as it is *supposed* to work. If the plan is followed, if all quotas are fulfilled, and if the administrators are vigilant, production should rise steadily and smoothly. Sometimes it does, but frequently there are situations that cannot be handled within the regular system.

Suppose work in a Volgograd machine shop has come to a halt because an order of necessary gear parts has not been delivered on time. It will probably take days or weeks for the manager's complaint to the local bureau of the Machine-Building Ministry to produce any results. Meanwhile, much of the shop may be idled, and the manager will be penalized for not fulfilling his monthly quota.

One solution, which many Soviet managers resort to, is to use part of the factory budget to set up a small section within the machine shop to make the needed gear parts. This is not really legal (since it is not included in the plan) but it is practical; it works. A second common solution is to make a private deal with the manager of another factory. He agrees to provide the required parts in return for some similar favor. This is also extra-legal, but in both cases the machine shop keeps running, and the production targets are met.

In fact, the Soviet economy would have stopped completely long ago if it were not for such extra-legal "private" activities. The central authorities realize this fact, and they therefore tolerate this type of private initiative despite its capitalistic overtones. In recent years, however, the Party press has attacked the growing number of managers who have shown this kind of initiative. As it turns out, some have stolen factory materials and either sold them for their own profit or used them to build themselves country houses. One incident involved a manager who, over several years, took thousands of pounds of raw leather, had it made into shoes by private shoemakers, and then sold the shoes in a market for personal profit. Stealing from the state has been a serious problem, and recently the death sentence has been ordered for such crimes (see Chapter 9).

Measuring Success

The measurement of success in Soviet industry presents some interesting difficulties. In the United States economy, those companies with the largest profits are usually considered the most successful. Success for a Soviet factory means fulfilling the plan. There can be complications, however, as illustrated in a short story by Zoshchenko a Soviet satirical writer (see Further Reading).

The story concerns an ordinary Soviet citizen who hunts through all the stores for an electric light bulb for his apartment. The smallest bulb he can find is of the several-thousand-watts variety, enough illumination for a blinding searchlight. It seems that the local electric company was given a production quota of x hundred thousand watts of light bulbs. Instead of producing thousands of the normal 75- and 100-watt bulbs, they saved a great deal of time and effort by making just a few gigantic bulbs. They met their quota with ease and were congratulated.

This story exaggerates only slightly. Similar abuses exist in many industries where the manager has an opportunity to make some of the production decisions. Since most factories manufacture a variety of items, it is not possible to give plans that are precise in every detail. Every manager knows that he will be judged almost exclusively by whether or not he meets the production targets set by Gosplan. He usually ignores other considerations, such as quality, and tries to find the easiest way to reach his quota. Regardless of how his production targets are stated, there will probably be a way to cut corners. If a nail producer is told to produce 100,000 nails, he may make them all of the smallest possible size, thus cutting the cost of raw material. Ordered to produce 10,000 rubles worth of nails, he may make a few very complicated, expensive ones. Or, if the quota is set in terms of so many tons, he may make large, heavy ones.

Consumer goods in particular suffer from the pressures of the production target system. The quality of many products is frequently below standard. Until very recently much of Soviet clothing has been lacking in style and comfort and often seemed ill-fitting. One likely reason is that, under an order to deliver 10,000 men's suits, the clothing producers have made them all of one size and from the simplest pattern in order to save time and materials. Up to the 1960's, people bought such merchandise because they had no other choice. In the past several years, however, consumer goods have become more available, and shoddy products have been piling up on store shelves. Literally billions of rubles' worth of goods are going to waste. Soviet citizens are beginning to demand style and fashion in clothes and appliances. The quality of consumer goods is now a major concern of Soviet economists and government officials.

A New Approach

Some Soviet economists in the past three or four years have been proposing some very radical solutions to some of the problems described above. One of the best known of these economists is Yevsey Liberman. Here, very briefly, is what Liberman and his supporters say about the crisis in the Soviet economy and what they suggest be done.

The main problem has to do with how success is to be measured in a centrally planned economy. Central planners can check and control only a few of the many aspects of a complex modern economy such as that of the Soviet Union. They can set production quotas for each factory in terms of volume, quality, or cost, and the factory may fulfill this quota. But does this mean success? Obviously not, if the Plan is fulfilled by making clothing that no one buys. Under the present system, fulfilling the Plan may not be the same thing as raising the general welfare or satisfying public demands.

What should be done? How should success be measured? On the basis of profit, Liberman suggests. The factory manager should be given considerable freedom to decide what to make, how much of each item to produce, how many workers to employ. He should work directly with stores to learn more exactly what people want and then he should make what is in demand. The central planners would then be able to judge his performance very simply. Did he sell what he made and did he make a profit? The planners would still lay down general guidelines, but most of the decisions would be up to the individual factory managers.

There has been great public debate in the Soviet Union over Liberman's proposals. Many officials resist such ideas; "profit," after all, is a word associated with capitalism. It is what the capitalists get by exploiting the workers. But there are indications that some leaders are willing to try this approach and to judge by practical results rather than by emotional prejudices. Even Lenin was willing to compromise with capitalism, as illustrated by the New Economic Policy (see Chapter 6). In 1965 it was decided to experiment with 400 clothing factories, allowing them to plan their own production and judging them mainly on the basis of profit.

Results of this experiment have been mixed, but generally successful. The reforms are supposed to go into effect in one-third of all industry in 1967. If these reforms are successfully extended to other industries, it will mean a very substantial change in the concept of a centrally planned economy. There has been a great amount of resistance to such moves from planners and traditional bureaucrats. But even they may eventually be forced to agree to such changes in order to make the increasingly complicated Soviet economy work.

The Party and the Economy

The Communist Party plays an essential role in the control of the Soviet economy. Many of the people mentioned so far, the planners, administrators, and factory managers, are Party members. Their first duty is to follow Party orders as established in the economic plan. Theoretically, they direct the enterprises in the national interest, not for personal profit or success. Experience has shown, however, that other controls are necessary. The fact that a factory manager is a Party member does not ensure his honesty.

Some members of every local Party group are responsible for all industry in their region. They check to be sure that managers are carrying out their plans correctly, that materials are shipped and delivered properly, and that there is no theft or embezzlement.

Close control over the finances of all enterprises is kept by the Party members in the Ministry of Finance and the State Bank. (All banks were combined after the Revolution, and since then only a single State Bank, controlled from Moscow, exists.) Each enterprise is allocated certain funds from the central budget to pay for wages, to purchase new machinery, and to buy supplies. The accounts of every enterprise are checked carefully to see that all money is being used properly. Nevertheless, the Soviet press is constantly exposing cases of collaboration in which Party members, managers, foremen, and trade union representatives have all combined to work for the success of their own enterprise rather than the national good. All kinds of illegal activities (misuse of investment funds, underpayment of workers, falsification of production reports) may be resorted to in an effort to meet the requirements of the government's economic plan.

Trade Unions

The Party is also very active in the trade unions. Soviet trade unions do not resemble those in the United States since their functions are quite different. All workers, technicians, and engineers in an industry are organized into a single union. The main purpose of the union is to organize everyone in the task of fulfilling the plan. Workers are grouped into brigades, which compete against each other to raise production. The most productive brigades and individual workers receive bonuses and are publicly acclaimed as models for all to follow. The title of "Hero of Socialist Labor" is frequently given for outstanding achievements.

All strikes are illegal in the Soviet Union. Collective bargaining does not exist, at least not in the form in which we know it. In the West, the main responsibility of the union is the welfare of the workers; in the Soviet Union, it is to help raise production. Often the union will protest if a manager is especially arbitrary, but generally speaking, the Soviet workers do not use their unions to press demands for pay raises and better working conditions. (For more on trade union activities, see Chapter 12.)

Agriculture

Forty-five per cent of the Soviet population still works in farming (compared to 7 per cent in the United States), and agriculture represents the weakest section of the economy. There are several explanations. First of all, most of the land is not very good. Only the Ukraine and parts of southern Russia are really fertile (see Chapter 3). Even under ideal conditions most of the land could never be as productive as the farmlands of western Europe and America.

Second, the Soviet leaders have given priority to investment in industry, not in agriculture. Soviet farming methods are more advanced than before the Revolution, but machines are still not used as much as in the United States. There are five million tractors in this country but only two million in the Soviet Union. Fertilizers have also not been used to the extent they are here. When the Soviet leaders decide to increase production of farm equipment and fertilizers, agriculture should develop more rapidly, although basic problems of climate and soil will remain. Some recent moves to increase investment in chemical plants should eventually mean a greater supply of fertilizers.

Many Western visitors to the Soviet Union feel that Soviet agriculture is

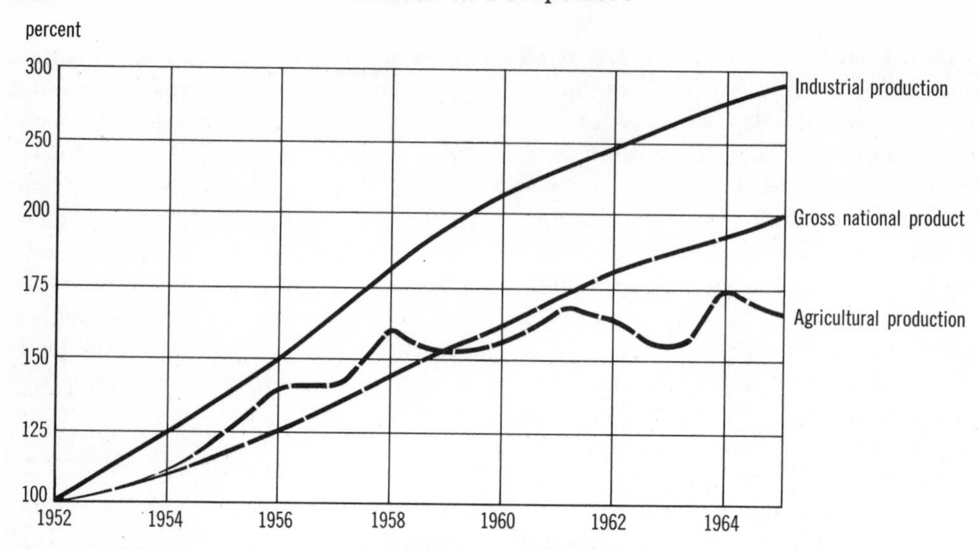

Graph showing the rise in Soviet industrial production, gross national product, and agricultural production since 1952

It is apparent that the total economy is being held back by the relatively slow growth in agricultural production.

unproductive because of its organization. There are no private farms; all land is organized into state or collective farms. Production quotas are set for each farm by Gosplan, and the produce is collected by the state for sale in the cities and towns. There are important differences between state farms and collective farms. These differences relate directly to the question of how Communist society should be organized.

The State Farm

The state farm represents the Communist ideal: an "agricultural factory." Marx was repulsed by the backwardness of rural life (see Chapter 2) and believed that an industrial society, if controlled by the proletariat, was on a higher level than an agricultural society. The Soviet government has tried to organize state farms like factories.

State farm workers are treated as factory workers; they work the land as an industrial laborer works in a factory. None of them owns any land, either privately or collectively. All receive a regular set wage and work regular hours. They do not keep anything they grow but buy all necessary produce with their wages. Many state farms are run as experimental stations, specializing in the development of new crops or breeds of livestock. They often employ a large number of agricultural specialists as well as plain workers.

There are now about 10,000 state farms. An average farm has some 600 workers and 20,000 acres. Many of these farms are located in the "virgin lands" of Kazakhstan, which has only recently been settled (see Chapter 7). The Soviet leaders constantly urge that new areas be organized into state farms and that peasants turn their collective farms into state farms. There is considerable resistance to this change, however, regardless of what the Soviet leaders say about its inevitability. Most Russian peasants prefer the collective farm, because of the small private plot of land they may keep.

Faces of typical Russian peasant women

Almost all of them wear the traditional scarf or babúshka. (Courtesy, Wide World Photos)

The Collective Farm

Collective farms (*kolkhozy*) account for almost 70 per cent of the total sown area. There are about 40,000 kolkhozy, varying in size from 100 to 1,000 households and from 2,000 to 12,000 acres. According to Communist theory, a *kolkhoz* is formed by the voluntary decision of the peasants to combine their individual farms for greater efficiency. They combine their land so as to be able to use machinery and produce more food.

Many Russian farms were, in fact, too small to be very productive when each family worked its own land. Only a small percentage of the land was fertile, and this was divided among a very large and rapidly increasing rural population. However, the decision to combine, to "collectivize," was not usually voluntary (see Chapter 7). The peasants were extremely possessive of their land, poor as it was. They had to be forced into the kolkhozy, and many who resisted were killed.

In theory, all members of a kolkhoz own the land together and can withdraw if they wish. No one ever does so, however. The kolkhoz represents an intermediate stage, a compromise between private and state farms.

At the time of collectivization it was necessary to make some concessions to the peasants. The most important concessions were those that allowed each household to keep a private plot of land, ranging from one-fourth acre to one acre, plus one cow and a certain number of sheep, chickens, and other animals. These private plots are called "survivals of capitalism." They are supposed to disappear in a communist society.

Most peasants, however, are very reluctant to give them up. They spend more time and energy cultivating their own plots than they spend working on the land of the kolkhoz. The peasants are allowed to sell the produce from their private plots in collective markets in towns and cities at whatever prices they can get. The significance of this private enterprise for the Soviet economy can be seen by the fact that over 30 per cent of the total agricultural output comes from these private plots, which represent less than 4 per cent of the total area under cultivation.

Recent Concessions to Peasants

After Khrushchev was removed, one of the first moves his successors made to raise agricultural production was to increase the size of the private plot allowed to each peasant. This illustrates an increasingly typical attitude of Soviet leaders. They are more and more willing to ignore the ideals of Marxism-Leninism (which would condemn such "private enterprise") and to do what is practical. It is obvious even to the Soviet leaders, however distasteful the fact may be to them, that the best way to increase food production is to allow individual peasants more freedom.

Every kolkhoz member is obligated to work the collective lands a set number of days per year, approximately a hundred. This is his first duty, and this work is supposed to be his main source of income. Most peasants, however, manage to spend a great amount of time on their private plots and earn most of their cash from them. Peasants from isolated regions often travel great distances to town and city markets to sell their produce from these plots. Despite all the time spent in travel they still make a profit. In the major cities, such as Kiev, Kharkov, or Moscow, one can actually see peasants who have come all the way from the warm Caucasus and other southern regions to sell oranges and other fresh fruits and vegetables. It seems incredible that an Azerbaijanian or Georgian peasant can fly a thousand miles to Moscow with a few sacks of oranges and fly home with a good profit.

Earnings on a Kolkhoz

No set wages are paid on a kolkhoz. Earnings depend on the harvest and on a complicated system of job classification. Every job is assigned a value in so-called "workday units," according to its difficulty and the skill required. One workday unit is equal to one day of average work requiring average skill. The job of harvester mechanic or tractor driver might rate 2 or 3 units, milking cows 1 unit, and cleaning the stables ½ unit.

At the year's end, the sum of all workday units of all kolkhoz members is divided into the total receipts of the farm: the cash paid by the state for produce, plus any produce left after deliveries to the state. (The money earned by the peasants from their private land is not included.) The result of the division is the value of one workday. It might be expressed as 1 ruble, 2 pounds of grain, and ½ quart of milk. Thus, the peasant who worked the equivalent of 300 workdays would receive 300 rubles, 600 pounds of grain, and 150 quarts of milk.

Peasant women selling their own produce in the central market in Moscow
(Courtesy, Wide World Photos)

Under Stalin, if the harvest were excellent, each member might earn a substantial amount; if it were poor, he might receive almost nothing. The state always took its share first, and the peasants divided the remainder. The state paid extremely low prices and constantly raised the quotas. In the years 1931 and 1932, when there was widespread drought, Stalin took such a high percentage of the harvest that several million people died of starvation in the following two winters. He was determined to build heavy industry at the expense of agriculture, even though it literally meant taking the food from the mouths of the peasants to give to the workers.

Khrushchev made some efforts to improve the lot of the peasants. State prices—those the state paid to the peasants for their produce—were raised to three or four times the level of 1950. But Brezhnev and Kosygin have taken considerably more significant steps. Beginning July 1, 1966, collective farmers began to receive guaranteed monthly wages and payments in kind, similar to those which state farm workers receive. Collective farmers are also supposed to be brought gradually under the system of pension payments that until now has applied only to nonagricultural workers. In addition, investments in agriculture for such items as farm machinery, fertilizer, and irrigation will be double in the period 1966-1970 what they were in 1960-1965.

By the time all of these measures are fully implemented throughout the country, a real start will have been made towards narrowing the gap between city and country living standards. At present, most peasants are able to afford very few of the consumer goods available to urban workers.

It is interesting to note that in the period of Stalin's rule, rural life was

Main street of Balyezino

Modernization has not yet reached all of Russia; many villages still have no paved roads. (Courtesy, Wide World Photos)

always described in Soviet art and literature in the most glowing terms. Bountiful harvests and dancing peasants were described again and again as typical of all collective farms. In 1962, two Soviet writers published stories which give a more honest impression of present day country life. The fact that these stories, both very critical, were printed in well-known Soviet magazines, shows how much things have changed since the days of Stalin. The first story, "Matryonna's House," by Alexander Solzhenitzen, is published in a collection of modern Russian literature, *Halfway to the Moon.* The second, "The New Life: One Day on a Collective Farm," by Fyodor Abramov, is available in paperback (see Further Reading).

Summary

The history of Soviet economic development is a mixture of success and failure. Despite the bureaucratic inefficiency of centralized planning, there have been some impressive accomplishments, especially in heavy industry. These achievements were built on the terrible sacrifices of the 1930's and 1940's. The human suffering of those decades was greater than that experienced by any other industrializing country. Nevertheless, Soviet growth has been rapid. In the production of many basic commodities, such as coal and steel, the USSR is approaching the United States.

Under the central control of the Party, the entire economy and the energies of the whole society can be directed toward a single goal. All resources can be concentrated on the one vital task of the moment. Americans were surprised by the tremendous speed with which the Soviet space program developed.

There is some reason to doubt, however, whether the Soviet economic system will retain the structure which Stalin gave it. This structure worked fairly effectively, although brutally, to build a strong industrial base. It seems unlikely that it will function as well when the economy begins to concentrate more attention on consumer goods and on a variety of goals. In particular, it is a matter of doubt how quickly it will be able to react to growing and changing consumer demands. If production is doubled within 20 years, as predicted, will the planning system break down under the added strain? One Soviet economist estimated that by 1980 the Gosplan bureaus would need 36 times as many employees as they have now, because the economy is growing so complex.

The strains within the Soviet economic system were becoming evident at the time of Stalin's death. Khrushchev reacted to the pressures for reforms by experimenting with various solutions. He gave individual factory managers more freedom to run their enterprises. He increased the use of cash incentives for workers and peasants, hoping that money rewards would produce better results than had Stalin's terror and labor camps. Brezhnev and Kosygin are continuing to experiment, searching for a way to reconcile the demands of central planning with the need for individual initiative.

PROJECTS

A. Research

(1) Describe ways in which the United States government exercises control over our economy and industries. A few examples might be: Pure Food and Drug Act; anti-trust laws; influence on prices of major items such as steel or aluminum; involvement in military defense; requirement of safety devices on automobiles.

(2) What per cent of the United States working force is involved in agricultural production? How many family farms are there and what part of the total production do they supply? Compare 1965 with 1900. (The United States Statistical Abstract, published by the government, would be a helpful source.)

(3) Compare Soviet state farms with big "industrial" fruit and vegetable farms in California.

B. Activities

(1) Draw a cartoon poking fun at some excesses of central planning.

(2) Describe how consumers' tastes and preferences influence what is produced in the United States. Take the extreme example of a "craze" or fad that is generated by a particular television series. Cite any current examples. What happens as the series becomes increasingly popular? Could something like this happen in the centrally planned Soviet economy?

(3) The Soviet economy is sometimes called a "command economy." Explain what this means.

(4) Take a look at all the products in the local supermarket. Where have they come from? How did they get there? What can you guess about the variety of products in a typical Soviet store? Why?

(5) Make a crossword puzzle using as many of the following words as possible. Try to give a short and accurate definition of each word.

Gosplan	consumer goods	enterprise
Politburo	bureaucracy	capital
ruble	exploit	investment
kopeck	trade union	bonus
kolkhoz	state farm	peasant
proletariat	technician	

C. Reading

Abramov, Fyodor, *The New Life: One day on a Collective Farm* (Grove Press, N.Y.).

Campbell, Robert W., *Soviet Economic Power* (Houghton Mifflin, Boston, Mass.)—Survey of the main features of the Soviet economic system.

Feifer, George, *Justice in Moscow* (Dell, N.Y.)—Read the description of an economic conspiracy by a group of workers in a government restaurant who constantly made a little extra money by watering down the coffee and cocoa (pages 297-322).

Nove, Alec, *Soviet Economy* (Praeger, N.Y.)—A detailed study of the Soviet economy.

Schwartz, Harry, *The Soviet Economy Since Stalin* (Lippincott, N.Y.)—A description of economic changes since 1953.

Solzhenitzen, Alexander, "Matryonna's Home," included in Blake, P., and Hayward, M., *Halfway to the Moon* (Anchor, N.Y.).

Wilcox, C.; Weatherford, W. D., Jr.; Hunter, H.; Baratz, M. S., *Economies of the World Today* (Harcourt, Brace & World, N.Y.)—A brief introduction to several different kinds of economic systems. See especially Chapters 2, 4, and 7.

Zoshchenko, Mikhail, *Scenes From the Bathhouse* (University of Michigan Press, Ann Arbor, Mich.) and *Nervous People* (Vintage Books, N.Y.)—Two collections of humorous satirical stories about Soviet life.

Chapter 11

EDUCATION AND CULTURE

It is possible to know about a country's history, government, geography, and economy but still not understand the country very well. All of this information only partially answers the question: "What is it like to live in the Soviet Union?" Many Americans can't tell you who their Senator is, how Congress works, what the Supreme Court does, or how much steel the United States produces. But they can describe daily life in the United States. This chapter and the next describe some aspects of everyday living in the Soviet Union, such common things as schools and cultural life, working conditions, unions, shopping, and religion.

Education

The importance of education in any country, and especially an underdeveloped one, cannot be exaggerated. At the time of the 1917 Revolution, Russia was underdeveloped in many ways. Less than 30 per cent of the population could read and write. In some areas, especially in Central Asia, only one-half of 1 per cent of the people were literate. In less than 50 years illiteracy has almost been wiped out. A great deal of energy and money has been put into Soviet education, and the progress has been great. Soviet space achievements are an obvious example of the results of the educational system.

Education is important to the leaders of a developing nation because no modern country can be built and run without thousands of educated and trained people. Government officials, engineers, industrial directors, teachers, skilled workers, and many other highly trained citizens are necessary to create a modern country.

Education is also important to the ordinary people of a developing nation. Americans take schools for granted and have trouble understanding how exciting education seems to people who have not previously had the opportunity for it. In a country where perhaps only 5 or 10 per cent of the people have had a chance to be educated, the idea of learning to read or to operate a machine in a factory or to use a slide rule is not only exciting but almost mysterious.

Education, as well as technical progress, comes to symbolize modernization in the minds of the people.

For many Westerners who have visited the Soviet Union recently and in the 1930's and 1940's, the most striking feature of Soviet life has been the widespread passionate desire for education. Although the Soviet Union is by now a modern country in most respects, there is still a tremendous interest and faith in education. Especially for the peasants and the non-Russian peoples of Central Asia, higher education and technical education represent the new life as well as the primary way to get ahead. For many people education is probably the most significant achievement of the Revolution.

Soviet schools and universities are administered by the national government. This is different from the American educational system, in which the states and local communities control the schools. As is true of the Soviet judicial system (see Chapter 9), however, this educational system is not unique. France and Germany both have centrally administered systems of education, in contrast to the American tradition of local control.

The Soviet concept of education is also different from the American; it is broader and more political. Every student is required to read the basic writings of Marx and Lenin. Education is not just going to school but includes Pioneer and Komsomol activities (see Chapter 8), part-time work experience, and learning correct political and social attitudes. Even more than in the United States there is emphasis on preparing the child to become a useful member of society.

Because the Soviet Union has been building up a modern industrial society, it is natural to expect that heavy stress has been put on technical and scientific education. It was important to train directors, engineers, and skilled workers to construct and man the new factories. Even for a student of history or literature, however, technical education has had a prominent role. This is partially the result of Marxist ideology, which attaches extraordinary significance to the industrial workers, the proletariat. A real Soviet citizen should know something about tools and basic industrial processes, even though he may become a musician. Some practical work experience is considered essential for every student.

Primary and Secondary Schools

The Soviet school system has changed several times in recent years. The basic system had consisted of four years of elementary school, four of middle school, and three years of high school, making a total of eleven. Eight years was the legal requirement for every student. This requirement could not always be carried out, especially in isolated rural areas, because of a lack of equipment and teachers. In some areas, students attended school for only four years. In 1965, the eleven year school system was reduced to ten years, and this figure was set as the eventual universal requirement. But for the forseeable future, most Soviet students will continue to receive only eight years of schooling.

Soviet students work much harder than most American students, take more subjects, have more homework, and begin to study sciences and foreign languages earlier than is the general custom here. Students go to school six days a week; they are in class four to five hours a day. All sports and other activities are after school. Homework

A Soviet elementary school

The younger boys and girls wear school uniforms such as these. (Courtesy, Wide World Photos)

begins in the first year. Foreign languages are taught from the fifth grade on. Biology, physics, and chemistry are begun in the sixth or seventh grades. Of the total classroom time, perhaps as much as 35 per cent is devoted to science and technology. Students are not separated according to ability, at least in theory. Everyone takes the same courses during the eight years. All students must meet certain standards set by the central government. If a student fails to do so, he repeats. In fact, however, in recent years there has been a tendency to group students according to ability, as is often the case in America.

After eight years the student has several alternatives. He can drop out and begin working. He can continue through secondary school, formerly three years, now two. This is an academic course, but a third of the time is given to "work-study," actual work learning a skill in a factory or on a farm. The student can also enter a *Tekhnikum,* a technical school where he can learn a specific skill, such as printing. The Tekhnikum is a four-year school. There are also trade schools that are more specialized than the Tekhnikums. Courses last from six months to two or three years, and the student learns one specific trade. Entrance to the trade schools and Tekhnikums is based on competitive exams.

Higher Education

For students who complete secondary school there are many institutions of higher learning, most of which have five-year courses. The most important are the universities, Technical Institutes, Agricultural Institutes, Medical Institutes, Law Schools, two-year Pedagogic Schools (for elementary school teachers), and five-year Pedagogic Institutes (for secondary teachers). Competition for entrance to these institutions is very keen. From three to eight students apply for each available place. (There has been much discussion in the United States about the increasing competition for entrance to "prestige" colleges. Many state colleges, however, still accept most applicants.)

Acceptance is based on examinations, Komsomol references, and practical work. Most students, about eighty per cent, are required to work for two years after secondary school before entering a university or institute. Only the brightest students, students in critically needed sciences, and children of important people go directly on to the university. (This is one place where the "pull" of Party membership sometimes helps.) Students from rural areas are at a disadvantage in the competition for entrance to universities and institutes, because the facilities and teachers in rural areas are usually much poorer than those in the cities. Khrushchev began a policy of giving preference to applicants who come from peasant families and families of poor urban workers.

Elementary and secondary education is free, of course, and there is also no tuition at any university or institute. All students receive scholarships, ranging from twenty-five to sixty rubles a month, for living expenses. The exact amount varies according to grades,

Moscow University, located on the hills overlooking the city

financial need, and the subject area being studied. In return, students are required to work for two or three years after graduation at a location which the government chooses, before they make their own choice of job location. The government feels that this is a reasonable demand in return for a free education. Thus, a doctor or a mathematics teacher might have to work in a small city in eastern Siberia for two years before settling in a more desirable place such as Moscow or Leningrad.

This system is an attempt to make sure that basic services are provided in areas that would not be able to attract skilled people easily. Many American college students are shocked by this system and critical of it. Soviet students on the whole find it natural and fair, although few look forward to spending two years in an isolated location. Some Soviets point out that their system ensures all graduates a job and criticize the lack of such a guarantee for American college graduates.

Part-Time Study

Part-time study is much more common in the Soviet Union than in the United States. Often a student will go to work after finishing high school or technical school and will continue his studies at night. Some factories permit workers to study one or two days a week. Perhaps half of the three million Soviet students in institutions of higher education are part-time. Study through correspondence courses is also more common than in the United States, especially in the vast undeveloped regions of Siberia. Correspondence study usually includes regular conferences with a local teacher, perhaps one evening a week or during one season of the year. This system, however, has not been very successful in overcoming the disadvantages which face students in isolated rural areas. These students still compare poorly with urban students on national competitive exams.

Special Features of Soviet Education

There are several unusual features of Soviet elementary and secondary schools that should be mentioned briefly. One is the emphasis on close contact between parents and teachers. The elementary and secondary school teacher must visit the home of each of her pupils at least once a year. In addition, parents' committees are elected at each school and meet frequently (every two weeks) with the teachers to discuss various problems. A great effort is made to involve the parents in the educational system. Subcommittees concern themselves with cultural and extracurricular activities such as concerts and theatres, with cafeteria and sanitary facilities, with discipline and moral training, and with other questions. An important purpose of this involvement of parents is to educate them to the value of school and the problems of teachers.

The emphasis given to the study of foreign languages, including ones seldom studied in the United States, is much greater in Soviet than in American schools. Most Soviet students begin to study a foreign language in the fifth grade. In some special language schools, however, they begin in the second grade and by the fifth or sixth year all subjects are taught in the foreign language. At the end of ten years the student is fluent in the language. There were over 500 of these special schools in 1963, each school concentrating on one language. Most schools gave instruction in English, French, Spanish, or German, but a few were devoted to

Chinese, Hindi, Arabic, Swahili, and other less frequently studied languages. The government hoped to have an additional 700 such schools in operation by 1966. These schools are not just for future language experts but for all interested students.

Boarding Schools

Boarding schools were begun in 1956 and are becoming increasingly popular. They were established mainly for orphans, children of widows, children from large families or from slum areas, and some delinquents. Children live in from Monday to Saturday and go home on Sundays. Enrollment is voluntary. Tuition ranges from nothing to thirty or forty rubles per month, according ability to pay. This includes all food and clothing. In 1961, 700,000 students attended such schools. By 1965, the enrollment had grown to nearly two and a half million, or 5 per cent of the total school population.

Specialized, intellectually elite boarding schools are also beginning to be established. So far there are only two such schools, in Novosibirsk and in Moscow. They are for scientifically bright students, from ninth grade on. The schools emphasize advanced work in mathematics and physics. Students are selected by national competitive examinations.

Also popular are the semi-boarding schools, or "prolonged day" schools. These are generally for children of families in which everyone works and there is no one at home to take care of the children after school. The children can be dropped at school early in the morning and they are cared for in the afternoons. They are fed supper and kept until evening when the parents have finished work and can pick them up again.

Position of the Teacher

As in the United States, Soviet teachers are not particularly well paid. Even with the 25 per cent pay raise of 1964, the average elementary teacher receives 80 to 100 rubles per month, the secondary school teacher 120 to 175 rubles. A skilled industrial worker earns from 100 to 200 rubles per month. The social position of the teacher in the Soviet Union is much higher than in the United States, however. The teacher is respected and admired by the public as a doctor or lawyer is in the United States.

Political Control of Thought and Culture

If an American went to live in the Soviet Union, the hardest thing he would have to adjust to would be the political emphasis in all aspects of Soviet life. Many Americans are concerned with political questions only when there is a big election or while reading the headlines in the morning newspaper. Soviet citizens, on the other hand, are almost constantly made aware of political affairs, while working, studying, or just relaxing. Marxism-Leninism not only provides the answers to economic questions but is supposed to provide the basis for understanding art, literature, science, sports, music, and all other aspects of life (see Chapter 2).

Sometimes one has to be very imaginative to see the connection between the ideas of Marx and Lenin and, for example, biology or music. The effort to fit every subject into a "Marxist" conception often has harmful effects and hinders progress. At the very least it results in the boring repetition of the same ideas and phrases.

Lysenko's "Biology"

Biology is a good example of a field that suffered from this attempt to interpret every aspect of life according to political ideology. Modern biology is based on the discoveries of Mendel, which showed that physical characteristics are inherited through the genes. Soviet biologists, however, were compelled to reject Mendel's findings in favor of the theories of one of Stalin's supporters, a man named Lysenko. His theory, called "inheritance of acquired characteristics," became the only acceptable one for Soviet biologists. Lysenko's theory stated that if a physical feature of a plant or animal was changed by its environment, this change would be inherited by succeeding generations. By changing the physical environment, one could quickly bring about important changes which would then be passed on. Genes were considered to be of little significance. Taken to its logical, but obviously absurd, conclusion, this theory would mean that if you cut off the tails of a few generations of cats, their kittens would eventually be born without tails.

Lysenko's ideas, though ridiculed by most Western biologists, could be made to fit in well with Marxist-Leninist theories and attitudes. Stalin felt that the Communists were creating a new kind of man, superior to previous men who lived under feudalism or capitalism. By changing one generation of people, through education and changes in the economic system, man would be perfected, and each succeeding generation would inherit this superiority.

But Lysenko's ideas caused the greatest harm in agriculture. By rejecting the long slow process of genetic changes revealed in Mendel's work, Lysenko promised quick results and overnight solutions to Soviet agricultural problems. His ideas never worked out in practice, but his attitude fit in very well with the spirit of the 1930's and 1940's.

Stalin gave Lysenko nearly total power over Soviet biology teaching and research. Textbooks described only the ideas of Lysenko. Biologists who continued to adhere to Mendel's theories lost their jobs and were often arrested. During the 1930's, many died in the purges. To disagree with Lysenko was considered unpatriotic, anti-Soviet, and anti-Communist.

After Stalin's death, Lysenko began to lose influence, but he regained considerable power in 1958. Khrushchev's attitude shifted back and forth. He did not support Lysenko as consistently as Stalin did, but he still hoped that Lysenko would magically solve Soviet agricultural problems. For example, Lysenko spent many years working, unsuccessfully, to produce grains which would grow in arctic regions. After Khrushchev's ouster, Lysenko was finally removed and his ideas exposed as the nonsense they are. Soviet biology textbooks are being revised and some anti-Lysenko biologists have been placed in important positions in universities and laboratories. But the process of "de-Lysenkoization" has not been completed. Many of Lysenko's supporters are still teaching and directing research. Their influence still hinders Soviet biology from catching up with the scientific progress of the past 30 years.

Ideological Culture

Soviet literature, art, music, sculpture, ballet, drama, and movies have also suffered from this perverted attempt to give all activities a Marxist-Leninist interpretation and content. It might be expected that the government would control such news media as radio, television, and newspapers. However, since culture reflects the economic system, according to Marx, this control must be extended to all forms of art as well. A socialist country must have socialist art.

One of Stalin's officials stated the government position on literature this way:

> "Our literature, our newspapers, must not stand aloof from contemporary tasks, but must help the Party and the people educate the youth in the spirit of dedicated loyalty to the Soviet system, in the spirit of dedicated service to the interests of the people."

Government influence has two aspects: there is censorship, which prevents certain kinds of works from being published; and there is positive direction, which suggests what kinds of works should be produced. For example, it has so far been impossible for a Soviet writer to publish a book that criticizes the 1917 Revolution. The case of the novel, *Dr. Zhivago,* by Boris Pasternak, a Nobel Prize winning poet, is a good illustration of how censorship works. In 1958 Pasternak submitted his novel to a literary magazine for publication. He was told by the magazine's editors that the novel was anti-Soviet, because it did not portray the 1917 Revolution favorably, and that therefore it could not be printed. The novel was smuggled out of the country and published in Europe, but it has never been published in the Soviet Union.

"Partiinost"

More important than this restrictive censorship, or rather, another aspect of it, is the attempt to put positive political and social messages into all works of art. There is a special Soviet term that is often used in connection with the arts, *partiinost;* "party-ness" is the literal meaning. A major concern of the government is whether or not a particular novel or ballet or movie has enough "party-ness"; in other words, whether it expresses the policies of the Communist Party. The specific meaning of "party-ness" varies, of course, depending on what concerns the Party most at any one time. If the problem of raising agricultural production is the major concern, then a novel that showed peasants struggling successfully to overfulfill their farm's quota of wheat would win high praise.

"Art Belongs to the People!", "Literature Belongs to the People!", "Music Belongs to the People!"—these are slogans that one sees and hears frequently in the Soviet Union. They mean that all art must be simple enough for the common citizen to understand. The artist or writer has a duty to produce works that are not too complicated or difficult for the ordinary man in the street. To do otherwise is to betray his country and his fellow citizens. Abstract painting, for example, is strongly condemned; pictures should be realistic and portray objects that are easily recognizable. Poetry should not be too difficult or obscure. Music should have nice melodies, not modern dissonances and strange rhythms.

Foreign as well as Soviet art must have the correct political message and should be simple in form. Every Soviet student reads the works of American writers such as Upton Sinclair, Jack London, and John Steinbeck, because they write simply and are critical of some aspects of American society. Steinbeck's *Grapes of Wrath,* a novel of social protest about farmers in the

1930's, is very widely read and praised. The works of writers such as William Faulkner, James Joyce, or Marcel Proust are seldom published because they are more concerned with the psychology of the individual than with social protest.

Art must not only be simple, it must be optimistic and didactic, that is, it should provide a moral or ethical lesson. The reader or viewer should be inspired by a book or painting to work harder and to act as a good Soviet citizen. A positive hero must be presented, a hero who will be an example to be imitated. If a book is pessimistic or critical, it might cause the reader to have doubts or to lose faith in Communism. Even if a book is critical of some aspect of Soviet life, it should balance this criticism with a solution to the problem described and it should have a happy and positive ending.

Means of Controlling the Artist

In what ways do these official attitudes and policies actually control and influence the Soviet arts? In the first place, the government owns all printing facilities, museums, concert halls, and the like. Through Communist Party members it can make sure that unsuitable novels, pictures, or symphonies are simply not published or produced. The government can decide which books are printed and in how many copies. For example, a difficult poet like Pasternak might have a collection of poems published in only 5,000 copies, whereas a hack poet who wrote doggerel praising Cuba and Fidel Castro might have his work published in 200,000 copies.

Another way in which Party influence is felt is through unions. We usually associate unions with factory workers, not with artists or writers. Soviet writers, musicians, and artists, however, are all members of unions. These unions meet regularly to discuss political and social, as well as artistic, questions and to hear speeches by Party and government officials. Khrushchev often spoke to groups of writers, usually to warn them when some writers seemed to be getting too critical. After the 1956 Hungarian revolt, in which many Hungarian students and writers participated, Khrushchev told the Writers' Union that the Hungarian government could have prevented the revolt by shooting a few writers before things had gotten out of hand. He indicated that he would favor that solution with Soviet writers if it seemed necessary.

A writer must be a member of the Writers' Union in order to have his work published and to receive payment for it. After the *Dr. Zhivago* incident, Pasternak was not arrested but was expelled from the union, which meant that he had no way to earn money by writing. The threat of expulsion from the Writers' Union has been used several times in recent years against some of the more outspoken young writers.

The Arts Under Stalin

The period of Stalin's rule was disastrous for Soviet literature and the other arts. Stalin insisted that literature serve the political needs of the government. Since the main tasks at that time were industrialization and collectivization, literature was supposed to be concerned with these subjects and to present the government's attitudes. Hundreds of novels were written about the building of new factories in Siberia, about mining new deposits of iron and coal, about heroic "Stakhanovite" workers, about devoted tractor drivers and milkmaids who overfulfilled their work quotas.

Not only was it risky for a writer not to glorify Soviet industrial progress, but it was also unwise to write anything that did not involve the aims of the Five-Year Plans. A simple love story of a boy and girl, for example, would be criticized as "anti-Soviet" unless the couple were also pictured as working 14 hours a day to produce more steel than the Plan required. An often repeated cliché has it that the typical Soviet romance involves a boy, a girl, and a tractor. Much of the literature of the 1930's suggests that this would indeed be the ideal relationship.

The "Thaw"

Stalin's death in 1953 set off a "thaw" in all aspects of Soviet life, especially in literature and art. The term thaw describes accurately the new feeling of life which swept through the Soviet Union after the winter of Stalin's reign. (The word was first used by the writer, Ilya Ehrenburg, who wrote a novel in 1954 called *The Thaw,* in which he implied that changes and reforms in Soviet society were necessary.)

One of the most significant features of the thaw in Soviet cultural life has been the gradual expansion of the areas of life that can be dealt with by writers and artists. Since 1953 writers have begun to examine such problems as agricultural backwardness, official bureaucracy, and anti-Semitism. They have also begun to write more honestly about the past. Until Solzhenitzen's novel, *One Day in the Life of Ivan Denisovitch,* there had been no mention of the labor camps in Siberia and the far North, although millions of people had spent years or died in them. The whole phenomenon of the purges has been written about with growing, but not yet complete, honesty. Many of the writers and artists who were destroyed by Stalin in the 1930's and 1940's have been "rehabilitated"; their reputations have been revived and their works are now published again.

One of the most important figures of the thaw is Ehrenburg. Several volumes of his memoirs have been published over the last few years. In them he mentions many Soviet writers who were victims of the purges. He tries to provide present day Soviet readers with a guide book to modern literature and art, Russian and European. Ehrenburg writes quite frankly of the terrible fear and silence of the purge years and of the cultural destruction that was caused by Stalin's policies.

Contemporary State of Literature

While older writers such as Ehrenburg are attempting to be more honest about the past, some of the younger writers are looking at the current scene more critically. Solzhenitzen and Abramov have already been mentioned. *Not By Bread Alone,* by Dudintsev, is a bitter criticism of Party and government bureaucrats. The poet Yevtushenko has raised the question of continued Soviet anti-Semitism, which is supposed to have been eliminated. Yevtushenko's autobiography is available in paperback and makes interesting reading. It is frank and critical. Because he feared that it would not be published in the Soviet Union, Yevtushenko took it with him on a trip to France and had it published there. This action naturally angered Soviet authorities, and he was strongly denounced. His poems were not printed in the Soviet Union for over a year; but he is now back in favor and is published again.

Other writers have been writing as if literature did not have to contain an optimistic political or social message. They are writing about people as they observe them, which often means unheroic people, living uninspiring and

Andrei Voznesensky, extremely popular young Soviet poet, talking with admirers
Poetry readings by Voznesensky, Yevtushenko, and others attract thousands of Soviet students. (Courtesy, Sovfoto)

sometimes sad or tragic lives. Some of the best poets are concerned with style and write very difficult verse that is not easily understood by all peasants and workers. Some artists have been experimenting with abstract art, instead of realistic, easy to understand pictures of workers and peasants. Abstract art is still officially prohibited, but many abstract paintings are done and sold undercover and interest is growing, even among Party members and government officials.

Popular Music

Jazz and rock and roll have long been criticized by Soviet officials as bourgeois and decadent. The only American jazz figure to tour the Soviet Union is Benny Goodman, who was popular here in the 1930's! In spite of, or because of, this official policy, Soviet young people are intensely interested in modern jazz and rock and roll. (Many Soviet young people listen eagerly to the evening jazz programs broadcast by the Voice of America and even record them on tape. They are usually uninterested in the political programs, tending to dismiss all government pronouncements as propaganda, whether Soviet or American.) In recent years some jazz has been permitted, and there are now many jazz groups in the major Soviet cities. Rock and roll and the "twist" have been approved recently, but the "official" versions bear little resemblance to the American originals.

Since Stalin's death, writers and artists have generally drifted into two camps, which might be called liberal and conservative. The liberal ones favor experiment, honesty, open discussion of more and more problems and viewpoints. The conservatives would feel more comfortable with Stalin's policies, which enforced a rigid conformity in what people wrote about and how they wrote. For them, literature and art should serve the Party and educate the people to the Party's policies and tasks. Over the last decade Soviet cultural life has shifted often between liberal and conservative tendencies. The long term trend is toward a freer, broader, more interesting literature and art, although there is still a distance to go, as the recent trial of Sinyavsky and Daniel shows (see Chapter 7).

Newspapers

It is illegal for a Soviet citizen to own a printing press. All newspapers and magazines are printed by the government or the Party. The news is presented in a very one-sided fashion. There is no attempt to be objective, only to present the correct Marxist interpretation of all domestic and foreign events.

The reporting about the United States consists mainly of countless articles about unemployment, juvenile delinquency, and racial discrimination. These are all serious problems, and the information presented is usually accurate as far as it goes. But the Soviet reader hardly receives a complete picture of life in the United States, and often he is aware of this. The constant repetition of the same themes has made many Soviets skeptical of anything printed in the newspapers. Both the skepticism and the boredom are expressed in a phrase that is often muttered by disgruntled Soviet students. It is a play on the meaning of the names of the two major Soviet Newspapers. *Pravda* is the paper of the Communist Party of the Soviet Union; *pravda* means "truth." *Izvestia* is the official government paper; *izvestia* means "news." The student saying is: "In *Pravda* there is no news, and in *Izvestia* there is no truth."

The average Soviet citizen has probably never seen a typical American or European newspaper. The only American newspaper on sale in the Soviet Union is the *Worker*, the paper of the Communist Party of the United States of America. The same is generally true of magazines. The selection of French, German, English, and other European publications is similarly slanted. Premier Kosygin was recently asked by a British journalist why non-Communist British newspapers were not sold in the Soviet Union. His reply is interesting.

"I cannot tell you now whether your newspaper could be sold here. We

> are not bound to sell your newspaper. It should first be considered whether it would be useful. We are not afraid of the influence of foreign newspapers on our people. You probably know that we are not jamming the radio broadcasts of the BBC and the Voice of America, and our people can buy radio sets with medium, short and long waves. We are not afraid of the foreign press, but for various other reasons their sale is not possible. Their content sometimes contradicts the views of our people, and therefore they often reject them. We have no demand for foreign newspapers."

Under an official government agreement between the United States and the Soviet Union, there is an exchange of two government-sponsored magazines, *America* and *Soviet Life*. Copies of *America* are sold out rapidly in the Soviet Union and are enthusiastically read, especially by younger people. *Soviet Life* can be found at most large newsstands in this country. In addition, *Pravda, Izvestia,* and other Soviet newspapers and magazines are sold in most large cities and are available in libraries across the country.

Entertainment

Perhaps the major Soviet recreation is reading. People on buses, subways, and trains always seem to have a book with them. The Soviets claim that of all books published in the world, over a fourth are published in the Soviet Union. (The Soviet definition of a book, however, includes what we would call pamphlets and brochures.) It is certainly true that people seem to be reading more there than in the United States. Books are generally inexpensive. A typical hard cover book costs from fifty kopecks to one ruble. (See the next chapter for a discussion of comparative prices.)

Movies are another inexpensive and extremely popular form of entertainment. Most films shown are from the Soviet Union and other socialist countries, although in recent years this has been changing. About a dozen American films are exhibited in the Soviet Union every year, under an exchange agreement. Movie houses are always jammed and tickets are bought before the showing, usually early in the day. Soviet movie theatres sell seats at five or six different prices, according to location, much like American legitimate theatres.

The ballet has traditionally enjoyed a prominent place in Russian cultural life. Many people feel that there is no ballet in the world to equal that of the best Russian groups. The most famous groups are the Bolshoi Ballet of Moscow and the Kirov Ballet of Leningrad. Some Soviets say that the group in Kiev is just as good as the first two. There are many other ballet companies throughout the country, and performances everywhere are usually sold out.

Tickets for the ballet, as well as for the theatre and for concerts, are inexpensive. Seats are usually available for less than a ruble, and at even lower prices for students. Before the Revolution, such cultural events were almost entirely for the aristocracy. Today plays and concerts are attended by large numbers of ordinary workers and peasants, for most of whom it is a relatively new and exciting experience. Moscow and Leningrad, as would be expected, are the major centers for drama and music, much as New York is in the United States. Cities such as Kiev, Kharkov, Volgograd, Tbilisi, Vilna, and others also have surprisingly

Restaurant of Moscow's Yunost Hotel, popular gathering place for young people
More such restaurants and cafes have been opened due to pressure from Soviet youth. (Courtesy, Sovfoto)

rich dramatic and musical seasons, often better than those in comparable American cities such as Atlanta, Cincinnati, Kansas City, Philadelphia, or Dallas.

An interesting feature of Soviet plays and concerts is that they usually begin at 6:30 or 7:00 in the evening. Performances are often four hours long. There are normally two or even three intermissions, during which the audience can get sandwiches, pastries, and drinks from buffets and snack bars. Intermissions at the Bolshoi Theatre in Moscow can also be spent wandering through several large corridors and side rooms set up with exhibitions of the past history and stars of the Bolshoi Ballet.

Sports

The Soviet Union is a very athletic nation. Soccer is the most popular and widely played sport, as it is in most nations of the world. Winter sports occupy an even greater number of ordinary citizens, from the very young to the very old. In many areas, winter may last five months or longer, with snow and sub-zero temperatures during the entire period. Skiing and ice skating are favorite activities. In some of the large city parks, the paths are deliberately covered with water, which, of course, freezes quickly. It is then possible to skate all over the parks on these frozen paths.

Swimming, track, gymnastics, hiking, and camping are also very popular activities, and people continue to participate long after they finish school. There are many sport clubs, often associated with factories. Soviet women participate in sports much more than American women do, as their performances at the Olympics indicate. In general, the Soviets are more of an outdoor people than we are, and a greater percentage are active participants in sports.

PROJECTS

A. Research

(1) Compare United States, Soviet, and French school systems. Who runs the schools? Who goes to school? Who pays? What subjects are studied?

(2) What kind of support does the United States government give to the arts? Are there subsidies for writers and artists? How does this situation differ from that in the Soviet Union? What are the advantages and disadvantages of each system?

B. Activities

(1) When you graduate from high school, what choices do you have for further education? What kinds of schools and training are available? How does this compare with the Soviet Union? Stage a debate on which country offers the greatest opportunity for further education.

C. Further Reading

Aksenov, Vasili, *A Ticket to the Stars* (New American Library, N.Y.)—A novel about rebellious Soviet youth.

Grant, Nigel, *Soviet Education* (Penguin Books, London)—A general description of the entire educational system.

Johnson, Priscilla, *Khrushchev and the Arts* (Harvard University Press, Cambridge)—A description of Soviet policy toward art and literature, including the reaction of Khrushchev to modern art.

Morton, Henry W., *Soviet Sport* (Collier, N.Y.)—A description of how sports activities are organized in the Soviet Union.

Nekrasov, Victor, *On Both Sides of the Ocean*—A Russian writer describes his travels in America and compares what he saw with his own country. He found many good things here and said so. He later got in trouble with the Party for this honesty. Published separately and in *Halfway to the Moon* (Anchor, N.Y.) edited by Blake and Hayward.

Rice, Tamara Talbot, *Concise History of Russian Art* (Praeger, N.Y.)—A broad survey, with excellent reproductions.

Tertz, Abram, *The Trial Begins* and *On Socialist Realism* (Vintage, N.Y.)—A short novel and an essay by Tertz-Sinyavsky, who was arrested in 1966.

Yevtushenko, Yevgeny, *A Precocious Autobiography* (Dutton, N.Y.)—By one of the exciting young poets, this book was first published in France.

Four Soviet Masterpieces (Bantam Books, N.Y.)—Four short stories by young Soviet writers. They are not "masterpieces" but are very interesting for what they reveal of Soviet life.

Chapter 12

DAILY LIFE IN THE SOVIET UNION

How much does your father earn? How much rent do you pay for your apartment? How large a scholarship do college students receive? What does a pair of shoes cost? How much for a pound of beef? For a shirt? For a dress? For a subway ride? For a car?

The American visitor to the Soviet Union is often beseiged by an endless stream of such questions. There is very keen interest in comparing prices and general living conditions. Soviet citizens are constantly being urged by posters and speeches to catch up with the United States in the production of meat, steel, milk, oil, corn, sugar, and the like. Ironically, although they are taught that the capitalist system is inferior to the socialist system, United States material achievements are frequently held up to Soviet workers as a goal to be equalled. At the same time, Soviet officials maintain that the quality of life in the Soviet Union is superior to the American way of life.

Comparing Soviet and American standards of living is dangerous and complex. Almost anything can be proven by citing carefully selected statistics. It is misleading to compare only isolated figures such as wages, the cost of food, or medical expenses. A great variety of factors must be taken into account. It is also necessary to remember that Soviets and Americans sometimes have different values and ideas about what is important.

One should also be aware that the ordinary Soviet citizen compares his living conditions with those of his father or grandfather. The progress since 1917, or since 1953, makes a more vivid impression on him than abstract comparisons with other countries.

Wages

Almost all Soviet citizens work for the government, either directly or in some government-owned enterprise. Many Americans also work for local, state, or federal governments: mailmen, policemen, public health officials. Even school teachers are considered public employees. Nevertheless, most Americans still work in privately owned factories, businesses, and other enterprises.

What the average worker, Soviet or American, cares about, however, is not only who employs him but how much he gets paid every Friday. The average American factory worker earns about $105 a week, or $420 a month. An American school teacher earns $400 to $800 a month.

Soviet wages are considerably lower. The average Soviet factory worker earns 100 rubles a month. (The official exchange rate puts the ruble equal to $1.10, but its real purchasing power is perhaps around fifty cents.) The lowest wage, for work requiring little or no skill, is 40 to 50 rubles per month. Highly skilled industrial workers, technicians, and engineers receive up to 200 rubles or more per month. Factory directors earn more, 200 to 400 rubles, plus bonuses for overfulfilling the Plan.

It is interesting to note that the spread in salaries from the lowest worker to the top manager in the Soviet Union is more extreme than in the United States. On the other hand, of course, Americans get property income and Soviet citizens do not; the income that an American executive receives from stocks and other investments is often larger than his salary. Soviet school teachers take home from 80 to 175 rubles, with secondary school teachers, who must have more education, receiving higher wages than elementary teachers. In the typical Soviet family, both the husband and wife hold full-time jobs.

The Soviet peasant or collective farmer is the poorest off. Until recently he received little or no cash wages, only wages in kind; that is, a share of the wheat, milk, corn, and the like, which was left after the farm delivered its quota to the government (see Chapter 10). The reforms of Khrushchev and his successors have eased this situation somewhat. Now at least some of the wages are in cash, and, on a successful collective farm, they might average 40 to 45 rubles per month. In addition, the peasants can sell produce from their own gardens in the city and town markets. But clearly, most Soviet peasants still stand well below their more prosperous city cousins.

Choice of Jobs

It is often said that Soviet citizens have no choice about where they work, that they have to do what the government tells them. This charge is no longer accurate. During the war and up to 1955, workers were "frozen" on their jobs and prohibited from changing. With the exception of recent college graduates, mentioned in the last chapter, Soviets are now free to work where they can find jobs. The "slave labor" camps of Stalin's time have been disbanded. To attract workers to such areas as Siberia, money incentives are now used. Wages in the Archangel area in the far north might be double those paid in Moscow.

The one restriction on movement from job to job is the availability of housing. Wartime destruction of housing in the western parts of the Soviet Union was extensive. In recent years much effort has gone into housing construction, especially construction of apartments using prefabricated concrete walls and floors. Even so, there is overcrowding in most cities, and the average family of four or five people would live in two or three rooms, possibly sharing a kitchen and bath with

Construction of a huge new hotel just off Moscow's Red Square
Soviet women share heavy work with Soviet men. (Courtesy, Wide World Photos)

another family. Because of this housing shortage, a worker in Kiev, for example, cannot change jobs and come to work in Moscow unless he already has a place to live. Such restrictions discriminate particularly against the peasants. Young peasants are often eager to escape the farm and come to the city, and they try hard to find ways to get around this rule.

The majority of collective farmers are women. Women work as tractor and combine drivers. They also work on construction sites, clean streets, drive buses, operate industrial machinery, and do many kinds of heavy labor that we consider suitable only for men. It is necessary for them to take such jobs because of the number of men lost in World War II. As was mentioned before, in the working age population there are about twenty million fewer men than women. Thus, if the work is to get done, women have to do a share of it. Soviet women are also doctors, lawyers, and hold high government positions.

Prices

Americans generally earn three or four times as much as their Soviet counterparts. More significant is what can be bought with these earnings. Is it harder or easier for a Soviet family to live on 100 rubles a month than for an American family to live on $400? To answer this question many factors must be considered.

The prices of most food products and clothing are higher in the Soviet Union than in the United States. But it is difficult to match up specific goods and services. There is greater variety in this country in quality of goods available and range of prices at which they are sold. The following rough table of comparative prices (in dollars) is for goods of adequate but not luxurious quality.

Product	*Price*	
	Soviet Union	*United States*
Food		
Hamburger, pound	$ .85	$ .50
Bread, pound	.09	.25
Sugar, pound	.40	.15
Orange, one	.40	.05
Cabbage, pound	.05	.10
Eggs, dozen	1.25	.60
Clothing		
Shoes, pair	$ 30.00	$10.00
Shirt	6.00	4.00
Dress	35.00	15.00
Man's suit	110.00	50.00
Overcoat	130.00	50.00

As you can see, prices of food and clothing in the Soviet Union are considerably higher than in the United States, even without taking into account the fact that Soviet wages are only about one-fourth of American wages. But housing and such social services as medical care and education have not yet been included. To put things in a slightly different perspective, one should note another interesting comparison. The Russian worker still has 85 per cent of his income left after paying for housing, transportation, medical and dental care, education, union dues, and income taxes; the American worker has only 40 per cent of his income left after paying for these things.

There is much less variety of food available in any one location in the Soviet Union than in the United States. Meat is expensive and is not eaten as often as here. Fresh vegetables and fruits are usually available only in the summer. Frozen foods are a rarity. Cabbage soup, potatoes, milk products, and bread are basic food staples. The average citizen gets plenty to eat, but the diet can become rather boring.

Clothing is one of the most expensive items in the Soviet family's budget. Shoes in particular, and synthetic fabrics such as nylon and dacron, cost much more than they do in the United States. Most of the clothing is not very fashionable, at least by Western standards. Only in the last two or three years has there been an effort to produce clothing that will be attractive to consumers. Fashion shows have become a regular feature at the big department stores in major cities.

Housing

While a greater percentage of the Soviet than the American family budget goes for food and clothing, much less goes for rent. In the United States it is thought reasonable to spend roughly 25 per cent of one's income for rent. Less than 5 per cent of the Soviet worker's wages is spent on rent. All apartment buildings are owned by the government, which sets the rents. Although housing is extremely crowded, rent seldom exceeds three to five rubles a month for a two or three room apartment.

Soviet family moving into a new apartment

New five- and six-story apartment buildings are going up all over Moscow and other cities, but the housing shortage persists. (Courtesy, Wide World Photos)

Most Soviets live in apartments, even in small towns. There are no suburban housing developments such as we have. In the countryside, peasants live in their own individual houses, which they have often built themselves. Because of the housing shortage, the government has encouraged this private initiative, although some officials object that it is a compromise with Marxist ideals. Government loans are available to individuals and to groups wishing the government to build cooperative apartment houses for their use. Soviet citizens are permitted to own their own homes but not to own a whole apartment building and rent to other families. They may not own land. They can use the land, which is owned by the government, but they cannot sell it.

Shopping

Shopping in the Soviet Union is a frustrating and time-consuming process, partially because of the relative scarcity of many consumer goods and partially because of the way the stores are set up. There are some department stores in the major cities, but no supermarkets. To shop for food for the day, it is necessary to go to the meat store, the bread store, the milk store, and the vegetable and fruit store; each store is separate from the others. There may be a line at each one, especially if a shipment of some scarce item, such as butter, has arrived. Some shopping has to be done almost daily, since many families do not yet own refrigerators. More refrigerators have been produced in recent years, but they are small and still not available in all parts of the country.

The only example of legal private enterprise still operating in the Soviet Union is the so-called collective market. In every city and town there is a market to which collective farmers bring the surplus produce from their private gardens and livestock. Fresh vegetables and fruits, eggs, milk, mushrooms, and sometimes meat are for sale. Prices are set by the individual farmers. These prices are often higher than those in the government-run food stores. But customers are willing to pay more because sometimes the collective markets are the only places where certain products can be found.

The situation is somewhat better for other goods. Most cities have department stores where you can get a great variety of products, just as you can in American stores. The most famous Soviet store is GUM (initials of the Russian words for State Department Store), located across Red Square from the Kremlin. Some consumer goods are

Typical Soviet apartment (right), flanked by the more imaginative Yunost Hotel

Interior view of GUM, major Moscow department store

Located on Red Square, it is actually a collection of hundreds of small shops and booths. (Courtesy, Wide World Photos)

still hard to find, however, because the demand is greater than the supply. If a particularly attractive or desirable product is for sale, it usually causes long lines of eager customers to form.

In an economy based largely on central planning rather than on supply and demand (see Chapter 10), it is inevitable that some items produced will not be wanted by anyone and that some items that people do want will not be produced in sufficient numbers. It is often difficult for the Soviet shopper to find exactly what he wants; for example, a sweater that is not only in the color he is looking for but is also the right size. Soviet stores seem to be jammed with crowds of excited, frustrated, often empty-handed shoppers, searching for certain items.

Taxes

Soviet officials point to the extremely low income taxes in the Soviet Union as another indication of the superiority of their system. It is quite true that income taxes have been reduced to almost nothing, especially in comparison to our income taxes. But, as always, it is misleading to compare two isolated figures. Soviet personal taxation takes another form.

All prices are set by the government planning agency. Often they are far above the production costs of an article. For example, a shirt may cost two rubles to manufacture but sell for five rubles. In the Soviet Union, most of the differential of three rubles will go to the government. (Sales taxes in the United States are similar, but much smaller.) The revenue from this tax, the "turnover tax," can then be used by the government in a number of ways. Some of it goes to provide social services for the individual, which are either free or inexpensive. Some of it may subsidize the production of another item, which can then be sold below cost. (To oversimplify, if a shirt cost two rubles to produce and sells for five, then it would be possible to produce a book for five rubles but sell it for only two.) The majority of the state's revenue goes into building new factories, into national defense, and into the space race.

Price Controls

By controlling prices, the Soviet government influences the kinds of things people buy and the way they live. For example, the government does not wish to produce many cars for personal use because to do so would require using materials which now go into the manufacture of other items considered more important. In order to check the ability of Soviet citizens to purchase a car, the price has been set extremely high, more than twice as much as an ordinary worker earns in a year. In addition, the central planning agency provides for the production of only 200,000 cars per year, although many more could be sold, even at these high prices. Thus the Soviet government discourages private transportation and encourages the use of a cheap system of public transportation. (This is an interesting contrast to our own government, which pays the bulk of the cost of new highways but provides relatively little financial support for public transportation, such as railroads.)

One of the interesting announcements made by Kosygin at the Twenty-Third Party Congress, in March, 1966, was that the government planned to increase production of passenger cars substantially in the next five years. Production of 800,000 cars per year by 1970 is planned. In addition, the Fiat automobile company of Italy concluded a deal to build an entire auto plant in the Soviet Union. Kosygin cited the great public demand for more cars as a reason for raising production. This kind of consumer pressure has been getting stronger and stronger in recent years and may become an important influence on Soviet policy in the future.

Social Services

Soviet citizens pay much less than Americans for a variety of social services. As mentioned, education is entirely free, from kindergarten through all universities and institutes. Most students at institutions of higher education receive scholarships to cover living expenses, at least partially. All medical care, except drugs, is also free. There is no charge for hospital or doctors' fees, even in case of long and serious illnesses. Education and medical expenses can use up a sizeable part of an American family's budget.

Public transportation is much more important and convenient in the Soviet Union than it is here because few people own private automobiles. Bus lines and subways are well-developed, efficient, and cheap. The fare is usually three or four kopecks. Trains in the Moscow subway run every 90 seconds; foreign visitors are impressed by the elaborateness and extreme cleanliness of the stations. Buses are almost all electric trolley buses; diesel buses are seldom used because of the air pollution caused by exhaust fumes.

Nurseries and child care centers are provided in most cities and large towns for children of mothers who work. This is necessary, since almost all women have jobs. (Only about 30 per cent of American women work.) These nurseries and centers are either free or charge low fees.

Every Soviet worker gets two to four weeks of vacation annually. The major

One of the ornate stations of the Moscow subway

Clean and fast, the subway was opened in 1935 and is a source of Soviet pride. (Courtesy, Wide World Photos)

factories and concerns have their own vacation areas to be used by their workers. For example, the villas and estates on the Black Sea that were owned by wealthy Russian nobles or businessmen before 1917 were confiscated by the government. Some have been made into public museums and parks. Others have been turned over to individual factories and enterprises. Soviet workers can spend a part of their vacation living inexpensively in these villas, which have been converted into resort facilities.

Many factories also run summer camps to which their employees can send their children. A factory in Leningrad, for example, might operate a camp in the forests on the Baltic Sea

A so-called "rest home" near Leningrad

Actually it is a vacation spot in the country owned by a Leningrad factory and used by its workers for part of their summer vacation.

A summer camp near Moscow for Pioneer-age children, 10 to 14 years old

(Courtesy, Sovfoto)

for children of its workers between the ages of nine and fourteen. Such a camp would be free, or very inexpensive.

Trade Union Services

Additional social services are provided by the trade unions. Soviet trade unions are quite unlike American trade unions. First of all, practically everyone who works belongs to some union, even secretaries, engineers, doctors, and artists (see Chapter 11). Second, Soviet workers are forbidden to strike, and their unions do not engage in collective bargaining about wages and working conditions with the factory directors. Soviet trade unions have two functions: to encourage workers to raise production and to administer certain social services.

Connected with most factories are various recreational facilities, such as gymnasiums, athletic fields, libraries, movie theaters. These are run by the trade unions. Some of the child care centers spoken of above are also operated by the trade unions.

Old age pensions and disability pensions are also administered by the trade unions. Pension arrangements are quite similar to the ones provided under our social security system. Soviet men can retire at 60, women at 55. The aged receive a pension usually equal to about half their normal wages.

Soviet trade unions generally provide a greater variety of services for their workers than do American unions. On the other hand, they are much less active than American unions in protecting workers' rights and pressing their grievances with management.

Religion

Karl Marx attacked all religion as "the opiate of the people." By this he meant that religion was used to take people's minds off their problems, to divert their attention, and to put them to sleep. Marx viewed religion as another part of the capitalist plan to deceive and oppress the masses. By promising a better life after death, religion caused people to accept their suffering here on earth. Marx felt that people should be concerned with revolution and change on earth rather than with the hope of heaven. In addition, science and industry had explained everything, according to Marx, and had made God "unnecessary."

Workers removing icons from a church
Stalin's program against religion included conversion of churches into recreation clubs.

Lenin and the other Russian Marxists accepted Marx's opposition to religion. It was easy to criticize the churches in Russia. Most Russians belonged to the Orthodox Church, which was the official state church. The cooperation of the church and the Tsar are described in Chapter 4. It should not be forgotten that the church was the largest owner of land and serfs prior to 1861. Russia's religious leaders were usually conservative or reactionary, supporting the autocratic rule of the Tsar and opposing all change. It is not surprising that Lenin and the Bolsheviks felt that the Revolution must destroy religion as well as the nobles and the capitalists.

Attempts to Destroy Religious Belief

After the 1917 Revolution, the Soviet government attempted to wipe out religion in Russia. Many churches were closed or turned into museums, recreation centers, or warehouses for grain. Antireligious propaganda was spread by newspapers and speeches, in youth groups and schools. Campaigns were organized to persuade people, especially young people, that science proved that God did not exist. Considerable social pressure and actual discrimination were employed against those who continued to believe.

The Soviet constitution guarantees freedom of religion and the freedom to disseminate antireligious propaganda. Significantly, there is no right to disseminate pro-religious propaganda. Although the cards are stacked in favor of the government, religion has not yet been destroyed in the Soviet Union. Some churches remain open. In Moscow, there are perhaps a hundred operating churches. That is not many for a city of seven million people, and they are always crowded, especially on religious holidays. Since the government controls all publishing, religious works such as Bibles and prayer books are seldom if ever printed.

In addition to the Orthodox, there are three other major religious groups: the Baptists, the Jews, and the Moslems. These groups encounter the same difficulties as the Orthodox believers. For instance, in Moscow there is only one synagogue open. The government places many obstacles in the way of religious Jews who want to bake Matzoh to celebrate holidays such as Yom Kippur. The Moslems, who live mainly in the Central Asian republics, are also persecuted. Many mosques have been closed, and traditional practices, such as requiring women to wear veils, have been forbidden.

In many ways the Baptists are today the most dynamic and vital of all Soviet religious groups. Their numbers have probably been increasing over the past several decades, rather than decreasing as is the case for other religious groups. (No accurate statistics are available on Soviet religion.) When entering a Baptist church, one notices immediately that there are more young people present than there are in Orthodox churches, synagogues, or mosques. The majority of believers in the Soviet Union are people over 50, predominantly women. It is rare to see more than a half dozen young people at a crowded Orthodox service. Older people also predominate at Baptist services, but there are many children and men and women between the ages of 20 and 50.

Plight of the Believer

To be a religious believer in the Soviet Union requires courage and sacrifice. In addition to bearing social and government pressure, it is necessary to give up certain rights. Obviously, all members of the Communist Party and the Komsomol must be atheists. To enter a university one must profess to be an atheist. No teacher can be a believer. In other work, even in factories, it is often difficult to advance very high if one is a known believer. This fact is recorded in one's work book, and supervisors hesitate to show favor or even tolerance for believers. (Each worker carries a work book in which is recorded every job he has held, with comments about his work: whether or not he gets drunk, is late for work, shirks hard work, and so forth.)

Another obstacle for religious believers is the feeling of isolation that the government creates. Not only are they isolated from the majority of people who accept the official atheist position of the government, but they are cut off from all religious groups outside the country. In recent years there have been a few visits to the Soviet Union by foreign religious leaders, but contact is very limited. Government restriction of such contact is especially severe in the case of the Jews. The existence of Israel as a Jewish homeland increases Soviet fears. The government fears that Soviet Jews might feel more allegiance to Israel than to their own country, and so Soviet-Israeli relations are kept at a minimum.

Future of Religion

Soviet officials maintain that religion is dying out, that only a few old people still believe, and that in a few years no believers will be left. They have been saying this for forty years, however, and somehow religion seems to survive. There are even indications in the Soviet press that some young people (including Komsomol members!) are being attracted to religion, perhaps out of curiosity or because of the monotony of Soviet life. There are also fairly frequent articles denouncing small semi-secret religious sects that have been

uncovered, often in rural areas. It is difficult to judge the strength of religion in the Soviet Union or its future. Suppression is rarely a successful way of dealing with people's beliefs, however, and it is doubtful that the government will soon reach its goal of totally eliminating religion.

Some Intangibles of Soviet Life

There are several characteristics of Soviet life that are difficult for Americans to understand. Western observers find some basic Soviet attitudes quite alien and opposed to their own education and experience. Yet it is important to recognize these different attitudes and to make an effort to understand them.

The Soviet emphasis on collectivism, rather than individualism, is one difference that profoundly influences the way of life in the Soviet Union. Most Americans are taught that progress has been made by individual initiative and that each person should look after his own good. The whole Soviet orientation is toward collective or public action and responsibility. The general welfare is usually placed above individual welfare. The individual Soviet citizen is taught to be aware of his responsibilities to his society and to be willing to sacrifice his own personal advantages for the good of the country.

Collective Incentives

Soviet workers are encouraged to raise production for the benefit of the country, not to make more money themselves. Increasingly, however, the government has realized that this idealistic appeal is less effective than the appeal of cash. Accordingly, workers are now often offered cash bonuses as incentives to produce more. These incentives are usually offered to groups of workers,

"Board of honor" containing the pictures of outstanding workers

Such displays are common in Soviet cities. Some boards also display pictures of negligent or lazy workers, drunkards, and trouble makers in the hope that public ridicule will cause them to reform. (Courtesy, Wide World Photos)

organized into *collectivs* or brigades. These work brigades are encouraged to compete against each other, the winners being awarded such titles as "Heroes of Socialist Labor." By such devices the government hopes to encourage workers to cooperate and struggle together for the common good, while at the same time holding out financial rewards to them.

Emphasis on one's social responsibilities is strong throughout the educational system and such groups as the Pioneers and Komsomol, as well as in trade unions. The effects can be seen in small ways. Soviet streets, for example, are extremely clean. Soviet visitors to New York or other United States cities are shocked at the dirt and the careless attitude of most Americans. It is considered very offensive to throw a piece of paper, a cigarette, or even a match in a Soviet street. If a person does so, it is almost certain that he will be stopped immediately by a passer-by and lectured on his bad manners. Many American tourists have received such lectures on proper behavior after casually tossing a bit of trash into the gutter.

Correcting Bad Manners

The favorite Soviet word for such bad manners is *nekulturny,* meaning "uncultured" or "uncivilized." It is a strong word and meant to embarrass. It is used to describe a great variety of actions and attitudes. A man sitting in a subway with his legs crossed so as to take up more room than usual would soon be advised that he is acting "uncivilized." To wear heavy make-up or to dance the twist is very *nekulturny.*

Many Americans might feel the same way about some of this behavior, but what is different in the Soviet Union is that such matters are considered the proper concern of the public. The following incident may illustrate why this sense of social or collective responsibility can have negative as well as positive aspects. A young woman may be walking along and be stopped by another woman and told that her slip is showing. But the young woman may also be treated to a long and hostile lecture on how uncivilized and improper this is and how we're building Communism here and it just won't do to have people walking around like that. Collective responsibility sometimes seems to be interpreted as the right or duty to be concerned with everyone else's affairs.

A "druzhinik", or part-time volunteer policeman

Wearing a red armband, he helps patrol the streets in the evening and handles minor disturbances. (Courtesy, Sovfoto)

The writings of Marx, Lenin, and present-day government leaders tend to strengthen this urge to concern oneself with one's neighbors' affairs. Marx stated that when the final stage of communism was reached, the state would wither away. No police or government would be needed; people would run things for themselves. He was rather vague about how this would actually work, and Soviet rulers since Lenin have been trying to find specific ways in which the "withering away of the state" could be started. Two recent experiments are cited as examples of how the state will be replaced by volunteer, unofficial citizens' groups. They are the *Druzhina,* or "police helpers," and the comrades' courts.

The Druzhina

Under Communism everyone is supposed to receive "according to his needs," so there will be no reason for crime and therefore no need for police. There may still be occasional cases of drunkenness, fights, and traffic problems, but these can easily be handled by volunteers from among ordinary citizens. Several years ago the Druzhina was started to handle just this kind of problem. They are volunteers who wear red arm bands and patrol the streets, mainly in the evenings. They are supposed to assist the regular police and to take care of minor instances of drunken fights, rowdy behavior, and other disorders. Often the Druzhina are active local Komsomol members.

In principle this seems like a reasonable and helpful idea. There are dangers, however, when a volunteer group like this is formed without clear duties or controls over it. The Soviet press has carried numerous articles warning local Druzhina groups about taking the law into their own hands and going too far. The case of a local band of Druzhina who went around the city ripping loud Western-style sport shirts off people's backs was mentioned in Chapter 8. In another city, local Druzhina opposed modern jazz as American and decadent. They carried their opposition to the point of breaking into private apartments where people were listening to jazz and destroying records and tapes.

Comrades' Courts

The comrades' courts are similar to the Druzhina and are subject to the same dangers. They are not part of the regular court system. They were established recently to handle cases of anti-Soviet attitudes and improper behavior rather than actual crimes. The purpose is to prevent crimes and to educate people to the proper Soviet ethics and ideals. These courts meet in apartment buildings, places of work, universities, and villages. Members of the court are elected for one year by the entire group. The defendant therefore is tried by people who know him, at least slightly. Typical cases involve drunkenness and public disorder, lateness for work, minor juvenile delinquency, neglect of children, minor damage of public property, violations of apartment or dormitory regulations, petty personal squabbles, and other antisocial activities. (Feifer's book, *Justice in Moscow,* has some interesting descriptions of cases handled by comrades' courts.)

Everyone in the apartment building or place of work can attend the court and is free to give his opinions about the case. The court can hand out such punishments as warnings, fines, wage cuts, or recommend that a case be turned over to a regular court if it seems more serious than originally thought.

The comrades' court is the model of the future under communism. The regular courts will be abolished and all disputes will be handled by local groups of citizens who will discipline themselves. Again, the danger is that without strict controls and regulations, these informal courts could be misused to attack anyone who seemed to be different. This is especially true since the cases do not involve actual crimes that break specific laws but rather involve attitudes and behavior, questions on which there is always disagreement.

National Pride

Developing countries are probably all somewhat defensive about their problems and extremely proud of their

An auto worker being read a public reprimand

This comrades' court meets in a Moscow automobile plant. (Courtesy, Sovfoto)

achievements. Because of feelings of inferiority, criticism, from outside or within the country, is often resented and suppressed. The Soviet Union is an example of this defensive attitude and as such might help us to understand better the countries of Asia, Africa, and Latin America.

Like so many Soviet excesses, this defensiveness was at its height under Stalin but still affects Soviet attitudes today. The early days are perhaps best characterized by the effort to prove that Russians had invented everything from the airplane to baseball. Ironically, because of the absurd lengths to which Soviet officials went to show superiority in every field, many people tended to dismiss as propaganda the authentic accomplishments of Russian scientists in the nineteenth as well as the twentieth centuries.

Even in recent years, during informal conversations, the mention of some Western achievement or product still evokes an immediate, "We have that too!" from Soviet citizens. There is an almost desperate need for citizens of a backward country to feel that they are catching up to other countries. At the beginning of the first Five-Year Plan, Stalin made a very revealing speech outlining why it was so important for the Soviet Union to industrialize and become a world economic and military power.

"One feature of the history of old Russia was the continual beatings she suffered for falling behind, for her backwardness. She was beaten by the Mongol khans. She was beaten by the Turkish beys. She was beaten by the Swedish feudal lords.

She was beaten by the Polish and Lithuanian gentry. She was beaten by the British and French capitalists. She was beaten by the Japanese barons. All beat her for her backwardness: for military backwardness, for political backwardness. She was beaten because to do so was profitable and could be done with impunity."

Konstantin Paustovsky, one of the liberal Soviet writers, recently described an incident that illustrates the continuing Soviet defensiveness and sensitivity. He and some other writers were traveling in Western Europe along with a group of important Soviet officials and bureaucrats. When one writer exclaimed that the sea had a magnificent color, an official snapped back, "Well, does the sea look worse back home? This comrade should be investigated."

Soviet space achievements and their on-again off-again lead in the race to the moon have been a real surprise for most Americans. It is difficult for us to realize how much these feats meant psychologically to the Soviet people. Here was clear evidence at last that they had surpassed the Americans and were now looked upon as world leaders, at least in one area. National pride is a powerful emotion, especially in a country that has only recently moved out of a state of backwardness.

It is dangerous to predict, but it seems possible that as the Soviet Union gradually reaches a level of material and technical equality with the United States, it may become less defensive and hostile and more relaxed and self-confident. This difference may be only a question of style and not involve any basic change in foreign policy or relations with the West. Hostility between the Soviet Union and the United States might nevertheless be decreased if the Soviets felt less pressure to prove themselves and defend national prestige.

PROJECTS

A. Research

(1) Compare the New York and Moscow subways, in terms of miles of track, number of passengers, frequency of trains, fare, and the like.

(2) Compare United States and Soviet housing. Find out if there is any government-owned housing in your city. Do most Americans live in private or in government-owned housing?

(3) Describe American trade unions. Who belongs? Are they growing or declining? Do all United States workers have a right to strike? What about government employees, such as postmen, teachers, policemen, and the like? What groups of American workers do not have unions? Would they be better off if they did have unions?

(4) Read the 1961 Program of the Communist Party of the Soviet Union. What is the picture of future Soviet life which is drawn? How is it similar to or different from the American ideal of a good life? (The

Program is available in *Essential Works of Marxism,* edited by Arthur P. Mendel. See *Further Reading.*)

(5) What percentage of Americans are religious? Compare the situation of an atheist here with that of a religious person in the Soviet Union. Are there any government restrictions or social pressures against an atheist in the United States?

(6) Find out about the condition of public transportation in the United States. There is much debate currently about whether the government should take over passenger service, since it is not profitable. Find out how much the government puts into building highways. Do you think more money should go into railroads, subways, and bus systems?

(7) What health services does the United States government provide? Who is covered by Medicare? How does this compare to Soviet medical care?

B. Activities

(1) Organize a debate about living standards in the United States and the Soviet Union. Which system provides more opportunity for all its citizens? One side could argue that the Soviet system guarantees certain things, such as health care, education, cheap housing, and the like, to even the poorest citizen. The Soviet government takes an active role in ensuring the public welfare. There are good ideas and arguments for this position in the Party Program. (Available in *Essential Works of Marxism,* edited by Mendel. See *Further Reading.*) The opposing side could argue that there is more opportunity in the United States; the majority of the people live much better than Soviet citizens, have more consumer goods and more economic freedom. One book both sides might read and incorporate into the debate is *The Other America* by Michael Harrington (Penguin Books, London), the book which touched off our current "war on poverty" program.

C. Further Reading

Bourdeaux, Michael, *Opium of the People: the Christian Religion in the USSR* (Bobbs-Merrill, N.Y.).

Feifer, George, *Justice in Moscow* (Dell, N.Y.)—Read Chapter 4, on the comrades' courts.

Mendel, Arthur P., *Essential Works of Marxism* (Bantam Books, N.Y.)—The texts, with commentary, of such major documents as the "Communist Manifesto," Lenin's "State and Revolution," the 1961 Communist Party Program, and various writings of Stalin, Mao Tse-tung, and others.

Miller, Wright, *Russians as People* (Dutton, N.Y.)—General impressions of Russian life and people.

Van der Post, Laurens, *Journey into Russia* (Penguin, N.Y.)—The best of recent "travel books" describing daily Soviet life.

Chapter 13

DIFFERENT PATHS TO SOCIALISM

Just as there have been significant changes within the Soviet Union in recent years, so there have been changes within the "socialist bloc," all the countries governed by Communist Parties. Fifteen years ago it was possible to speak with some certainty about world communism. Today one must be careful to specify which variation of communism one is referring to. This chapter will look at the recent disintegration of the communist movement, particularly the Sino-Soviet (Chinese-Russian) split. The first chapter of this book discussed the modernization of developing nations and the appeal of the Soviet example of rapid industrialization. Basic to the Sino-Soviet rivalry is the question of which country offers the best model for developing nations to follow and which country best understands the current world political and social situation.

The Monolithic Bloc

Until after World War II, all Communist Parties conformed exactly to the Soviet Communist Party, in organization and ideology. This was natural, since only the Soviet Communist Party had been successful in gaining power. The other parties therefore looked to Moscow for guidance and obeyed orders faithfully. Stalin was the acknowledged leader of all communists in all countries. When Stalin spoke, everyone eagerly repeated what he said. Statements of all Communist Parties, whether in Chile, France, India, or the United States, were almost word-for-word repetitions of the latest Soviet statements. Typical of this situation is the definition of a communist that Stalin gave in 1927: "An internationalist (communist) is one who unreservedly, without hesitation, without conditions, is ready to defend the Soviet Union."

After World War II, communist governments came to power in Eastern Europe (Albania, Bulgaria, Czechoslovakia, East Germany, Hungary, Poland, Rumania, and Yugoslavia) and in China. Until Stalin's death, however, the communist movement (except for Yugoslavia) remained united, and the individual ruling parties continued to follow the Soviet lead, imitating Soviet governmental organs, economic patterns, cultural policies, and even architectural styles.

Even where the Soviet experience had been unsuccessful there was pressure for the other countries to conform to Soviet patterns. Thus, collectivization of agriculture was pushed through, even in countries such as Poland, where public opposition was intense and where it led to food shortages. (Collectivization has since been reversed in Poland and Yugoslavia.) The "satellite countries," as they were soon called in the West, obediently echoed all aspects of Soviet foreign and domestic policies. One reason for this was that most of the European Communist Parties had come to power in the wake of the Red Army, which remained as an occupation force for some years (see Chapter 7).

The Yugoslav-Soviet Split

Yugoslavia and Albania were the only exceptions to this pattern in Eastern Europe. Yugoslavia, Albania, and China, in fact, were the only countries where the local Communist Party took power without help from the Soviet Red Army. During the Second World War, Tito and the Yugoslav Communist Party had taken a leading role in the partisan struggle against the Nazis. As World War II was ending, Tito and the communists won power in a civil war with little but moral support from the Soviet Union.

In 1948, the Yugoslav Communist Party, headed by Tito, refused to follow Moscow's lead and declared itself independent of the socialist bloc. It announced that it would follow an independent foreign policy and pursue its own independent course to socialism. That there was another way to build socialism than by simply copying the Soviet model was a heretical notion. Stalin was outraged and denounced the Yugoslavs but took no further steps. He was reluctant to risk war at that time, and in any case, Yugoslavia was separated from the Soviet Union by several hundreds of miles. Although the Soviet Union cut off all economic and military aid to Yugoslavia, the United States and other Western countries gave aid in order to support Yugoslav independence.

The Sino-Soviet Split

China is the most significant example of an independent communist seizure of power, and it is the Chinese rivalry with the Soviets that is of major importance today. The Chinese Communists, led by Mao Tse-tung, fought a long civil war with Chiang Kai-Shek's Nationalist government and finally pushed his army out of China in 1949. Since then Chiang and his supporters have ruled the island of Taiwan as the Nationalist Republic of China. (A mutual defense pact exists between Chiang's government and the United States.) Many people, including Stalin, were surprised by Mao's victory. He did not anticipate the early and total defeat of Chiang Kai-Shek and probably was not very enthusiastic about having a neighboring communist country with three times the population of the Soviet Union. Nevertheless, the Soviets gave economic, technical, and military aid to the Chinese and relations were outwardly friendly and cooperative for nearly a decade.

It is difficult to say exactly when the Sino-Soviet split began. Tensions existed for years under the surface. Open debate and disagreement started only

Nikita Khrushchev and Mao Tse-tung in a friendlier period, 1959
The Soviet Premier is leaving Peking after the tenth anniversary celebration of the Chinese Communist revolution. (Courtesy, Sovfoto)

around 1960. The Chinese now say that Khrushchev's secret speech to the Twentieth Party Congress in 1956 (see Chapter 7) marked the beginning. In any case, there is no doubt that the Chinese strongly disagreed with the speech, its denunciation of Stalin, and its liberalizing implications. They were angry that Khrushchev had consulted neither them nor other Communist Parties before launching his policies of de-Stalinization and peaceful coexistence with the West. At the time, however, all conflict was hidden from public view.

The Issues at Stake

In the next few years the Sino-Soviet rift gradually broadened and came into the open. A number of specific issues lie at the center of their disagreements. There is still a wide range of opinion in the West as to which issues are the most significant. China and the Soviet Union are in direct conflict over: (1) Soviet refusal to help China get nuclear weapons and regain Taiwan; (2) the possibility of peaceful coexistence with the West; (3) the amount of support to be given to "wars of national liberation," wars fought by a people against a foreign power that rules their country directly or controls its government covertly; and (4) which nation is more faithful to Marxism-Leninism and therefore the true leader of the communist bloc and the model for developing countries.

As a closer examination of these issues will show, the Chinese and the Soviets have come to view the contemporary world very differently. They interpret certain key events in conflicting ways and draw quite different conclusions. When the Soviets developed the hydrogen bomb and inter-continental ballistic missiles (ICBM's) in 1958, they and the Chinese proclaimed that the world balance of power had now shifted in favor of the communist bloc. Or, as Mao put it, "the East wind had prevailed over the West wind." The Chinese assumed that this development meant that communist policy would now become more aggressive. Specifically, they hoped to receive nuclear weapons, or at least Soviet military support, in order to drive Chiang Kai-Shek and the United States Navy from Taiwan. They were surprised and angered when this support did not materialize.

The Chinese therefore began their own nuclear development program and managed to build and explode an atomic bomb by 1965. They had become a nuclear power but only by diverting much energy and money from other important programs.

Conflict over Peaceful Coexistence

The Chinese were even more upset when it appeared that Khrushchev seriously intended to pursue a policy of peaceful coexistence and to try to relax tensions with the United States. Since 1956 Khrushchev had repeatedly stated that war between capitalist and socialist countries was no longer inevitable. He had also said that it might be possible for some countries to move peaceably from capitalism to socialism, without a violent revolution. The Chinese charged that this was "revisionism"—a betrayal of the ideas of Marx and Lenin. Khrushchev, however, continued to speak of the possibility of avoiding war and even made a goodwill trip to the United States in 1959 (a trip which, it later became known, the Chinese opposed.)

Until 1963 neither the Soviets nor the Chinese criticized each other by name. The Chinese always attacked the Yugoslavs when they meant the Soviets, and the Soviets attacked the Albanians, meaning the Chinese. (The Albanians were the first, and for a while the only, supporters of the Chinese.) The hostility between the two countries came out bitterly at the Twenty-Second Party Congress in Moscow in 1961. Although many Communist Parties supported Khrushchev's criticisms of the Albanians (meaning Chinese), several parties significantly remained silent; the North Koreans and the North Vietnamese were two. In the next few years their silence was to change into open support for the Chinese position. If you look at a map of Asia, you can perhaps see why.

Border Incidents

In the early 1960's Soviet economic aid and technical assistance to China was cut down and then almost entirely ended. (China later complained that the Soviet Union had always been stingy with her and much more generous to noncommunist countries such as India and Egypt.) During the same period rumors began to circulate in the West of border incidents between the two countries. China and the Soviet Union have a common border of three thousand miles in Central Asia. People of the same ethnic background live on both sides of the border. Recently the Soviet press has carried reports of shooting incidents and of refugees fleeing China and asking for asylum in the Soviet Union. The Chinese have made similar counter-charges. There have been newspaper reports in the Soviet press about Chinese and Soviet troop movements and warnings to Soviet citizens to be vigilant. (See Map 11.)

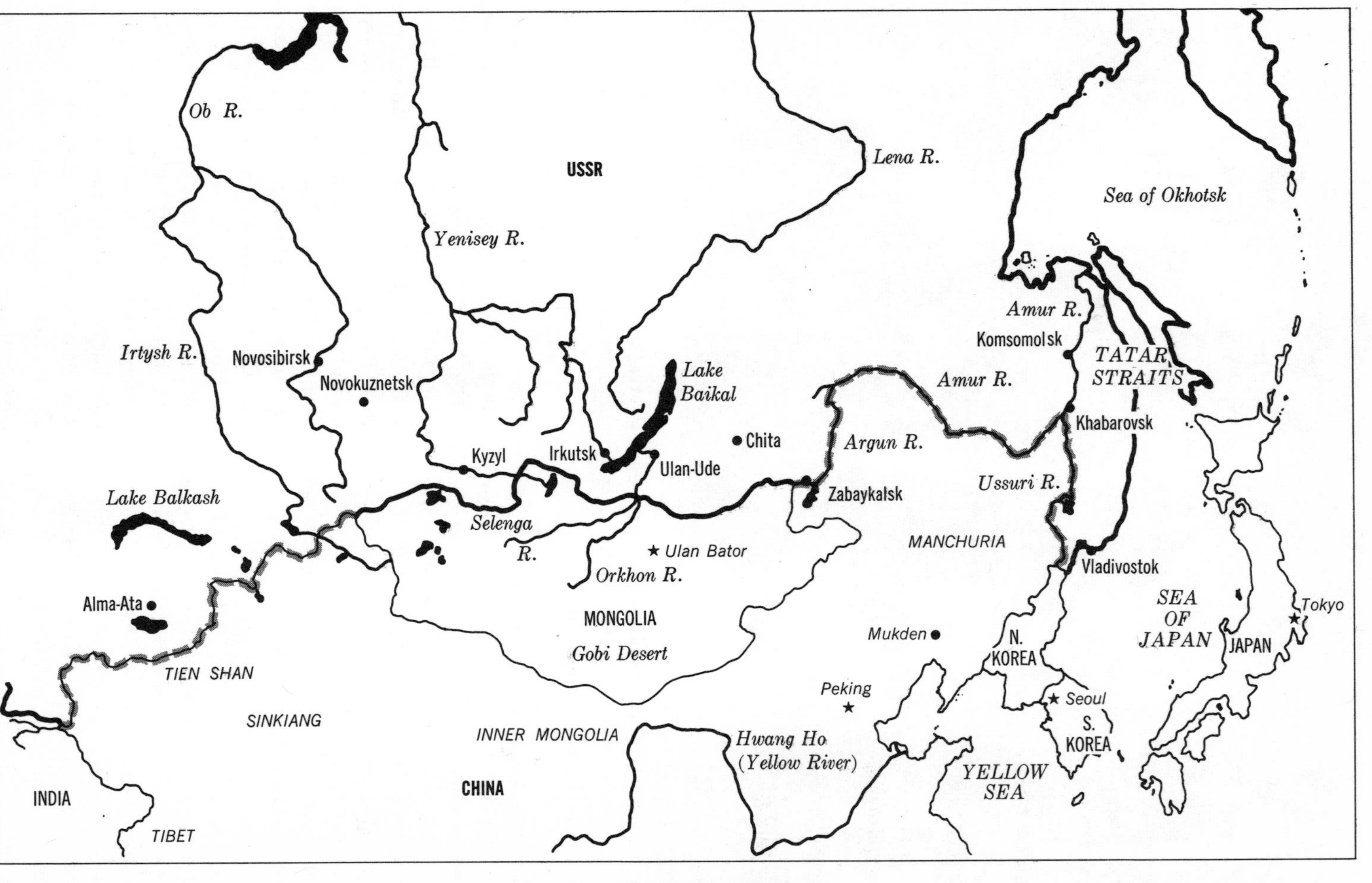

Map 11 The Sino-Soviet Border

Chinese students reading quotations from Mao Tse-tung in front of Lenin's Tomb
Soviet police (left, rear) eventually broke up this demonstration. (Courtesy, China Photo Service)

So far it is difficult to say how serious all this is. It is certainly an exaggeration to predict an outbreak of serious fighting. It has been pointed out, however, that Chinese maps show some borders in Central Asia and Siberia as undefined. Some maps even state ominously that the borders "have not yet been permanently fixed."

The Turning Point

The autumn of 1962 marked a turning point in Sino-Soviet relations. Two events sharply widened the conflict: the Cuban missile crisis and the Chinese-Indian border war. Khrushchev provoked strong criticism from the Chinese by first attempting to put missiles into Cuba and then removing them under pressure and threats from the United States. According to the Chinese, Khrushchev forfeited all right to leadership of the bloc by these acts. It was a foolish risk to put the missiles there in the first place, the Chinese charged, and cowardly and humiliating to then withdraw them. By doing so, the Soviets had not only blundered but betrayed the Cubans and all other developing nations.

Even more of a shock to the Chinese was the Soviet attitude toward the Chinese war with India over their common border in the Himalaya Mountains. The Soviets not only did not support the Chinese but remained neutral and even sold weapons to the Indians. Among the weapons were MIG fighters that were newer than and superior to any that the Soviets had ever given to China! From late 1962 on, the Chinese were convinced that the Soviets were no longer willing to support the world revolution and that China should take over as the leader of the socialist bloc. They had hardened in the opinion that they were the only true Marxist-Leninists.

Two World Views

The Chinese and the Soviets still speak the same ideological language: both see the world through the eyes of Marx and Lenin; both see socialism inevitably replacing capitalism throughout the world. There are many areas of general agreement. Nevertheless, there are significant differences in the way they interpret the current world situation, and each side gives special emphasis to different aspects of it, drawing separate conclusions.

Brezhnev and Kosygin realize that nuclear weapons have changed the nature of international relations. Lenin wrote that wars were inevitable while capitalism and socialism both existed. But war could now mean total destruction, with little to be gained by the victors, as leaders in both Russia and the West realize. Khrushchev revised Lenin and stated that war was no longer inevitable. He emphasized a policy of peaceful coexistence, meaning competition between East and West by all means short of war. Khrushchev also stated that it is now possible for a country to become socialist without any revolution, peacefully, through elections.

This viewpoint is obviously a cautious one, and for good reasons: The Soviet Union has made great material progress in this century, despite two destructive wars, and has too much to lose in another one. Soviet officials state their support for "wars of national liberation" and emphasize the importance of independence for all former colonies in Africa, Asia, and Latin America. The Soviets have often given aid to national groups fighting for independence, such as the Algerians. But Soviet leaders are aware of the possibility that a war of national liberation could expand into a general nuclear war and give less emphasis to such wars than do the Chinese.

The Soviet view is that although wars of national liberation can be used to weaken the West and drive Western influence out of the developing countries, the West will finally be defeated through economic and social competition. The socialist bloc will build a stronger and better society that the world will see and acknowledge to be the superior of the two. As the Soviets see it, this path to victory may be longer, but it is less risky and just as inevitable.

It is difficult to assess the true Chinese attitude concerning an all-out war against the West. Chinese statements have asserted that such a conflict is inevitable; her attitude toward the West has been consistently belligerent and menacing. Mao's words, however, have not been matched by deeds.

China, to be sure, is more willing to run the risk of all-out war than is Russia. She has attacked India, invaded Tibet, committed thousands of troops during the Korean War. Furthermore, Chinese provocation in Laos, Cambodia, and Indonesia is a matter of record. Yet there is no doubt that China greatly fears a direct confrontation with the West. (For example, it has never directly attacked Taiwan.)

Her internal problems are legion, her

nuclear stockpile is extremely small, and she cannot count on the support of other Communist countries in such a struggle. Furthermore, the Sino-Soviet split poses important questions for China as to whether Russia might ultimately profit from China's involvement in a costly war. While strong statements may still be expected from Peking, it is likely that China will continue to support wars rather than fight them.

The Chinese, it should be noted, insist that the development of nuclear weapons is not the most important fact of recent history. They feel that the most significant aspect of today's world is the movement of the colonial nations of Asia, Africa, and Latin America toward independence. They compare the present world situation with their own struggle for power in the 1930's and 1940's. In those years the Chinese Communists gradually gained control of the rural countryside, surrounding and finally seizing the cities. By analogy today, the developing nations represent the "countryside" and the developed nations of Europe and North America represent the "cities." By winning the developing nations, through "wars of national liberation," the "cities" will eventually be conquered.

In the Chinese view, everything should be done to aid the struggle against the capitalist and colonial powers. Wars of national liberation should be supported in Angola, in Vietnam, in South Africa, in Venezuela. By this method the West will be defeated, not by economic competition. According to the Chinese, there is not as much risk in this tactic as the Soviets fear; the West will not use nuclear weapons in a local war, and, in any case, the balance of power is now against the West.

Chinese "Revisionism"

It is interesting to note how far this Chinese point of view has strayed from the original theories of Marx and Lenin. The class conflict, in Chinese eyes, is between the colonial or imperialist powers, and the national liberation forces of Asia, Africa, and Latin America. There is no mention of a struggle between bourgeoisie and proletariat, since the people of Asia, Africa, and Latin America are almost all peasants. The Chinese brand of communism is based not on the urban, educated, well-organized proletariat of Marx but on the peasant. The Soviet view described above is still closer to original Marxism, since it continues to see the main struggle as between the economic systems of socialism and capitalism. In the Chinese view, the peasants and the underdeveloped countries of the world have replaced the proletariat and are struggling against the wealthy, developed nations, who now represent the bourgeoisie. Thus, not only Khrushchev but Mao also has made significant revisions in the ideas of Marxism-Leninism.

Competition for the "Third World"

Chinese-Soviet rivalry has become increasingly noticeable in the developing countries. Both sides offer economic and military aid (for example, in Vietnam) and encourage anti-Western leaders. Each side claims to have the most to offer in the way of foreign aid and example to be imitated. Both the Chinese and the Soviets denounce each other and distort each other's policies in an attempt to win influence. The Chinese accuse the Soviets of "selling out" to the West, of placing their own national welfare above the cause of world revolution, of wanting to concentrate on making the Soviet Union richer rather than on defeating imperialism. The Soviets counter by accusing the Chinese of being reckless, of wanting to provoke a war, and of throwing around violent words without backing them up with actions. Although there is an element of truth in all of these accusations, none of them is entirely accurate.

The question of race has also come up in the Sino-Soviet conflict. The Soviets have accused the Chinese of racism, of trying to turn the colored peoples of Asia, Africa, and Latin America against them because they are white. Again, this is only a partial truth. The Chinese have made no open racist statements. They have, however, argued against including the Soviet Union in conferences of Afro-Asia nations on the grounds that the Soviet Union is a European country. This is intended to play on the emotions of leaders of newly independent nations that have only recently gained their freedom from European colonial powers such as England, France, and Belgium. The Chinese also hint that as members of a non-white race they can understand the situation and problems of developing nations better than the Russians can.

In this connection it is interesting that there have been complaints from African students who have accepted scholarships to study in China and in the Soviet Union about racial discrimination in both countries. Some students have left disenchanted with Soviet or Chinese society because of hostility toward them and unpleasant incidents. At least one African student has been beaten to death by Soviet toughs. Evidently, neither the Soviet nor Chinese system has been more successful than the American in wiping out racial prejudice.

The Appeal of Communism

What is the appeal of communism today in the developing nations? Few of these countries have much industry or a large proletariat. The majority of their populations are peasants. The appeal, then, is not that of traditional Marxism in advanced European countries. Young Asian or African students are nevertheless attracted to communism as a model for rapid modernization, as a way to organize a society in order to pull it into the twentieth century. The tendency is to imitate certain aspects of the communist system, such as one party dictatorship, state ownership of the economy, and central economic planning. The doctrines of Marx and Lenin as a whole do not apply.

In one sense, the Chinese example has more interest and appeal than the Soviet, and the Chinese emphasize this. China is still an economically backward, largely agricultural country that has just begun to industrialize. Considerable progress has been made in a few years, especially in certain fields; the recent development of nuclear weapons is a good example. Nevertheless the Chinese experience is still much closer to that of the backward nations of the "third world" than is the Soviet experience. The Soviet Union, rapidly growing wealthy and enormously powerful, has considerably less in common with the "have-not" nations than does China.

Both China and the Soviet Union are looked to by many people in the developing nations because of their active support of the struggle against colonialism. Both of them argue that the major problem of the world today is the achievement of independence for Portuguese Angola, black South Africa, black Rhodesia, and the few other remaining colonies. Furthermore, they often back

Chinese Red Guards demonstrating outside the Soviet Embassy in Peking, January, 1967

They are protesting the "revisionist" policies of the Soviet Government and the alleged mistreatment of Chinese students by a Moscow crowd a few days earlier. (Courtesy, China Photo Service)

up their arguments with military aid for rebel groups. Western nations, while often sympathetic to the idea of independence, are not so prone to actually support the overthrow of existing institutions.

Despite communist support for national independence, and the appeal of their system as a model for rapid modernization, many leaders of the third world have begun to look more critically at Soviet and Chinese intentions. Some countries have curtailed the activities of communist diplomats and foreign aid technicians who were interfering in domestic political matters. Guinea expelled some Soviet officials; Burundi sharply reduced relations with China. Nkrumah of Ghana and Sukarno of Indonesia have been removed from power by military leaders who were concerned by the amount of Soviet and Chinese influence that these leaders allowed. Some African leaders have expressed their reluctance to exchange one imperialism (of the West) for another (of the East). To these leaders, Sino-Soviet competition in Africa has unpleasant similarities with the competition among European countries in the nineteenth century to divide up the continent into colonies. The appeal of communism in the developing countries may eventually not be as great as we fear.

Developments in Eastern Europe

The Sino-Soviet split is only one example of the disintegration of the world communist movement, although it is the most extreme and important example. With the exceptions of Yugoslavia and Albania, none of the East European countries has declared itself independent of the Soviet Union and in opposition to it. But in varying degrees, each of the "satellite" nations has taken steps to assert its national independence and to discover its own path to communism. The East European countries no longer blindly imitate and obey Moscow. They do not always follow the "line" laid down by the Soviet leaders, and the Soviets no longer try to force them to. There is a renewed sense of nationalism in East Europe, and significant differences among the communist governments there.

Soviet rule of East Europe has never been entirely secure. The Yugoslavs were the first to break away. Unrest in East Germany and Poland led to riots in 1953, which were crushed by force. In 1956, the Hungarian Revolution broke out, led at first by people who wanted to liberalize communist rule and remove Soviet troops from Hungary. The revolt turned into an effort to take Hungary entirely out of the socialist bloc. This secession could not be tolerated, and the Soviet Army finally suppressed the revolution. A bloodless revolt in Poland in the same year led to a change in the government, in which Stalinist leaders were replaced with more liberal nationalistic leaders. Among the reforms carried out was the reversal of collectivized agriculture; most Polish farmland was returned to private ownership.

Different Roads to Reform

The lesson learned in Eastern Europe was that armed rebellion would be crushed by Soviet force and that gradual reforms offered the only real possibility of regaining a measure of national independence. Reforms have accordingly taken place at varying degrees of speed, with some countries becoming much more "liberal" and de-Stalinized than the Soviet Union, whereas others have continued to imitate the Stalinist system even after the Soviet Union itself has changed. It is instructive to look briefly at some of the ways in which the countries of East Europe now differ from the Soviet Union.

It was pointed out earlier that agriculture in Poland and Yugoslavia is now mainly in private hands, not collectivized. In other areas as well, these two countries, especially Yugoslavia, are more liberal than the Soviet Union. For example, abstract art and Western experimental literature and music are allowed. Polish and Yugoslav artists and writers are much freer than their Soviet counterparts, although still restricted and censored in part. Noncommunist Western newspapers and magazines, such as the *New York Times, Time,* and *Newsweek,* are on sale in Polish and Yugoslav cities, and now in Rumania as well. They are not available in the Soviet Union or in other East European countries. The Catholic Church is still strong and very popular in Poland. Yugoslavia's foreign relations are quite independent from, and often in conflict with, Soviet policy.

Soviet citizens are extremely restricted in their freedom to travel. Only official delegations and a very few tourists, mainly government and Party members, are allowed to travel in the West. By contrast, there are almost no travel restrictions for Yugoslavs; both Hungarians and Czechs can obtain passports without great difficulty.

In Hungary and Czechoslovakia, economic reforms have moved even further away from central planning than in the Soviet Union and in the direction of a market economy based partially on profit. In Hungary a great effort has been made to involve non-Party people in the government and economy. In contrast to the Soviet system, anyone can be a farm chairman or factory manager, positions that the Soviets almost always fill with dedicated Communist Party members.

Rumanian Assertions of Independence

Rumania has been the most outspoken in asserting her independence of the Soviet Union over the past two or three years. Rumanian nationalism has worked against Soviet control in several ways. Most important, Rumania refused to agree to coordinate her economy with the economy of the whole bloc. She insisted on developing her economy separately, without regard for what would be best for the bloc as a whole. This daring defiance of Soviet wishes was successful, probably because the Soviet leaders did not want to have another crisis to deal with while they were having trouble with China and with the United States.

In addition to this economic independence, Rumania also asserted cultural independence of the Soviet Union. The teaching of Russian was eliminated from the schools. The Russian book store and publishing house in the capital of Bucharest was closed. Institutions and streets named for Russians were renamed for Rumanians. It is important to remember that Rumania is still governed by a communist dictatorship and that there is little political or social freedom. Its economy, moreover, is still highly centralized and "Stalinist." But it is no longer simply a "satellite" of the Soviet Union and it would be a mistake to treat it like one. In 1966, Rumanian leaders even went so far as to propose the dissolution of the Warsaw Pact, the East European equivalent of NATO.

Reactions to Khrushchev's Ouster

One measure of the weakening of Soviet control over other Communist Parties is their reaction to Khrushchev's ouster. Instead of simply swallowing the line and repeating everything the new leaders said, some national parties protested and asked for explanations. Party leaders from many countries went to Moscow to find out what had actually happened. More surprisingly, Brezhnev and Kosygin felt the necessity of making a trip to Poland to explain the reasons personally to the Polish leader Gomulka. Even after public and private explanations, some leaders made further comments of disapproval. The Italian Communist Party, for example, voiced dissatisfaction with the sudden way Khrushchev had been ousted and even compared it unfavorably to democratic elections in the West! Clearly the day is past when all communists accept without question what comes from Moscow.

Looking Ahead

The communist movement today is in a state of serious disorder. At least three countries—the Soviet Union, China, and Yugoslavia, claim to be building Communism with a capital "C," each insisting that their version is closest to the original ideas of Marx and Lenin. Each of the other ruling Communist Parties has also departed in some degree from Soviet practice and is asserting national independence. The confusion is even greater among Communist Parties that are not in power.

By 1964, some parties, mainly in Asia, had broken openly with the Soviet Union and were supporting China—the parties of Japan, Malaysia, New Zealand, North Korea, and Indonesia, among others. (The Indonesian Communist Party, once the third largest in the world, was almost entirely destroyed after the army took over effective power from President Sukarno in 1965.) Other parties split and two new parties were formed, one pro-Soviet, the other pro-Chinese. This happened in India, for example.

A more recent trend is toward a "neutral" position, supporting both the Chinese and the Soviet parties, refusing to choose sides. Cuba, Rumania, Japan, North Korea, and North Vietnam have taken this independent attitude, and others are hinting at a similar shift. It is clear that the Soviet proposal to "excommunicate" the Chinese from the communist movement is not popular with all other parties. Many of the smaller parties are distressed by the Sino-Soviet dispute and wish to stay out of it.

It is dangerous to predict the future of the communist movement, or to predict whether the breakup of the movement will make it more or less difficult to deal with. For many years there will probably be three general tendencies, none of which will dominate. The Soviets will attempt to regain as much control over the movement as possible. The Chinese will attempt to replace the Soviets as the new world leaders. Neither attempt is likely to succeed. The third tendency will be that of increasing nationalism within the communist movement, with each national party paying respect to Marxism-Leninism but insisting on its own interpretation. What the policy of the West should be —which tendency, if any, we should encourage—is another and a difficult question. We must, however, be aware of the changes that have occurred and are occurring in world communism and attempt to understand them.

PROJECTS

A. Research

(1) What has the United States government's attitude been in recent years toward the countries of Eastern Europe? Do we recognize all the governments? Do we trade with each country or favor certain ones? Do we give foreign aid of any kind to some or all East European countries?

(2) Take a single country, such as Hungary, Poland, or Yugoslavia, and find out more about the way of life there; how does it differ from life in the Soviet Union? *The New York Times* often has articles on contemporary life in these countries.

(3) The Chinese effort at rapid industrialization in the late 1950's, known as the "Great Leap Forward," was a partial failure and had to be abandoned. What were some of the reasons for its failure?

B. Activities

(1) Imagine you are the American Secretary of State trying to justify giving foreign aid to Rumania or Czechoslovakia before the Congress. What arguments would you give to support your policy? How could such a policy benefit the U.S.? What objections might some Congressmen raise?

(2) Write the statement which the Chinese, or the Soviet, government might make on the occasion of breaking formal diplomatic relations. What reasons might be given by each side? What are some of the charges they might make against each other?

C. Further Reading

Crankshaw, Edward, *The New Cold War: Moscow vs. Peking* (Penguin Books, London)—Brief survey of the Sino-Soviet split.

Ionescu, Ghita, *The Break-up of the Soviet Empire in Eastern Europe* (Penguin Books, London)—Review of Soviet relations with Eastern Europe over the past twenty years.

Kennan, George, *On Dealing with the Communist World* (Harper & Row, N.Y.)—A short book by a former U.S. ambassador to the Soviet Union and Yugoslavia who suggests changes in the way we act toward communist countries.

Mrozek, Slawomir, *The Elephant* (Grove Press, N.Y.)—A collection of amusing satirical stories by a contemporary Polish writer about life in a communist country. Especially good stories are: "The Elephant," "Children," "The Trial," "The Lion," and "The Co-operative."

Rothschild, Joseph, *Communist Eastern Europe* (Walker & Co., N.Y.)—A brief outline of recent and current East European history. Good maps, economic and political facts, and biographical sketches.

Zagoria, Donald S., *The Sino-Soviet Conflict* (Atheneum, N.Y.)—The best description of the early years of tension, up to 1961.

Problems of Communism is a magazine published by the United States Information Agency six times a year. It contains many interesting articles on current developments in Communist countries. Most libraries subscribe. A year's subscription costs only $2.50 and can be ordered through the Government Printing Office in Washington, D.C.

APPENDIX

Soviet Statistics

Area: 8,650,000 square miles

Population: 233,000,000 estimated, Jan. 1, 1967
53% urban, 47% rural

Ten largest cities (Estimated, Jan. 1965):

Moscow	6,427,000
Leningrad	3,636,000
Kiev	1,332,000
Baku	1,137,000
Tashkent	1,090,000
Gorky	1,084,000
Kharkov	1,070,000
Novosibirsk	1,027,000
Kuibyshev	950,000
Sverdlovsk	917,000

Major rivers:

Yenisei	3,550 miles
Ob	3,200 miles
Lena	2,980 miles
Amur	2,780 miles
Irtysh	2,700 miles
Volga	2,300 miles
Dniepr	1,400 miles
Don	1,325 miles

Lake Baikal (world's deepest lake): 5,710 feet deep

Caspian Sea (world's largest inland sea): 152,500 square miles

Major mountain ranges:

Caucasus
Pamir
Tien-Shan
Altai
Ural

Highest peak: Mount Communism, 24,595 feet

Transportation facilities:

Railroads	80,400 miles
Paved roads	180,000 miles
Inland waterways	87,000 miles

Education:

Elementary and secondary school students	46,400,000
Teachers	2,200,000
Trade school students	1,600,000
Technical college students	3,325,000
Students in 754 universities and other higher institutions (1,700,000 of these are evening or correspondence students)	3,608,000

Major holidays:

January 1	New Year's Day
May 1-2	May Day (traditional Socialist labor day)
November 7-8	Anniversary of 1917 Bolshevik Revolution
December 5	Constitution Day

Employment (Percentage of total working force):

Agriculture	34%
Industry, Construction	34%
Education, Health	13%
Transport, Communication	8%
Other	11%

Number of collective farms (kolkhozy):	37,618
Number of state farms (sovkhozy):	10,075

Important dates and events

Late 9th to mid 12th century	Kievan period
1237-40	Mongol invasion
1480	End of Mongol rule
15th century	Rise of Moscow
1547-84	Reign of Ivan the Terrible
1667-71	Revolt of Stenka Razin
1696-1725	Reign of Peter the Great
1703	Founding of St. Petersburg
1773-74	Revolt of Pugachev
1812	Napoleon invades Russia, is defeated
1825	Decembrist revolt
1854-56	Crimean War
1861	Emancipation of serfs by Alexander II
1881	Assassination of Alexander II
1883	First Russian Marxist group founded: "Liberation of Labor"
1891-1905	Trans-Siberian railroad built
1898	Russian Social Democratic Labor Party founded
1903	Social Democratic Party splits into Bolshevik-Menshevik factions
1905	"Bloody Sunday"; demonstrations, strikes,

	peasant rebellions; Soviet of Workers' Deputies established in St. Petersburg; October Manifesto of Tsar Nicholas II
1906-1911	Stolypin land reform
1914	World War I begins
1917, Mar. 2	Nicholas II abdicates; Provisional Government formed
1917, Apr. 3	Lenin returns to Russia
1917, July 7	Kerensky becomes Prime Minister of Provisional Government
1917, Oct. 25-26	Bolsheviks overthrow Provisional Government
1918, Mar. 3	Brest-Litovsk Peace Treaty
1918, Mar. 10-11	Capital shifted to Moscow
1918-1921	Civil War
1921	New Economic Policy begins
1924, Jan. 21	Lenin dies
1927	Trotsky expelled from Party
1928	End of New Economic Policy; first Five-Year Plan begins
1929	Collectivization of agriculture begins
1936-38	Mass purges
1939	Non-aggression pact with Germany; Soviet invasion of Poland
1939-40	Soviet-Finnish war
1940, Aug.	Trotsky murdered
1941, June 22	Hitler invades Soviet Union
1942-43	Battle of Stalingrad
1945	Defeat of Germany; Soviet forces enter Berlin
1948	Tito leads Yugoslavia out of Communist Bloc
1949	First Soviet atomic bomb exploded
1949	Communists win civil war in China
1950-53	Korean War
1953, Mar. 5	Stalin dies; Malenkov becomes Prime Minister; Khrushchev becomes First Secretary of Party
1953, Aug.	First Soviet hydrogen bomb exploded
1954	Ehrenburg's novel, *The Thaw*
1956	20th Party Congress; Khrushchev's secret anti-Stalin speech
1956, Oct.-Nov.	Hungarian revolt
1957, Oct.	Russians launch first satellite, Sputnik I
1958	Khrushchev becomes Prime Minister
1959	21st Party Congress
1959, Sept.	Khrushchev visits United States
1960, May	Russians shoot down U-2 spy plane
1960, Sept.-Oct.	Khrushchev visits United States
1961, Apr.	Russians launch first manned satellite; Yuri Gargarin, pilot

1961, Aug.	Berlin Wall built
1961, Oct.	22nd Party Congress; Sino-Soviet split becomes apparent
1962	Incidents reported on Sino-Soviet border in Central Asia; Soviet aid to China is stopped
1962, Oct.	Cuban missile crisis
1963	Russians and Chinese begin public attacks on each other
1963	Rumania asserts independence of Soviet Bloc in economic affairs
1964, Oct.	Khrushchev ousted from power; Kosygin becomes Prime Minister; Brezhnev becomes First Secretary of Party
1966, Mar.-Apr.	23rd Party Congress

INDEX

Y, Z

$5.00